China's Energy Relations with the Developing World

CHINA'S ENERGY RELATIONS WITH THE DEVELOPING WORLD

Edited by

Carrie Liu Currier

and

Manochehr Dorraj

continuum

NEW YORK • LONDON

2011

The Continuum International Publishing Group
80 Maiden Lane, New York, NY 10038
The Tower Building, 11 York Road, London SE1 7NX

www.continuumbooks.com

Library of Congress Cataloging-in-Publication Data
China's energy relations with the developing world / edited by Carrie Liu Currier and Manochehr Dorraj.
p. cm.
Includes bibliographical references and index.
ISBN-13: 978-1-4411-7555-7 (hardcover : alk. paper)
ISBN-10: 1-4411-7555-5 (hardcover : alk. paper)
ISBN-13: 978-1-4411-4104-0 (pbk. : alk. paper)
ISBN-10: 1-4411-4104-9 (pbk. : alk. paper)
1. Energy policy–China. 2. China–Relations–Developing countries.
3. Developing countries–Relations–China. I. Currier, Carrie Liu.
II. Dorraj, Manochehr. III. Title.

HD9502.C6C4845 2010
333.790951–dc22

2010021988

ISBN: HB: 978-1-4411-7555-7
PB: 978-1-4411-4104-0

Typset by Newgen Imaging Systems Pvt Ltd, Chennai, India
Printed and bound in the United States of America by Sheridan Books, Inc

Contents

Notes on Contributors

Gabriel Collins is a former ONA Research Fellow at CMSI and is now a private sector commodity market analyst focusing on China and Russia. Collins is an honors graduate of Princeton University (A.B. Politics) and is proficient in Mandarin Chinese and Russian. His primary research areas are Chinese and Russian energy policy, maritime energy security, Chinese shipbuilding, and Chinese naval modernization. Collins' energy and shipping related work has been published in such venues as *Oil & Gas Journal, Jane's Intelligence Review, Geopolitics of Energy, Proceedings, Naval War College Review, The National Interest, Hart's Oil & Gas Investor, LNG Observer, and Orbis.*

Carrie Liu Currier (M.A., Ph.D. University of Arizona; B.A. University of Michigan) is an Associate Professor of Political Science and the Director of Asian Studies at Texas Christian University. Her research interests are focused on China's economic reform policies to understand how developing countries are adapting to the demands of globalization. She conducted survey research in China in 2001–2002 that examines labor market reform and its impact on women's public and private sphere activities in Beijing, and has written several articles based on her survey and interview data. She has also written articles on population policy in China, and Chinese foreign policy with the Middle East, with an emphasis on both the arms and energy connections between China and Iran. Her publications include several articles in the *American Journal of Chinese Studies, Asian Journal of Women's Studies, Journal of Chinese Political Science, Journal of Women, Politics and Policy,* and *Middle East Policy.* She has also contributed chapters to books on China that examine China's regional strategies with the Middle East and the gendered effects of market reform in China. The courses she teaches include Chinese Domestic Politics, Chinese Foreign Policy, Feminist International Relations

Theory, Global Political Economy, International Relations of East Asia, and introductory courses in Asian Studies and in International Relations.

Manochehr Dorraj is a Professor of Political Science at Texas Christian University. He holds a Ph.D. from the University of Texas at Austin. His research focuses on developing nations in general and Middle East and North Africa in particular. He teaches courses on International Relations, Globalization, Politics of Developing Nations, and the Politics of the Middle East and North Africa. He has published extensively on Third World and Middle East development issues and their foreign relations. His publications have appeared in such Journals as *Central Asian Survey, Journal of Developing Societies, The Muslim World ,The Review of Politics, Social Compass, Middle East Policy, The Digest of Middle East Studies, Arab Studies Quarterly, The Whitehead Journal of Diplomacy and International Relations, Comparative Studies of South Asia, Africa and the Middle East, and Journal of Chinese Political Science.* Among his publications are: *The Changing Political Economy of the Third World, Middle East at the Crossroads: Internal Dynamics and the Foreign Policy Challenges.* With Carrie Liu Currier he has published the following: *"Lubricated With Oil: Iran-China Relations in a Changing World" (2008), "In Arms We Trust: Strategic and Economic Factors Motivating China-Iran Relations" (2010), Recasting the Silk Road in a New Era: China's Expanding Regional Influence in the Middle East" (2010).*

Andrew S. Erickson is an Associate Professor in the Strategic Research Department at the Naval War College and a founding member of the department's China Maritime Studies Institute (CMSI). He is an associate in research at Harvard University's Fairbank Center for Chinese Studies, a fellow in the National Committee on U.S.-China Relations' Public Intellectuals Program (2008–2011), and a member of the Council for Security Cooperation in the Asia Pacific (CSCAP). Proficient in Mandarin Chinese and in Japanese, he has traveled extensively in Asia. Erickson received his Ph.D. in international relations and comparative politics from Princeton. His research, which focuses on East Asian defense, foreign policy, and technology issues, has been published widely in such journals as *Orbis*, *Journal of Strategic Studies*, *Joint Force Quarterly*, and *Proceedings* (forthcoming). Erickson is co-editor of, and a contributor to, the Naval Institute Press book series, "Studies in Chinese Maritime Development": *China Goes to Sea* (forthcoming 2009), *China's Energy Strategy* (2008), *China's Future Nuclear Submarine Force* (2007); as well as the Naval War College Newport Paper *China's Nuclear Modernization.*

Jean A. Garrison is a Professor of political science and Director of International Studies at the University of Wyoming. She received her Ph.D. in Political Science from the University of South Carolina. Her research interests focus on American foreign policy with an emphasis on U.S.-China relations, energy security, presidential foreign policy advisory systems, bureaucratic politics, and group decision-making dynamics. She is the author of three books *China and the Energy Equation in Asia: Determinants of Policy Choice* (Boulder, CO: First Forum Press, a Division of Lynne Rienner Publishers, 2009), *Making China Policy: Nixon to G.W. Bush* (Boulder, CO: Lynne Rienner Publishers, 2005) and *Games Advisors Play: Foreign Policy in the Nixon and Carter Administrations* (College Station, TX: Texas A&M University Press, 1999), and numerous articles in journals such as *Asia Policy, Asian Affairs: An American Review, Asian Perspective, International Studies Review, Foreign Policy Analysis,* and *Political Psychology.* During 2004, Jean received a prestigious Council on Foreign Relations International Affairs Fellowship and served in the Office of Chinese and Mongolian Affairs with the U.S. State Department's Bureau of East Asian and Pacific Affairs. In 2007–2008 she spent a sabbatical leave, in part, as a visiting fellow at The Maureen and Mike Mansfield Foundation in Washington, D.C. completing her book manuscript focusing on China's quest for energy security in Asia. Her future work will focus more specifically on climate change as an energy security issue. Her areas of teaching include American foreign relations, U.S.-China relations, Energy Security, and Comparative Foreign Policy.

Gregory Gleason is a Professor of Political Science and Public Administration at the University of New Mexico. He leads seminars on security studies at the George C. Marshall European Center for Security Studies in Garmisch, Germany. Gleason is currently on leave from the University of New Mexico, where he has taught international relations since joining the university in 1988. Prior to that Gleason taught at the State University of New York at New Paltz and the University of Miami in Coral Gables, Florida. Gleason's academic work has focused on international relations in former communist countries. He is the author of Federalism *and Nationalism: the Struggle for Republican Rights in the USSR* (1991), *Central Asian States: Discovering Independence* (1997), and *Markets and Politics in Central Asia* (2003) as well as scholarly articles in *Asian Perspective, Communist and Post-Communist Studies, Europe-Asia Studies, International Studies Perspectives, Problems of Post-Communism*, and other journals. Gleason has served as a consultant to Lawrence Livermore National Laboratory, Sandia National Laboratories, the Asian Development Bank, and the U.S. Agency for International Development.

Gleason's research has been sponsored by the National Science Foundation and the National Academy of Sciences as well as other public and private foundations. Gregory Gleason completed his Ph.D in 1984 at the University of California (Davis) on the subject of cotton production in the USSR.

Lui Hebron is currently Assistant Professor of Global Studies and Maritime Affairs. Professor Hebron holds a Doctorate in Political Science from Florida State University, a Master's in International Affairs from American University, and a Bachelor's in Political Science from the University of Florida. Prior to joining the faculty at Cal Maritime, he has taught at Eastern Washington University, Florida International University and Iowa State University. In addition, Dr. Hebron was the Director of the International Affairs Program at Eastern Washington University and Associate Director of Gordon Institute for Public Policy at Florida International University. Professor Hebron teaches courses in Comparative Politics (Asia and China), International Relations (Globalization, International Political Economy and U.S. Foreign Policy), and Methods (Research and Design). His research focuses on the areas of political economy (Globalization), international relations (ethnicity, conflict, and war), and Asian studies (Pacific Rim and China). Dr. Hebron's publications include *Globalization: Debunking the Myths*, Prentice-Hall, 2009 co-authored with John Stack; *The Ethnic Entanglement*, Praeger Publishers, 1999 co-edited with John Stack. His current book-project, *Globalization and China: Political Economy's Odd-Couple* is under contract with CQ Press and is scheduled for a 2010 release date. Dr. Hebron has also published several chapters in edited volumes as well as numerous journal articles.

Gregg B. Johnson is currently an Assistant Professor of Political Science at Valparaiso University. Professor Johnson holds a Doctorate in Political Science from the University of Arizona, and a Bachelor's in Political Science and Spanish from the University of Michigan. He teaches course in Comparative Politics focusing on Latin American Politics, Political Parties, Political Institutions, and Political Economy. Professor Johnson's research focuses on the political economy of economic reform, executive-legislative relations, legislative politics in both Latin America and the United States, and the intersection of public opinion and political institutions. His research has appeared in journals such as the *American Journal of Political Science*, the *Journal of Politics in Latin America*, *American Politics Research*, the *Journal of Legislative Studies*, as well as in edited volumes in both the United States and Latin America.

Jesse T. Wasson is currently a Political Science doctoral candidate at the State University of New York at Buffalo. His dissertation is entitled, "Political Institutions, Veto Players, and Intra-industry Variation in Protection: Explaining Tariff Rates and Policy Change in Developed Democracies." Mr. Wasson's research interests straddle comparative and international political economy, including topics such as trade policy and the impact of resource scarcity on interstate conflict. His research has appeared in *American Politics Research.*

Jian Yang is a Senior Lecturer in International Relations at the University of Auckland. He received his BA and first MA from Chinese universities and his second MA and PhD in International Relations from the Australian National University (ANU). Yang is Chair of the Auckland Branch of the New Zealand Institute of International Affairs, a member of the New Zealand National Council of CSCAP (Council for Security Cooperation in the Asia-Pacific) and an Associate Editor of *The Journal of Human Security.* He teaches *International Relations in Asia Pacific, Politics of Northeast Asia, International Relations Theory, Great Power Relations,* and *China and the World.* His research focuses on China's foreign relations, foreign policy making, Asian security, environmental politics, human security, and Chinese politics. He has published extensively on China's foreign relations, particularly its relations with other great powers and various Asian countries. He is the author of *Congress and US China Policy: 1989–1999* (2000). He has also published a number of articles in various journals, including *Pacific Affairs* (China's FTA strategy), *Pacific Review* (China in the South Pacific), *China: An International Journal* (Sino-Japanese relations), *Contemporary Southeast Asia* (The impact of Sino-Japanese relations on Southeast Asia), *Journal of Human Security* (China's environmental politics) and, *Political Science* (Congress and China's MFN status). One of his most recent book chapters is "The Rise of China: Chinese perspectives," the lead chapter in *The Rise of China and International Security* (London; New York: Routledge, 2009). He is currently doing research on China's involvement in the South Pacific.

Zhao Hong is visiting senior research fellow at East Asian Institute, National University of Singapore. He obtained his Bachelor of Economics from the University of International Business and Economics, Master of Economics and Ph.D. from Xiamen University, China. His publications have appeared in international journals such as *The Journal of East Asian Affairs, The Copenhagen Journal of Asian Studies, East Asia: An International Quarterly, Contemporary Southeast Asian Studies.* His current research interests include the political economy of China and Southeast Asian countries, Asian economic community, China and India's energy strategies.

Charles E. Ziegler is Professor and University Scholar in the Political Science Department at the University of Louisville. He is founder and Director of the Institute for Democracy and Development, and founder and administrator of the Center for Asian Democracy. A specialist on Russia and Eurasia, Ziegler is co-editor (with Judith Thornton) of *The Russian Far East: A Region at Risk* (University of Washington Press, 2002), and author of *The History of Russia* (Greenwood Press, 1999), *Foreign Policy and East Asia* (Cambridge University Press, 1993), and *Environmental Policy in the USSR* (University of Massachusetts Press, 1987). In addition, he has written over fifty book chapters and articles for such professional journals as *Comparative Politics, Political Science Quarterly, British Journal of Political Science, Problems of Post-Communism, International Politics,* and *Pacific Review.* Ziegler has held an International Research and Exchanges Board Advanced Individual Research Opportunity grant, a Senior Fulbright Fellowship to Korea, an International Affairs Fellowship of the Council on Foreign Relations, and the Hoover Institution National Fellowship. He currently serves as Executive Director of the Louisville Committee on Foreign Relations. Recent papers include "Russia and China in Central Asia," forthcoming *Sino-Russian Relations in the Early 21st Century*; "Russia and the CIS in Asia: Axis of Authoritarianism?" Asian Survey (January/February 2009); "Competing for Markets and Influence: Asian National Oil Companies in Eurasia," *Asian Perspective* (Spring 2008); "Russia and the CIS in Asia: Putin's Final Year," *Asian Survey* (January/February 2008). He is Project Director for a State Department funded program on building civil society in Kazakhstan, and a consultant to the Ph.D. program at Eurasian National University in Astana. Ziegler received his Ph.D. from the University of Illinois.

Acknowledgments

The idea for this volume evolved out of a series of panels the editors organized on China's energy relations for the International Studies Association. We are grateful to our contributors for their prompt responses to our deadlines and their cooperation and patience. We would especially like to thank Continuum's political science acquisition editor Marie Claire Antoine for her stewardship of our book project from beginning to end, and Muralidharan and his team of editors for their fine work in finalizing and seeing the manuscript through publication. We would also like to thank the following individuals for all of their assistance and support at various stages of this project: Jaime Flores, Margaret Allyson, Tammy Harding, Darla Scroggins, and our current and former students at Texas Christian University. While we take full responsibility for any errors of facts or any shortcomings, the credit should go to our contributors for any merit that the present volume may have.

PART I

Theoretical and Historical Overview

CHAPTER ONE

The Strategic Implications of China's Energy Engagement with the Developing World

Carrie Liu Currier and Manochehr Dorraj

Introduction

Communist China's preoccupation with ideological concerns such as exporting socialism, supporting radical regimes, isolating Taiwan and combating US "hegemony" and Soviet "revisionism" during the 1950s through the 1970s, has now been replaced with the primacy of enhancing China's economic interests. Indeed, the issues that inform China's foreign policy are multi-pronged. Since China embraced marketization reforms in 1978, the situation has become even more complex with increasing domestic pressures placed on the communist regime to continue the path of economic growth and enhance the status and importance of China globally. China is simply interested in becoming fully integrated in the ascendant institutions of the global economy and global governance, and it aspires to be regarded as a responsible stakeholder by the global community. These goals are intricately tied to the continued growth and development of the Chinese economy, which is also necessary to provide legitimacy and stability to the communist regime. Thus, the economic rise of China has become one of the most carefully watched developments in recent years. However, scholars differ considerably on their assessments of China's future path—with assessments ranging from a "coming collapse" or sounding an alarm over the "rise of China." In spite of these differences, what remains clear is that the development of the Chinese economy has significant implications on domestic stability, its foreign policy, and the rise of China as a global power.[1] Furthermore, positive outcomes in these areas are contingent upon the continued success of its reform and opening policies.

Over the past three decades China has employed its diplomacy rather effectively to support these aforementioned economic goals and maintain a sense of national and economic security. Its permanent seat on the Security Council of the United Nations is just one of the high visibility positions China has used to assert greater influence in the international system. In the UN and other institutions, China has become the self-proclaimed champion of the developing world, using its position and its economic prominence to give a voice to less-developed states in institutions that are largely dominated by Western interests. In addition, China has created new institutions like the Shanghai Cooperation Organization, it has offered notable humanitarian assistance in the underserved areas of Africa, and it has engaged in trade and infrastructure development in countries that are largely ignored by Western powers. For most of the developing world, China enters the scene without the history of colonial domination Western powers have, and offers a foreign policy outlook that embraces multilateralism over hegemony and maintains respect for sovereignty and non-intervention. Thus it emerges with a relatively clean political slate, while offering much needed economic assistance. For those states cast aside by the United States, it serves as a strategic ally, and for most states of the developing world it serves as a valuable model.[2] Therefore, China's relationships with the developing world are among some of the most important in the world today and are watched closely by some of the established powers like the United States.

In recent years, the United States has begun to experience challenges to its status as a hegemon, with a weakening of the dollar, a troubled domestic economy, and loss of political capital as a result of its military involvements in Iraq and Afghanistan. For these reasons China's rise brings a great deal of concern to the United States, and the fear is China's relatively clean slate and economic prosperity will enable it to fill a political vacuum in the wake of declining US influence throughout many parts of the world.

Although some would argue military modernization is of greatest concern when examining the dangers China poses to the international system, there is little disagreement China will not pose a real military threat to the United Sates for some time.[3] The Chinese simply cannot keep pace with the sophisticated technology and the enormous defense budget of the United States, approved at over $700 billion USD in FY2010. Thus, militarily the China threat is more of a long-term fear than a short-term reality.

However, one issue of great concern both in terms of domestic and international security is energy. By all accounts China's pursuit of energy is scrutinized by many states, but it has significant implications specifically on the United States.[4] As a result of the global recession, major producer states like Saudi Arabia exported more oil to China than to the United States, representing a "fundamental shift in the geopolitics of oil" with China becoming the fastest-growing oil market in the world.[5] The increase in demand by China and other rapidly developing countries will not only affect global energy prices, but also cause further strains on already scarce resources. For the United States, this may lead to higher prices for consumers in an already wounded domestic economy struggling with a weakened dollar. For the Chinese, the United States' recession combined with China's current state of economic prosperity presents opportunities for them to fill an economic void in global energy markets.

As prosperity continues to trickle down throughout China, it is clear global energy markets will feel increasing pressures from growth in domestic demand. However, global energy markets largely dominated by US and Western investments are difficult to break into for a relative newcomer like China. Therefore, the combination of US-related factors and Chinese growth is enough to create a situation ideal for Chinese expansion. In addition the developing world, home to many newly discovered energy reserves, represents a unique opportunity for China, given their need for outside investors in the exploration and development of their energy resources. The intersection of these factors is the focus of this book, which seeks to understand and explain the strategic implications of China's energy engagement with the developing world.

In this book, we explore all of the aforementioned issues related to China's pursuit of energy security and how they structure China's relationship with other states. The chapters contained in this edited volume analyze China's expanding energy relations with the regions of the Middle East, Central Asia, Russia, Africa, Latin America, and other Asian states, with an emphasis on China's relations with the developing world. The strategic ramifications of China's quest for energy security, its expanding influence in the developing world, and its impact on China's relations with the United States and other great powers are examined in each of the regional chapters. The goal is to examine the historical development of China's relationship with key states in the region, determine the types of energy contracts or cooperative agreements that exist, and to examine trends for the future. Additionally, special consideration is given to the role the United States has in shaping the relationship between China and states in each of the regions. The result is a comprehensive evaluation of China's energy relations with the developing world and an analysis of the changing world order in light of the emerging Sino-US energy rivalry.

China's Expanding Energy Demands

As Ziegler suggests in the concluding chapter of this book, China is currently at a crossroads between the developing and developed worlds. This unique position presents it with many opportunities and can also make it appear threatening with respect to how it engages the rest of the world. Much of this perceived threat can be attributed to China's economic modernization, with many states fearing China's expanding economic appetite will lead to the depletion of resources (both renewable and non-renewable). In addition, many states fear the Chinese will simply overtake the global economy with their cheaper goods, their expanding investments abroad, and their seemingly endless supply of Yuan. Its rapidly growing economy and its success in weathering global economic crises (the 1997 Asian Financial Crisis as well as the current crisis associated with the weakening US dollar and global recession) have led many to wonder, what will happen if China continues on this current path? What does China's economic rise mean to the rest of the world? And can China's economic development be sustained? These questions are largely dependent on how the Chinese Communist Party (CCP) manages the economy and how successful China is in expanding its economic reach without threatening the rest of the world. One of the biggest pieces of this equation is the quest for energy security, which is largely driven by its desire to meet the needs of its domestic population and to secure resources for its continued economic development.

Examining the Chinese economy over the past thirty years shows just how rapidly China has begun to develop and what this means for energy markets. In 1980, China's Gross Domestic Product (GDP) was a mere $775 USD per capita. By 2010 this amount had reached $6,500. Compared to the 1980s the Chinese economy has experienced a 30 percent expansion, and no other industrial nation in the world can match this impressive rate of growth.[6] China's trade volume overtook Japan in 2005 and it is projected to surpass Germany and Japan as the second largest economies in the world by 2022.[7] Some analysts project that with the present annual rate of growth of approximately 10 percent, by 2010, China's GDP may even overtake that of the United States.[8] These estimates demonstrate China's expansion of its industrial base, manufacturing, construction, and transportation, all byproducts of the economic growth discussed above, have increased the demand for energy exponentially.

China's domestic oil and gas reserves (respectively, 2 percent and 1 percent of the world total reserves) sufficiently provided for the domestic energy consumption up until 1994. At this time, China became an oil importer, and its economic growth brought rapid increases in energy consumption. From 1994 to 2005, China went from being self-sufficient to dependent on imports for one-third of its total consumption. Domestic production was quickly outpaced by more than 8 percent growth averaged by the economy, with no slowdown in sight. In 2000, consumption was 4.8 million barrels a day, by 2009 it had reached 8.5 million barrels a day, and in the next two years demand is expected to grow by 900,000 barrels a day.[9] By 2003, energy shortages in China "forced authorities to ration power in key industrial areas, and Beijing abruptly halted exports."[10] And by 2004, China managed to surpass Japan as the world's number two oil importer.[11] Thus demand has already outpaced supply and is a growing concern for China's continued economic development.

The increase in demand is a product of China's economic growth. This unprecedented growth of the Chinese economy over the last thirty years has created a middle class and a class of *rich nouveau* who clamor for the amenities of modern life, most significant among them, private housing and automobiles. With more than one-third of its population now living in urban areas, and holding industrial, manufacturing and service jobs, private housing has witnessed increasing popularity. This in turn has ushered in a higher demand for appliances that are reliant on electricity and gas and other facilities that increase energy consumption. Despite its impressive production capabilities, China has not been able to keep pace with these increasing demands for electricity. For example, the overall electricity-generating capacity of China was estimated to be 510.2 KW in 2005. By 2006, the demand for electricity expanded by almost 16 percent to approximately 602.8 KW.[12]

Another part of increasing demand is China's tremendous growth in its automobile industry. Car sales in 2004 for example, were about 5 million, making China the largest market after the United States and Japan.[13] In early 2006 this number reached 11.5 million, and by early 2007 China was estimated to have 23 million cars.[14] China's automobile market is the second largest in the world and according to some estimates, China could have as many as 130 million automobiles by the year 2030.[15] The Chinese are buying cars at a rate of 19 percent a year and are expected to have more cars than the United States by the year 2030.[16] Cities like Beijing have experienced rapid booms in car ownership, with estimates increasing from 1 million cars in 1997, to 2 million in 2003, and 3 million by 2007.[17] These increases present long-term challenges to China's energy consumption and infrastructure more generally.

Another source of Chinese increasing demand for oil and gas is due to the fact that until recently coal has been responsible for two-thirds of the energy supply. But with the escalating levels of pollution in major Chinese cities induced by the burning of coal, China has come under increasing pressure internationally and domestically to reduce its emissions of carbon dioxide and sulfur dioxide in the atmosphere. According to *The New York Times*, "the increase in global-warming gases from China's coal use will probably exceed that of all industrialized countries combined over the next five years, surpassing by five times the reduction in such emissions that the Kyoto Protocol seeks."[18] Indeed, the current distinction of China as the second leading pollutant after the United States in the world has accentuated the political pressure on the Chinese government to look for alternatives to their massive reliance on coal as the major source of energy. These developments partially explain China's search for the long-term supply of oil and gas sources that generate much less carbon monoxide compared to coal.[19]

These changes have increased China's demand for energy substantially. From 1993 to 2002, China's demand for oil grew close to 90 percent while the domestic production grew at less than 15 percent. By 2004, Chinese demand for oil increased to 6 million barrels per day. According to the US Department of Energy, from 2001–2005, China alone has been responsible for a 40 percent of global growth demand for oil.[20]

China's continued economic development and quest for energy has implications on how other states perceive the rise of China. China's automobile market is expanding, its population is demanding more amenities, and its overall consumption patterns appear to be unsustainable given domestic resource constraints. These factors suggest China's development will be of concern to both developed and developing states for some time, as they view China as either an ally or a strategic competitor. How China engages those states and tries to alleviate their fears is one of the biggest challenges facing the regime today.

Theoretical Framework

China scholars have long debated the question of whether China is a status quo or a revisionist power, particularly as it finds itself increasingly at odds with US interests in the international realm. As China continues to develop economically, analysts speculate on the likelihood that China will emerge as a revisionist power and a serious challenger to US hegemony. The expectation is that an economically more powerful China will succumb to the structural realities of the system and seek to change the balance of power in its favor. In many respects this question is limiting since it forces one to generalize Chinese foreign policy behavior into a single categorization without adequately considering the contextual factors that may lead it to pursue different policies depending on the time and the actors involved. Those claiming it is revisionist underestimate the importance China has placed on becoming a responsible international stakeholder as it joins more international organizations. Furthermore, such depiction also ignores China's foreign policy behavior and rhetoric—advocating non-intervention and valuing the principles of sovereignty—all of which suggest that in fact China is more of a status quo rather than a revisionist power. However, a closer examination reveals a more nuanced picture, illuminating how the Chinese clearly adapt to the changing international climate in order to uphold their status as an international stakeholder and have pursued policies that are consistent with international norms and their social interactions with other states while pursuing their national interest. Examining China's relationships with the developing world, China has a clear interest in furthering relations on the basis of its energy needs, but its ties are also complicated by the US's current interests and exploits in the various regions. While China may claim to be a status quo power, others, most notably the United States, will perceive the rise of China as a threat to their own power or to the stability of the international system.

Some scholars contend that China will not be content until it establishes itself as a hegemon, and in the meantime it will continue to boost its military capabilities, work on economic growth, and seek strategic alliances with states to balance the United States' power. Moreover, China would behave in a way that indicates it is not satisfied with the rules of the current international system and will attempt to change them to ones that are more favorable to its own interests. Other scholars contend, "rising power leads to a growing geopolitical appetite and a likely change towards revisionism."[21] This revisionism is dangerous as it will likely lead to conflict with other states, such as the United States. So far as China's role and relationships with states in the developing world is concerned, some scholars see China's efforts to reach out to certain states as an attempt to balance against US interests in the region. China's pursuit of stronger relationships with oil-rich states like Iran, Saudi Arabia, Venezuela, Sudan, and Kazakhstan is indicative of its concerns about securing energy resources to fuel its rise as a regional and global power. It also presents those states with an alternative to the United States, particularly at a time when the United States' image in the developing world is suffering as a result of the ongoing wars in Afghanistan and Iraq. However, China has not pursued these relationships in ways that run counter to international norms nor has it served as an obstacle to the United States' interests, a point we will return to in the second section of the book as we examine China's energy connections in more detail with the various regions.

As China continues to develop and its energy needs expand, geo-economic interests will be a priority, thus better relations with oil-rich states in many parts of the world will be important. Moreover, the economic benefits China sees in each region extend beyond just oil and gas to also include trade in other commodities and the migration of Chinese laborers. However, in spite of the fact that China is seeking a stronger economic presence in much of the developing world, it has also modified its relationships with several states in response to US pressure. This can be seen in China's willingness to support three sets of US-sponsored UN sanctions against Iran for its nuclear program, its diplomatic efforts in Sudan to quell human rights criticisms just prior to the Olympics, and even holding back on developing its relationship with Venezuela to avoid further alienating the United States. In each case China has been willing to sacrifice certain economic and energy interests in an effort to maintain its more significant relationship with the United States.

In each of the chapters the contributors examine the role of these geo-economic interests and how norms, tied to China's increasing role in the global community, have encouraged Chinese foreign policy to be flexible in the different regions and avoid serious entanglements or conflicts with other global powers. A closer examination of some of these individual relationships will demonstrate how China has responded to pressures by the United States as well as the international community, modifying its foreign policy behavior in ways that are still consistent with its overall goals to never seek hegemony, uphold principles of sovereignty, engage in peaceful development, and to be a responsible stakeholder in the international system.

To illustrate these issues, the chapters of this volume are divided into three sections, Theoretical and Historical Overview, Regional Case Studies, and Challenges for the Future. In these sections the authors examine China's relationships with key states within the region, examining both the historical relationship and how it has evolved particularly in the reform era (post-1978). Each of the regional chapters examine the areas of concern in the contemporary relationships and how relations differ among states within the region, as well as outlining some of the key similarities across states. They also examine the various energy contracts and cooperative agreements that have been established and identify important trends that are emerging, with special attention to how energy relates to economic relations in general with the region. Finally, the authors address the role that the United States and other industrialized states play in China's energy relations with the developing world. An analysis of this relationship would not be complete without considering how China situates itself in light of the evolving structure of the international system and how other states try to respond to the changing global dynamics.

Historical Overview

In the first section of the book, the authors provide an overview of the two issues at the core of the book—China's relationship with the developing world and the domestic and international factors driving China's quest for energy security. In the chapter by Lui Hebron (Chapter Two), he examines the evolution of China's "grand strategy," and the interplay between both opportunities and constraints at the domestic and international levels as it relates to the developing world. He offers a historical overview of Chinese foreign policy, to show how it has evolved. More specifically he outlines three shifts in China's international relations toward the developing world. First is the rejection of foreign influences and subjugation that is associated with the "century of shame and humiliation," characterizing pre-1949 China and shaping Mao's foreign policy outlook. Second, is the post-reform era thinking of Deng Xiaoping, encouraging marketization and more economic openness that had China moving away from its more isolationist policies and allowing economic interests to serve as a catalyst for greater involvement in the global order. Finally, the post-Cold War era represents new challenges and opportunities in Chinese foreign policy, where China was thrust into a leadership position both regionally and internationally. This development has set the stage for more competitive relationships with the United States, Russia, the European Union, and its Asian neighbors. However the different periods have some significant shifts in terms of which issues were more pressing, given China's goals. It is clear that in spite of some of these changes, China's grand strategy has largely focused on improving its global position and demonstrating it can be a model or voice for the developing world.

With the historical and theoretical background to foreign policy laid out by Hebron, Jean A. Garrison's chapter (Chapter Three) analyzes the various domestic debates surrounding China's quest for energy security. Garrison argues that the fundamental challenge for China is that its search for energy resources still does not adequately secure its current and future energy needs. Her chapter examines some of the national security debates over energy shortages, addressing such issues as: domestic consumption practices, clean energy, and sustainable development. Some of the key areas of concern are moving away from energy-intensive industries, the expanding transportation sector, and the pressures they place on energy demand. Each represents dilemmas many emerging economies face; however, the situation is made more complex in the Chinese context given the structure of the central government and the challenges it creates for coordination among bureaucracies and to policy implementation. Moreover, she suggests neoliberal perspectives better explain China's quest for energy security, rather than assuming its development represents a zero-sum game for all other actors. When the United States, Western states, and other emerging powers may only be viewing China as a competitor for scarce resources, they miss out on opportunities for collaboration and enhanced global energy sustainability. Therefore, her detailed analysis of the domestic realm offers insight into how energy security is conceived, and suggests that China represents less of a threat than states are willing to currently accept. These two chapters thus offer the contextual framework needed to study and understand China's foreign relations within the various regions in terms of the evolution of China's overall strategy toward the developing world, its energy demands, and the quest to secure energy resources.

Regional Case Studies

The five chapters in this second section address China's relationship with developing states in the Middle East, Central Asia, Africa, Latin America, and Asia. Within these regions, the role of key competitors like the United States, Russia, Japan, and the European Union are also examined as relevant. Beginning with the Middle East, the chapter by Manochehr Dorraj and Carrie Liu Currier (Chapter Four) examines the strategic implications of China's relationship with states such as Iran and Saudi Arabia, the two largest energy producers in the region. These relationships are complicated by the United States, which has strong ties to Saudi Arabia and has worked hard to isolate Iran given its recent nuclear pursuits. At times this places China in direct competition with US interests, and has placed the PRC in a difficult position in terms of trying to pursue its own domestic and foreign policy objectives without intervention or pressure from the United States. Their chapter examines precisely how China has adjusted its policy in the region according to its strategic interests and the changing global environment, with the decline of US political capital in the region related to the ongoing wars in Iraq and Afghanistan.

In Chapter Five, Gregory Gleason examines the triangular relationship among China, Russia, and the Central Asian countries. His chapter discusses the conflicting and complementary stakes between China and Russia in consuming, transporting, processing, and marketing Caspian energy resources. Particularly since newly accessible oil and gas reserves in Azerbaijan, Kazakhstan, Turkmenistan, and Uzbekistan involve shipments through third-party countries before reaching the market. Chapter Six by Zhao Hong assesses China's expanding ties with Africa, including initiatives taken by Chinese companies to develop the oil industry. China's investment in Africa has been the subject of much international scrutiny as of late, particularly its relationship with Sudan. In spite of its expanding economic presence in Africa, China is still a relative newcomer to the oil industry in the region, where many Western companies are already well established. Thus China's entrance into the market is often mistaken to be of the "zero-sum competitor" mentality rather than seen as an opportunity by the United States, as discussed in Garrison's chapter. However, Zhao shows that China's expansion into Africa does not pose a real threat to Western companies or Western interests. Its ties to "rogue" regimes are not unconditional or made recklessly and China's pursuit of economic relations in the region are part of its long-term goals of securing energy, and serving as an economic partner to and assisting in the development of the world's most underdeveloped states.

Latin America represents yet another region where China's expanding influence has garnered international attention, especially in its relationship with Venezuela. In Chapter Seven, Gregg Johnson and Jesse Wasson assess China's perception as a direct energy competitor to the United States in the Americas. Their chapter deconstructs the debate surrounding the expansion of Chinese energy companies in Latin America and argues that the size and scope of China's agreements with many Latin American countries are actually quite limited. The largest challenges are the technical demands of extracting energy resources in the region, given the costs of transportation and the distance to Asia, the limits to foreign investment in most Latin American states, and the region's politics. The combination of these issues also supports the point that currently China is not a strategic competitor to the United States in the region, and its increasing presence is consistent with its grand strategies of expanding ties to developing countries and trying to diversify its access to markets.

The final regional chapter by Jian Yang (Chapter Eight), assesses China's competition for resources with two other Asian powers—Japan and India. The oil and gas resources in the East China Sea are of increasing interest to many Asian states, and it is an area where the two largest oil importers, China and Japan, find themselves in direct competition. In contrast, the

Sino-Indian energy relationship is more promising in terms of the potential for cooperation. India has already cooperated with China in a number of oil and gas projects in countries like Kazakhstan, Sudan, Syria, and Iran. In both of these cases China's strategy is consistent with what we see in other regions—China's pursuit of energy is extremely important and it is willing to put aside some of its historical tensions with these states to facilitate a greater sense of energy security.

Challenges for the Future

In the final section of the book, the contributors bring us back to the themes addressed in the beginning of the book—what will it take for China to secure energy resources and how does it affect the position of China with respect to the rest of the world. In Chapter Nine, Andrew Erickson and Gabriel Collins examine not just the quest to secure energy resources, but also China's efforts to diversify its sources. In recent years, China has been increasingly concerned about the transit of oil through the Strait of Malacca, the main point of sea transit for oil resources to all of Asia. Fears over vulnerability to seaborne energy interdiction and susceptibility to foreign pressure have given China reason to pursue pipeline agreements with states in Central and South Asia. Erickson and Collins analyze some of the pros and cons to pipeline construction with Russia, Kazakhstan, Pakistan, and Burma, as well as determining what impact China's development of its maritime capabilities will have on its sense of energy security. In the end, they argue China must proceed with caution when trying to enhance its "security," a concept that brings both economic and military pursuits to mind, since their strategies to enhance economic security are easily perceived by other states as threatening and masking a latent desire to become a hegemon. As we have seen in earlier chapters, this fear of a more powerful and rising China is one that the PRC continually faces, and it's in neither side's interest for a modern-day security dilemma to arise between the United States and China.

Bringing all of these themes together, the chapter by Charles Ziegler (Chapter Ten) assesses what China's quest for energy security will mean to the international system and the potential for great power realignment. This concluding chapter discusses how China is at a crossroads of development and re-examines China's motives for engaging states in the different regions. As the individual regional chapters have demonstrated, China's increasing presence in the developing world is not a reason for alarm by the United States and other great powers. China's grand strategy is primarily concerned with guaranteeing the continued growth and development of its economy. Moreover, China is interested in becoming a responsible stakeholder and a valued member of the international community. It is not seeking to create a revisionist world order which aims for Chinese hegemony. Only by understanding the domestic factors motivating Chinese foreign policy and taking a historical look at China's policy with the developing world can fears about the rise of China, particularly as it relates to a zero-sum game, be re-evaluated.

As this volume will demonstrate, in many ways the idea of energy security is a myth. There is no real security in the pursuit of energy resources nor in the diversification of those sources. It's a constant quest. China is undertaking this quest while trying to balance a variety of domestic and foreign policy goals, all of which are designed to fuel its continued economic prosperity. The future of China's energy security and its relations with the developing world is still somewhat uncertain, and a lot depends on how other states will respond to a rising China. Those that see it only as a competitor, like the United States, are missing important opportunities to engage China as a strategic partner and to reap the long-term economic and environmental benefits by engaging in more cooperative endeavors. Those that are willing to embrace China's increasing interest and investment in the developing world do so with caution, but are the beneficiary of some of the economic and diplomatic rewards that come from having the Chinese as an ally. A sober assessment of the relationships that China has cultivated in the developing world is important to how we understand both the global quest for energy as well as the possibilities for a changing world order. China may not be poising itself to be the new hegemon, but its rise is causing us to rethink the current power structures and the important role it would play in the developing world in general and the global energy markets in particular.

Notes

1. A. Goldstein (2005) *Rising to the Challenge: China's Grand Strategy and International Security* (Stanford, CA: Stanford University Press).
2. J. Eisenman, E. Heginbotham, and D. Mitchell , eds (2007) *China and the Developing World: Beijing's Strategy for the Twenty-First Century* (New York: M.E. Sharpe), pp. 3–25.
3. S. L. Shirk (2007) *China: Fragile Superpower* (New York: Oxford University Press), pp. 105–139.

4. M. T. Klare (2009) *Rising Powers: Shrinking Planet: The New Geopolitics of Energy* (New York: Macmillan). See also M. T. Klare (2001) *Resource Wars: The New Landscape of Global Conflict* (New York: Metropolitan).
5. J. Mouawad (2010) "China's Rapid Growth Shifts the Geopolitics of Oil," *New York Times*, March 20, 2010, pp. B1–B2.
6. *Energy Information Administration*, "China Country Analysis Brief," May, 2007. www.eia.doe.gov/emeu/cabs/China.html, accessed February 5, 2009.
7. "China and its Region: Reaching for a Renaissance," *The Economist*, March 29, 2007.
8. "A Less Fiery Dragon?" *The Economist*, November 29, 2007.
9. Mouawad, 2010, B2.
10. P. S. Goodman (2004) "Booming China Devouring Raw Materials," *The Washington Post*, May 21.
11. C. E. Zeigler "The Energy Factor in China's Foreign Policy," *Journal of Chinese Political Science*, Vol. 11, No. 1, Spring, 2006, pp. 1–4.
12. *Energy Information Administration*, May, 2007.
13. Zeigler, 2006, p.7.
14. *Energy Information Administration*, May 2007.
15. F. Leverett and J. Bader (2005–2006) "Managing China-U.S. Energy Competition in the Middle East," *The Washington Quarterly*, p. 189.
16. G. Luft, (2007) "Fueling the Dragon: China's Race into the Oil Market," *Institute for the Analysis of Global Security*. December 1. < http://www.iags.org/China.htm>.
17. Presentation by Max von Zedwitz (2009) "Innovation and Research/Development in China," January 29.
18. D. Barboza and K. Bradsher (2006) "Pollution from Chinese Coal Casts a Global Shadow," *New York Times*, June 11.
19. Zeigler, 2006.
20. Leverett and Bader (2005–2006), p. 190. See also F. Leverett and P. Noel (2006) "The New Axis of Oil," *The National Interest*, No. 84, Summer, p. 66.
21. J. W. Legro (2007) "What China Will Want: The Future Intentions of a Rising Power," *Perspectives on Politics* 5:3, 518.

CHAPTER TWO

The Evolution of China's Grand Strategy with the Developing World

Lui Hebron

China will always be a member of the developing world, and strengthening solidarity and cooperation with the other developing countries is the cornerstone of China's diplomacy.

—China President Hu Jintao 2005[1]

Introduction

In a little more than fifty years, China has transformed itself from a politically weak and economically backward country to a powerful and influential actor in regional relations and global affairs. Yet, despite its impressive domestic economic achievements and growing international political clout over the past half century, the People's Republic of China (PRC) continues to refer to itself as the "world's largest developing country."[2] Given the fact that in some academic and policy circles the PRC is already being viewed as the next superpower, Beijing's continuing self-portrait as a developing state seems rather odd, if not disingenuous, and raises some fundamental questions about the China's attraction to and kinship with the Global South: What does the Middle Kingdom[3] hope to gain by identifying itself as a Third World state? Why does the developing world have such a prominent role in China's foreign policy? What are the implications of China's grand strategy with the countries of Africa, Asia, Latin America, and the Middle East for international peace and stability?

This chapter provides a general overview of the changing nature and conditions of Chinese foreign policy making with the developing world since the founding of the modern Chinese state on October 1, 1949. A fundamental feature guiding the evolution of China's grand strategy is the inextricable interplay between opportunities and constraints (challenges and threats) at both domestic and international levels. Specifically, due to the complex interrelationship between Beijing's economic goals and strategic objectives on one side and its changing role in both the world economy and global balance of power on the other, we can differentiate three distinct policy epochs in China's foreign relations with developing states in the last half century: (1) an ideologically guided and strategically oriented program under Mao Zedong; (2) a shift toward a more pragmatic and economically centered directive under Deng Xiaoping; and (3) an economically based and strategically motivated course of action in the post-Cold War era.

Understanding China's grand strategic behavior (i.e., shifting patterns of interests in and policies toward the developing world) requires a comprehensive examination of the fundamental principles that inform and guide Beijing's policy makers on how they are to coordinate the country's competing strategic and economic considerations. By examining Beijing's effort to balance strategic goals and threats with the demands of its economic objectives and needs, this conceptually focused, historically based chapter offers the contextual framework with which to study China's foreign relations with the developing world and to assess what elements are most pertinent for understanding its policy making—particularly as the Middle Kingdom re-emerges as a major power.

Taking our cue from Michael Hunt's perspective that "[h]istory is essential and central, not optional and incidental, to an understanding of Chinese foreign policy,"[4] this study begins with a brief overview of China's external relations from the founding of the Middle Kingdom under the Qin Dynasty through the establishment of the PRC and Communist rule. The next three sections examine the evolution of Chinese foreign policy toward the developing world from the radical and revolutionary-tinged activism and interventionism of the Mao era, through the dramatic shift toward a more moderate, reasonable, and responsible country among the community of states under Deng's leadership, to the proactive, multipolar-centered and institutionally grounded rhetoric and behavior of the current post-Cold War period. The chapter concludes by addressing the future direction of China's Third World policy and the implications of Beijing's continuing engagement with the states of the Global South for international relations.

Imperial/Republican China: Hegemony, Isolation, Colonialization

A crucial factor shaping China's approach to international affairs and its foreign policy with developing states is the Middle Kingdom's historical experience with the outside world as well as Beijing's changing power and interests. China's Imperialistic past provides insight into Beijing's current foreign policy making and behavior. An examination, therefore, of Beijing's external relations and, specifically, its "memories" of China's foreign interactions throughout its history, allows us to put into context the elements (i.e., hopes and fears, opportunities and constraints) that are necessary for attaining a more textured and nuanced understanding of China's foreign policy rhetoric and behavior.

Beginning with the unification of the Chinese state by the Qin Emperor in 221 BC, the Middle Kingdom has been acknowledged to be one of the world's great civilizations. Some of China's more notable contributions to mankind include the civil service system, paper, the printing press, gunpowder, the compass, porcelain, cannons, the wheelbarrow, textile fiber, and the water clock just to name a few. In addition, Chinese scholarship in medicine, mathematics, and the sciences were many centuries ahead of European scholars. Without question these achievements, which were accomplished well ahead of the other great civilizations of the world, had a profound influence in both the orientation and execution of Chinese foreign policy making.

In its foreign relations, the Chinese Imperial Court instituted a Tribute System in which its weaker (inferior) neighboring states were required to pledge loyalty and obedience (including military service for the Emperor) to the Middle Kingdom in exchange for political recognition and protection from China. Indeed, owing to Chinese perception of its "cultural superiority," non-Han peoples were all considered to be "barbarians." The height of Chinese Imperial power was perhaps achieved during the Ming Dynasty when during the course of the seven expeditionary voyages by Admiral Zheng Hu Chinese ships made ports of calls in Southeast and South Asia, the Middle East and the Eastern coast of Africa, maybe even as far as the Cape of Good Hope.[5] China's abundant natural resources, combined with its economic power via its Eur-Asian overland trade, led the Imperial Court to believe that other countries had nothing of value to teach the Middle Kingdom, and that withdrawal from the political global stage would be Beijing's best course of action for maintaining its power and prestige.

To a large extent Chinese foreign policy was subordinate to domestic concerns, and dependent on China's internal situation. For Beijing, the more pressing danger and persistent threat to the Middle Kingdom's sovereignty and territorial integrity emanated primarily from internal sources—corruption, incompetence, palace intrigue—rather than from foreign powers. The fact that China has had sixteen dynasties[6] (fourteen of which were headed by Han peoples/tribes) since its founding is a manifestation of this internal threat, and the reason why Chinese leaders focused their attention and energies on internally generated dangers.[7] Interestingly, even when it was forced to submit to non-Han peoples, the Yuan (Mongol) Dynasty and Qing (Manchu) Dynasty, it was the foreign invaders who assimilated to Chinese (Han) civilization and culture rather than the other way around.

China's historical sense of its "cultural superiority" was shattered with the advent of the so-called "hundred years of humiliation," beginning with the Middle Kingdom's defeat at the hands of the British in the first Opium War (or the First Anglo-Chinese War) of 1839–1842 and lasting until Chiang Kai-shek's Kuomintang or Nationalist troops were driven out of the mainland to the island of Taiwan by Mao's Communists in the Civil War of 1946–1949. During this hundred-year span, the country endured the precipitous erosion of the Middle Kingdom's domestic sovereignty and territorial integrity (i.e., dismantling and colonization) to the British, Portuguese, Russians, and Japanese. From the traumatic memory of these darkest days of Chinese history the Communist Party vowed that it would never again allow China to become weak and vulnerable to foreign powers and threats that led to decades of humiliation, division, and war. When he proclaimed the founding of the PRC on October 1, 1949 at Gate of Heavenly Peace, Mao Zedong declared not only that "The Chinese people have stood up," but also that "No one will ever insult them again." In similar manner, Mao and the Communist Party set about enhancing the PRC's diplomatic influence, economic competitiveness, and military preparedness—basically those areas that define a country's power.

Projecting this brief historical overview of China's foreign relations to the current setting, we can extrapolate two core elements (one internal and one external) which transcend time and space that have conditioned Beijing's decision-making calculation and strategic behavior. And in so doing, we can derive the general principles that have guided Chinese foreign policy with the developing world since the founding of Communist China.

Domestically, the security (non-invasion and/or subjugation by a foreign power) of China's territory and the preservation of Chinese sovereignty (non-interference in internal affairs), and the continuation of Communist Party rule lies at the forefront of Beijing's calculation when formulating its foreign policy choices. Placed in this context, the Communist Party understands that the legitimacy of its power and authority to govern is contingent on the Party's ability to institute and maintain a stable political and social order, to acquire and augment a strong military, and to embark on a robust and prolonged period of economic development and growth.

On the global stage, the structure of the international order as well as China's relationship with the major superpowers are the key components that guide Beijing's international relations policy. The implications of these two components for China's foreign policy makers are two-fold: First, how China defines its interests and goals, and adjusts its strategy and tactics is strongly influenced and determined by the structure of the international order. If Beijing perceives the current order as advancing and/or complementing its goals, then the Communist Party will find neither reason nor need to challenge the prevailing arrangement. If, on the other hand, the Chinese leadership views the present structure as hindering and/or prohibiting China from reaching its objectives, then it can be expected that the Middle Kingdom will call for and work toward the restructuring of the existing system. Second, the Communist Party is mindful of the fact that the speed in which Beijing is able to return the Middle Kingdom to its place as a major power in regional and world politics depends to a certain degree on how friendly or hostile the United States, the Soviet Union/Russia, and/or other major powers are to China's rise. Will China's re-entry to the great power club be welcomed as a valuable addition for global governance or begrudgingly accepted as a *fait accompli?*

Since the relationship between these two contextual orientations shapes the formulation of Chinese foreign policy, they are critical for understanding China's relations with the developing world for each contributes to the general principles, if not core determinants and driving forces, that direct Chinese foreign policy makers. How China defines its national interest (the continuation of its internal sovereignty, the preservation of its territorial integrity, and maintenance of social stability in the domestic realm and the reinstatement of the Middle Kingdom's great power status on the international stage) has been stable and consistent. However, due to the changes in both the international system and with China itself, how Beijing tackles these goals and objectives has changed over time as evident by the variations in its declared policies and also its actual behavior. Moreover, the changing content and relative weight of these internal and external factors help to explain the direction and variation in Beijing's international relations. As we will see below, during the Mao, Deng, and post-Cold War eras we can clearly delineate how and why economic (at both the domestic and international levels) and strategic objectives have taken turns at being the primary force of Chinese foreign policy.[8]

Mao Era (1949–1976): Nationalism, Realism, Marxism-Leninism-Maoism

Learning from Beijing's previous error in withdrawing and isolating itself from international relations that eventually led to the Middle Kingdom's "century of humiliation," China's new Communist rulers took a more active and engaged role in foreign affairs. With the re-establishment of national independence in 1949, Chinese foreign policy under Mao Zedong was designed to achieve the Communist Party's fundamental strategic and economic goals of safeguarding the country's national security. The resulting policies revolved around two main goals—(1) to secure and strengthen the authority and legitimacy of the Communist Party, and (2) to enhance China's international status and position. The hallmarks of Chinese foreign policy under Mao included the rejection and revolutionary transformation of the bipolar order and its international organizations, hostility and partnership toward both superpowers, and close collaboration with the Third World.

In pursuit of its strategic and economic goals, Beijing's relationship with the United States and the Soviet Union shifted between the two superpowers. For most of the 1950s China followed a "leaning to one side" strategy in which the PRC closely aligned its economic development and foreign policy with that of the Soviet Union while taking a hostile orientation toward the United States. Initially, Mao had hoped to develop a good relationship with the United States, but was rebuffed by the Truman Administration who favored Chiang Kai-shek's Kuomintang regime and also did not have much confidence in the long-term prospects of the Communist Party. During this time period, US policies toward China can best be described as involving the use of political isolation, military threats, and economic blockades. To offset US attempts to isolate communists elsewhere, Beijing turned to the only other country that had the economic capacity to aid with China's nation-building and economic development.[9]

During the 1960s and the inauguration of the Sino-Soviet rift, China shifted to "the Double Anti"[10] or the Revolutionary Self-Reliance[11] strategy which entailed the "simultaneous pursuit of the anti-imperialism struggle against the US and the anti-revisionist struggle against the Soviet Union."[12] Under this orientation, China now viewed both superpowers with hostility. Already locked in an ideological war with the United States, by the end of the 1950s China broke away from the Soviet sphere of influence as it challenged Moscow for the leadership of the communist bloc and began to vie with the Kremlin for the hearts and mind of the Third World. As China's relationship with Asia, Africa, and Latin America became stronger, Beijing assumed a larger leadership role as an active partner of the neutral and non-aligned movement.

The nadir of Sino-Soviet relations occurred in March 1969 when their ideological and political split spread to include territorial issues and armed conflict broke out at Zhenbao/Demansky Island and quickly expanded along the Amur (Heilong) and Ussuri (Wusuli) rivers into Central Asia. This bloody clash which very nearly brought the two neighbors on the brink of an all-out war was also to some extent the culmination of centuries of Beijing's built-up frustration at Russian/Soviet illegal seizure of Chinese territory through a series of "unequal treaties" between 1700 and 1900. Fortunately, a meeting between Chinese Premier Zhou Enlai and Soviet Premier Aleksey Kosygin later that year in September prevented further military escalation.

Prompted by this latest Sino-Soviet border dispute, China once again switched its foreign policy orientation in the early 1970s. During this time period, the PRC's foreign relations operated under the "Theory of Three Worlds"[13] and practiced "Triangular Diplomacy."[14] According to Mao's Theory of the Three Worlds, the global order can be categorized as composed of three distinct power centers. Occupying the top echelon are the two imperialist states of the First World, the Soviet Union and United States, bent on global domination. At the other end of the spectrum are the developing countries of the Third World challenging superpower hegemony. Finally, the developed states of Europe plus Japan are the second-tiered countries of the Second World.[15]

Predicated on balance-of-power theory, the underlying mechanism of triangular diplomacy involved playing off one superpower against the other. From Beijing's perspective, the deepening Sino-Soviet split combined with the emergence of Sino-American rapprochement provided Mao with the opportunity to use the United States as a counterweight to the Soviet Union. Using these two theoretical orientations as its guide, Beijing normalized relations with the United States and ushered in the period of Sino-Soviet-American triangular diplomacy through the end of the Cold War. Viewing the Soviet Union as the greater threat to China's security, Beijing partnered with Washington in a policy of strategic cooperation to contain Moscow.

As for the Third World, inasmuch as China saw the United States as the head of the industrialized West, Beijing fancied itself as a leader among those in the developing world. Viewing the decolonization process as a major opportunity to appeal to newly independent states as prospective allies, Beijing embarked on a new phase in its external relations which at once centered on building and/or strengthening its relationship with developing states as well as seeking a more prominent and active leadership role among the Third World vis-a-vis the United States and the Soviet Union by challenging the bipolar hegemonic world order. In this regard, China's relationship with the United States and the Soviet Union can best be described as complex and contradictory, one that encompassed hostility, tension, and conflict as well as detente, friendship, and cooperation depending on the situation. For most of the 1950s and 1960s, therefore, Sino-American relations had a distinctly anti-American orientation which by the 1970s and 1980s had morphed into a pro-American perspective. Sino-Soviet relations had a similar pattern, though in reverse—adulation in the 1950s, rejection in the 1960's, and anti-Soviet throughout the 1970s and 1980s. Portraying itself as the "world's largest developing country" and repeatedly invoking the Middle Kingdom's similar historical (colonized) experience with the newly independent states of Asia, Africa, Latin America, and the Middle East, China spearheaded a policy agenda pushing for "anti-imperialist" solidarity among its fellow Third World states. By mobilizing the developing countries to take on a more independent international role, Beijing hoped to balance, if not break, the systemic domination of the two superpowers. By assuming a more pivotal role in the world-wide socialist revolution, China hoped to enhance its international stature as well as gain the Third World's endorsement for Beijing's "the Rest versus the West approach."[16]

Beijing's anti-colonial rhetoric translated into an ideological crusade and policy agenda that included both military aid in support of "national liberation" movements as well as diplomatic initiatives calling for greater economic cooperation among the members of the developing world.[17] In executing this policy orientation, Beijing was able to reconcile its strategic and economic agenda with the bipolar world order by positioning the PRC as the leading advocate of the Third World in its grievances against both the capitalist imperialism of the Western camp and the socialist hegemony of the Soviet bloc.

On the diplomatic front, Chinese foreign policy had a leading and ultimately substantial role in the creation of several significant initiatives and organizations in support of Third World interests and objectives. Specifically, the "Five Principles of Peaceful Coexistence"—mutual respect for territorial integrity and sovereignty, mutual non-aggression, non-interference in internal affairs, equality and mutual benefit, and peaceful co-existence—initially set forth by Premier Zhou Enlai has become widely accepted as norms for relations between countries. Originally expounded to guide Sino-Indian relations, the Five Principles eventually became an integral part of the 10-point Final Communique of the 1955 Bandung Conference in Indonesia.[18] Aimed at promoting Asian-African economic and cultural solidarity and opposition to colonialism (neocolonialism), an important outcome of the Conference was its articulation of the developing state's need to improve their relative position in the world economy by adopting a less dependent economic relationship with the developed, industrialized countries. China's significant influence and substantial contribution at the

Conference marked the PRC's newly acknowledged role as a major actor on the world stage among the nations of the Third World.

The success of the Bandung Conference, in turn, laid the foundation for the establishment of the Non-Aligned Movement (NAM) in 1961 in which Third World states jointly declared their intention to maintain a neutral and non-aligned position in the East-West conflict.[19] Furthermore, it can also be argued that the Five Principles, in particular its advocacy of "equality and mutual benefit," was an instrumental force that eventually culminated in the Third World's Declaration for the Establishment of a New International Economic Order (NIEO) in 1973.[20] Incorporating many of the proposals discussed at the United Nations Conference on Trade and Development (UNCTAD), the NIEO evolved into a set of propositions put forward by developing countries calling for a restructuring of the international economic system that sought greater participation from and benefits to Third World states.

Militarily, Beijing put into action Mao's "new democratic revolution" which aimed at overturning the developing world's condition of impoverishment and victimization as a consequence of Western and Japanese imperialism. Mao's strategy hinged on the notion that Beijing could forge these supposedly feeble states—the decolonizing nations in Asia, Africa, and Latin America—into a united and empowered revolutionary movement capable of reconstructing the international system to be more attuned with their interests and needs. Beijing's sponsorship of Third World radicalism and support for communist insurgent groups encompassed material assistance (economic aid) and military support (arms and military advisors) to radical regimes and guerrilla campaigns across the globe.

In the final analysis, Beijing's efforts and tactics to recruit and influence Third World regimes' policies and behavior to be more in alignment with China's interests and goals during the Mao years proved to be largely ineffective. Lacking the requisite instruments (generous economic assistance and advanced military armaments) normally extended to client states, Beijing did not have much leverage, and hence was not able to lead and/or remake the Third World into an alternative power center in international relations. Moreover, China's strategy was poorly executed (disorganized), and to a certain extent, contradictory, with many of its partner states openly questioning the veracity of Beijing's avowed support of the Five Principles of Peaceful Coexistence—particularly the non-interference in each other's internal affairs component—in light of the Communist Party's support of "national liberation struggles" directed at toppling those democratically elected Third World regimes allied with the Imperialist West.[21] Hence, by the end of the

Mao era, the glaring deficiencies in outcomes of China's revolutionary-driven foreign policy rhetoric and behavior in its external relations prompted the PRC to conduct a reassessment of its foreign policy orientation and instruments that resulted in a shift toward a less ideological and more pragmatic perspective and policy directive emanating from Beijing.

Deng Epoch (1978–1989): Internationalism, Liberalism, Globalization

The evolution of Chinese foreign policy from one that was ideologically oriented in the 1950s, 1960s, and 1970s to a more pragmatic approach in the 1980s and onward transpired over two phases. The first took place with the commencement of Deng Xiaoping's economic reforms in 1978 and the implementation of the "Four Modernization" strategy. This strategy included the modernization of agriculture, industry, national defense, and science and technology. The second began in the early 1990s and developed mainly in response to the newly established post-Cold War order. This section will examine Chinese foreign policy during the early Deng era while the next section will address China's relations with the developing world during the current post-Cold War order.

With the rise (rehabilitation) of Deng Xiaoping and his focus on building up the economy, China in the late 1970s and early 1980s enacted a new foreign policy course of action. Beijing abandoned the ideological and revolutionary directed components of its external relations and reset its foreign policy rhetoric and behavior toward a more pragmatic orientation. In so doing, Chinese foreign policy making shifted its objectives away from challenging the bipolar system and attempting to restructure the current world order and toward building mutually beneficial international relationships through diplomatic engagement and securing a peaceful global milieu via the support of international organizations. Under this framework, conflict and confrontation with the capitalist international economy were replaced with cooperation and accommodation in its relations with the two superpowers and the developed, industrialized world specifically, particularly in the issue-based areas of investment and trade.

The consequences of China's two-fold reorientation toward domestic development and integration into the global market had both political and economic implications for the developing world. Politically, Beijing tempered its collective action with Third World states. As Chinese foreign policy increasingly focused on establishing diplomatic, economic, and cultural relationships with the advanced industrialized West, Beijing became less and less interested in seeking alliances with other developing states aimed at the restructuring, if not overthrow, of the prevailing global structure. Indeed, as a result of its more constructivist approach, Beijing subsequently not only renounced its support of Third World revolutionary movements in favor of ironing out a separate working relationship with the global status quo and increasing its commitment to multilateral institution, but embraced much of the current world order's principles, rules, and norms for the conduct of international relations. As China increasingly focused its attention on fostering its connections with important economic partners, markets of the capitalist industrialized countries, and the ascendant institutions of the global economy (i.e., the World Bank and the International Monetary Fund), its relationship with the Third World became subordinated to joining these International Organizations.

Economically, Deng's "Four Modernization" strategy placed China as a direct competitor to other developing countries in their search for foreign investments, technological knowledge, management expertise, natural resources, as well as access to the developed world's markets. During this time period, China not only began accepting long-term foreign loans and portfolio investments, but it also became the primary destination for foreign direct investments, taking around 80 percent of total investment going to the developing world for the Asian region.[22] Moreover, despite promulgating the virtues of greater group action and collaboration among developing states, in reality most Third World states had little to offer China in terms of trade benefits and/or high-tech cooperation. As a result, China's economic development and growth prerogatives and its desire to become a major trading nation trumped Beijing's objective to maintain a united, collective front with the developing world.

Nevertheless, since China's foreign policy was now predominantly directed and judged by the progression of the PRC's economic development and growth, Beijing began to aggressively market Chinese manufactured products to many developing states. Furthermore, the Communist leadership had no inhibition in embarking on a military transfer and sale program of conventional armaments, nuclear knowledge, and missile technology that was desired by many Third World states such as Algeria, Pakistan, Iran, Iraq, Saudi Arabia, and Syria.

As the primary architect of the country's foreign policies from 1978 until the early 1990s, Deng discontinued China's support for national revolutionary movements in the Third World while enlarging the degree and range of its integration with the First World. Directed by China's drive for economic growth and development, Chinese foreign policy under Deng's stewardship exhibited a distinctively status quo orientation. In the beginning, rather than leading and exhorting Third World states to restructure the prevailing world order, China embraced the system. Furthermore, China established greater cooperation with the First World than with the Third World — indeed, Beijing became the developing world's largest competitor for the developed world's investments and trade.[23] Lastly, Beijing practiced a duplicitous policy of benign neglect of the Third World's efforts to challenge the First World on the one hand, and active engagement with individual developing states that can contribute to the PRC's economic growth and development on the other. Nevertheless, with the restructuring of the world order, came the now familiar reorientation of Chinese foreign policy toward the developing world.

Post-Cold War Order (1989–Present): Nationalism, Internationalism, Interdependence

The years between 1989 through 1991 marked a watershed period in Chinese foreign policy due to domestic disturbances and international events. The confluence of a dramatically restructured international order, the controversial resolution to the Tiananmen Square demonstrations, and the increasing demands to maintain the torrid pace of economic growth and development, all conspired to force Beijing to once again re-evaluate and fundamentally alter its strategies and objectives in its international relations. In both the domestic and international political realms, two dramatic events during both the late 1980s (the violent suppression of the student movement in June, and the fall of the Berlin Wall in November in 1989) and the early 1990s (the collapse of the bipolar world order, and the Persian Gulf War in 1991)—led once again to a drastic shift in Beijing's relationship with the developing world.

Domestically, the Tiananmen incident nearly toppled the Communist Party by exposing the deficiencies of the Market-Leninist system under which state-society relations operated. Heralded by Communist Party rulers as "building socialism with Chinese characteristics," this experiment in political, economic, and social engineering combines the iron fist political rule of Leninism with the wide-open economic hyper-permissiveness of free-market capitalism.[24] By 1989, the marriage between open laissez-faire free-market capitalism and a political system tightly controlled by the Communist Party Central Committee was not working. Despite ten years of economic reform, the benefits of the Chinese economy's growth and development were not being widely shared. Similar to the Imperial periods, the main problem lay with China's corrupt, opaque, and insufficiently accountable ruling regime. The Communist Party's response, however, was not a movement toward greater political liberalization and openness, but rather based its legitimacy and continued authority on its ability to make the benefits of China's phenomenal economic achievements more inclusive. This policy orientation, in turn, required China to become even more integrated into the global economy.

On the global stage, the combination of the widespread condemnation of Beijing's role in the Tiananmen Square massacre by the Western powers, and the unexpected lifting of the iron curtain resulting from the implosion of Communism led not only to Beijing's international political isolation, but also to the ascension of China as America's new primary antagonist and chief challenger to its hegemonic status in the post-Cold War world order. As a result of the Tiananmen Square massacre, the international perception of China's leadership literally transmuted from that of a dynamic, modernizing government to a pariah regime, one that spot-lighted the most brutal and horrific scenario of state-society conflict of non-democratic rule.[25]

Of further concern for Beijing was the glaring trend that despite its rapidly growing power and influence and continued integration into the world economy, China found that it did not have a seat at the table when it came to policy-making forums and organizations that deal with the major strategic and economic decisions that determine international relations. Hence, despite the fact that China was the world's third largest economy and had become one of the largest trading states, it was not invited to join the Group of Seven nor was it extended membership to the World Trade Organization. Additionally, despite having the world's third largest military, the decision to expand NATO was made without consulting Beijing. But perhaps even more troubling for China's military was that the Persian Gulf War demonstrated to Beijing and the rest of the world that the United States had developed overwhelming superiority in its conventional forces—in terms of military capability, America was second to none. Finding itself on the outside looking in, the Chinese government felt vulnerable in the face of the emerging economic and military realities of the global system.

As in previous occasions when China was confronted with the prospect of international isolation, and specifically in direct response to the diplomatic quarantine spearheaded by the United States resulting from the Tiananmen massacre, the Communist Party looked to the Global South for support. Specifically, it launched its own diplomatic campaign by courting those abandoned or neglected areas of the Global South with the purpose of establishing greater solidarity with its fellow developing world brethren in

Africa, Central Asia, Latin America, and the Middle East. From 1988 to 1994 alone, China normalized diplomatic relations with eighteen developing countries, including the successor states of the former Soviet Union. Later the PRC also established partnerships in 1996 with Russia, Kazakhstan, Kyrgyzstan, and Tajikistan to institute the Shanghai Five, an annual forum devoted to resolve border disputes through confidence-building mechanisms. The successful summits of the Shanghai Five eventually led to the establishment of the Shanghai Cooperation Organization (SCO) in 2001, with the inclusion of Uzbekistan. The SCO was further enlarged in 2005 when Pakistan, Iran, and India were granted observer status, and it continues to be an organization of growing importance.

By once again becoming one with the developing world and adopting a more multilateral foreign policy orientation, the Communist Party endeavored to not only break US containment strategy, but by implementing policies designed to promote a multipolar international environment, Beijing was implicitly also questioning the legitimacy of American unipolarity by challenging the authority of a US-led hegemonic order. Deng himself led the "call to arms" when he declared in response to Western economic sanctions imposed on China after the Tiananmen Square incident: ". . . we cannot simply do nothing in international affairs; we have to make our contribution. In what respect? I think we should help promote the establishment of a new international political and economic order."[26]

Economically, as China's economic development marched forward, Beijing has increasingly found itself confronted by a new set of challenges and needs. Hence, in contrast to the external political forces directing China's diplomatic and strategic relations with the developing world, Beijing's renewed interest in the Global South from an economic standpoint is being directed by its ever greater consumption needs. Its increasingly sophisticated and expanding economy—specifically, the country's internal need for markets, energy, and raw materials—has fed this growing consumption. The reasons for China's renewed interest in these regions, therefore, have a practical purpose—to attain and expand new export markets for its products, to find and acquire new sources of raw materials to fuel its surging economy's demand for natural resources, and to secure access to new energy suppliers to provide power for its industries—promote its growth.

From the mid-1990s onward, Beijing has been able to develop closer economic ties by successfully negotiating numerous bilateral and multilateral treaties with a number of developing countries in Asia, Latin America, Africa, and the Middle East.[27] These economic partnerships have greatly expanded China's market, trade, and investment opportunities. In terms of commerce, China's total trade with the developing world grew 88 percent faster than its trade with the developed states between 1999 and 2003,[28] and between 2000 and 2008 the PRC's exports to LDCs increased steadily from 43 to 49 percent.[29] Moreover, thanks to its intensified management of diplomatic relations with key suppliers, Beijing has been able to secure stable access to scarce raw materials by concluding a series of agreements for energy and other natural resources.[30]

In both diplomatic and economic terms, China's deeper engagement with the states of the developing world serves Chinese interests by advancing Beijing's strategic and economic objectives. Strategically, by securing the Global South's support in global governance organizations, Beijing is able to promote more of a multipolar world structure that will bring about a more "equitable" international order and thereby constrain the United States' global power. Economically, China's effort to secure access to energy and other crucial natural resources due to its growing dependence on oil/gas imports and to diversify supply sources as well as ensure access to overseas markets for its products has raised the relative importance of Beijing's relations with the developing world.

Conclusion

Before we speculate on the prospective direction and policy choices of China's foreign relations toward the developing world, two consistent trends can be drawn from our historical examination of Beijing's interaction with the outside world. First, it should be noted that throughout our discussion of the various eras, from Mao to the current Post-Cold War period, Chinese foreign policy making and behavior has operated under a consistent and relatively coherent grand strategy that reflects Beijing's efforts to balance its strategic and economic considerations. Second, developing states are an integral part of China's grand strategy since they are a central component for achieving Beijing's economic and strategic goals and objectives to become a rich and powerful country.

Anticipating the direction and/or behavior of Chinese foreign policy has not only been a challenging endeavor, but has also often proven to be a hazardous enterprise, replete with twists and turns in response to the perceived needs of Beijing's shifting policy goals and for dealing with the changing global milieu. Nevertheless, based on Beijing's previous rhetoric and behavior as well as the historical strategies that China has employed in its relationship with the developing world, we can deduce the future direction of the Middle Kingdom's grand strategy toward the Global South by formally addressing the questions posed at the beginning of this chapter.

What does the Middle Kingdom hope to gain by identifying itself as a Third World state?

From Beijing's perspective, the Third World helps with China's aspirations to become a global superpower by validating the Middle Kingdom's economic development model. A recurring theme of Mao's Third World foreign policy was his goal for the PRC to be the paradigm that the globe's downtrodden and oppressed would use to break away from their plight. To some extent, modern-day China has achieved Mao's vision and objective. For China's consistently high annual growth rate, which in turn has delivered millions of people from abject poverty, no doubt has been a source of inspiration and perhaps blueprint for developing states in the midst of their own desperate drive to escape from Third World status. Moreover, not only has Beijing provided for much needed inflow of capital into states and parts of the world that might otherwise either be deemed ineligible by Western governments or neglected by transnational corporations, but just as significantly China's willingness to help with infrastructural projects and/or give development assistance without preconditions or sermons, is greatly welcomed by unstable regimes trying to establish legitimacy for their rule.

Substantively, China's investments and trade have brought numerous tangible benefits for many developing states such as the construction of schools, hospitals, roads, rail lines, and other infrastructure frequently at the local community level. As Mark Leonard, a reporter for *The Guardian* observed in 2004: China's model is seducing leaders in countries as different as Vietnam (which is taking business tips from the thoughts of the former Chinese President Jiang Zemin), Brazil (which is sending study teams to Beijing), and India (Ramgopal Agarwala, an eminent sociologist, observed: "China's experiment should be the most admired in human history. China has its own path.").[31]

As Beijing had hoped, its comparatively generous terms of trade agreements, its no-questions-asked investments, and its extremely close bilateral relations with its key partners has permitted China to parlay its economic achievements into a valuable diplomatic asset with a large and growing section of the world increasingly seeing the Middle Kingdom as a progressive and constructive member of the global community. In fact, a 2005 survey gauging the pulse of society toward globalization in twenty-three countries (including twenty-one democracies) found that China was viewed as having a significantly more positive impact in the world than the United States.[32]

Supporting this result was a 2005 US State Department survey that found that a significant majority of Southeast Asian states anticipate and/or expect that China would be their nations' "most important economic partner in five to ten years."[33]

Why does the developing world have such a prominent role in China's foreign policy?

Beijing's relations with the Third World have been accorded high priority since the founding of the PRC in 1949. With the expansion of China's international economic interests, the relative importance extended to the developing world has risen accordingly for the Global South, helping Beijing reach its economic goals and objectives. Specifically, the PRC's need to secure access to energy and other essential natural resources necessary to maintain its economic growth makes Beijing's relationship with developing states a critical element of China's future.

To be sure, China has shown a disturbing tendency to work with "rogue" and/or "pariah" states. The economic policies and political principles of Beijing's resource diplomacy show it has no inhibitions in concluding trade and investment agreements with autocratic governments and/or brutal dictatorships such as Zimbabwe, Burma, and Sudan. At the same time, Chinese policy with the Global South is constantly under review, with the Communist Party not hesitating to make dramatic shifts or even reversals in policies, whenever Beijing concludes that a change in direction is what is needed to achieve its objectives. It is not out of the question, therefore, for China's resource diplomacy to become more in alignment with global norms. The Communist Party has repeatedly shown itself to be amenable to and capable of reassessing and revising their priorities and interests in their foreign affairs. Indeed, Beijing could in time come to the realization that the benefits of continuing its relationship with pariah states is not worth the costs to its international reputation.

What are the implications of China's grand strategy with the countries of Africa, Asia, Latin America, and the Middle East for international peace and stability?

Without question China's deepening engagement with Third World states will have a profound impact on both the structure of the international system and the prospects for global stability in the coming years. For as its influence on regional and global affairs continues to grow, its policy choices to preserve its interests and prosecute its goals will no doubt increasingly affect the dynamics of the international community. As China progresses toward superpower status, however, it is still desperately trying to convey to the world that it is a force for good—not evil. Since the late 1990s, China's international reputation as a responsible and valued member of the global community has arguably not been higher than at any other point in the long history of the PRC.

The reason for China's success lies squarely on Beijing's understanding that maintaining a peaceful international environment that allows China to further integrate in the world economy is the best long-term strategy for reaching major power status. Even with all of its economic accomplishments, China remains a developing country and will remain as such in the foreseeable future. A long-term peaceful international environment conducive to continued economic growth is therefore critical if China is to carry out its socialist modernization program. Furthermore, this strategy supports and complements the leadership's domestic objective of maintaining Communist Party rule by building an advanced economy and raising living standards.

While peace and development will continue to be China's primary strategic orientation, with the PRC continuing to work with the existing system, we can also expect Beijing to increasingly try to modify the system to better reflect its interests as well as its greater power and influence. But even in this regard, Beijing understands that the international goodwill toward the PRC is tenuous at best and could quickly dissolve if they attempt to take a militant posture in its attempt to restructure the international order. According to a 2001 study by Michael D. Swaine and Ashley J. Tellis, "Chinese-state initiated revisionism [of the international system] will be minimal."[34] This description establishes China as a status quo power and reinforces the primacy of its economic and political interests in its foreign policy toward the developing world.

Notes

1. Hu Jintao, "From the Glorious Past to a Bright Future: Building a New Type of Strategic Partnership Between Asia and Africa" (speech delivered at the 2005 Asian-African Summit, Jakarta, Indonesia, April 22–23, 2005).
2. For the purpose of this study, developing world/state, Third World and Global South will be used interchangeably.
3. China is called Zhongguó in Mandarin Chinese. The first character zhong means "central" or "middle," while guó means "kingdom" or "nation." Hence, the term is often translated into English as the "Middle Kingdom."
4. Michael H. Hunt, *The Genesis of Chinese Communist Foreign Policy* (New York: Columbia University Press, 1996), p. 3.

5. Inexplicably, it was during the height of China's power during the Ming dynasty, when the Chinese naval power was the largest and strongest in the world, that the Middle Kingdom withdrew from the global stage and instituted a policy of self-imposed isolation.
6. As a point of reference, the Japanese have only had one ruling dynasty since its founding.
7. Chinese dynasties are founded and maintained via the "Mandate of Heaven." Analogous to the Western concept of the "Divine Right of Kings," the authority and legitimacy of an emperor's right to rule is granted from "The Gods." And for so long as the Emperor is able to successfully care for his people (provide for their physical and economic security) then he has the "Mandate of Heaven." However, once the Emperor fails to fulfill his responsibilities to care for his people, then he "loses" his mandate and someone else, someone more capable who can fulfill this role is then granted the "Mandate of Heaven."
8. Michael D. Swaine and Ashley J. Tellis (2000) *Interpreting China's Grand Strategy, Past, Present and Future* (Santa Monica, CA: Rand).
9. The Sino-Soviet Treaty of Friendship, Alliance, and Mutual Assistance was signed on February 14, 1950.
10. Chen Bojiang, "Changes in China's International Strategy and Goals for the New Millenium" Institute for the Study of Diplomacy, Georgetown University, May 1998, http://www.ciaonet.org/wps/bog01/.
11 Yafeng Xia, "The Cold War and Chinese Foreign Policy" e-International Relations July 16, 2008 http://www.e-ir.info/?p=518
12. Humayoun Khan, "A Historical View of China's Foreign Policy Towards Big Powers" www.issi.org.pk/journal/2006_files/no_2/article/a4.htm - 68k
13. Chen Bojiang, "Changes in China's International Strategy and Goals for the New Millenium" Institute for the Study of Diplomacy, Georgetown University, May 1998, http://www.ciaonet.org/wps/bog01/
14. Yafeng Xia, "The Cold War and Chinese Foreign Policy" e-International Relations July 16, 2008 http://www.e-ir.info/?p=518
15. "Chairman Mao's Theory of the Differentiation of the Three Worlds is a Major Contribution to Marxism-Leninism" Peking Review 20:45 November 4, 1977, 10–41.
16. Peter Van Ness (1998) "China and the Third World: Patterns of Engagement and Indifference" in Samuel S. Kim, ed. China and the World 4th ed. (Boulder, CO: Westview Press), 154.
17. Thomas W. Robinson (1994) "Chinese Foreign Policy from the 1940s to the 1990s" in Thomas W. Robinson and David Shambaugh, eds.

Chinese Foreign Policy: Theory and Practice (New York: Oxford University Press).

18. The participants of the Bandung Conference included delegates from twenty-nine Asian and African nations. List the participants here.
19. Nazli Choucri, "The Nonalignment of Afro-Asian States: Policy, Perception, and Behaviour" *Canadian Journal of Political Science / Revue Canadienne De Science Politique*, 2 (1) March 1969, 1–17.
20. Jagdish N. Bhagwati, ed. (1977) *The New International Economic Order: The North-South Debate* (Cambridge, MA: MIT Press).
21. Peter Van Ness (1970) *Revolution and Chinese Foreign Policy: Peking's Support for Wars of National Liberalization* (Berkeley: University of California Press).
22. Foreign Direct Investment in Emerging Market Countries. Report of the Working Group of the Capital Markets Consultative Group September 2003.
23. Foreign Direct Investment in Emerging Market Countries. Report of the Working Group of the Capital Markets Consultative Group September 2003.
24. For more information on Market-Leninism please refer to Lui Hebron Globalization and China: Political Economy's Odd Couple Washington, DC: CQ Press expected 2010.
25. "Washington was particularly critical of China after the 1989 Tiananmen incident, urging it to implement human rights protections and to evolve into a liberal democratic state" (June Teufel Dreyer "Chinese Foreign Policy" The Newsletter of FPRI's Wachman Center Footnotes Vol. 12, No. 5, February 2007).
26. Deng Xiaoping, "Seize the Opportunity to Develop the Economy" People's Daily http://english.peopledaily.com.cn/dengxp/vol3/text/d1170.html.
27. Strategic partnerships have been signed with Brazil (1993), Venezuela (2001), Mexico (2003), South Africa (2004), Argentina (2004), India (2005), Kazakhstan (2005), Indonesia (2005), Nigeria (2006), and Algeria (2006).
28. IMF, Direction of Trade Statistics.
29. 2008 International Trade Statistical Year Book Volume I Trade by Country http://contrade.un.org/pb/.
30. Countries hosting significant Chinese energy investment include Kazakhstan, Nigeria, Iran, Sudan, Angola, Russia, Ecuador, Venezuela, and Brazil, among others (Brian Bremner and Dexter Roberts, Adam

Aston, Stanley Reed, and Jason Bush, "The Great Oil Hunt" Business Week No. 3908, November 15, 2004, 60–62).

31. Mark Leonard, "How China Is Wooing the World" *The Guardian* September 11, 2004 http://www.guardian.co.uk.
32. Program on International Policy Attitudes (PIPA) "In 20 of 23 Countries Polled Citizens want Europe to be More Influential than U.S." Institute for Agriculture and Trade Policy April 6, 2005 http://www.iatp.org/tradeobservatory/headlines.cfm?refID=70011.
33. "Asian Views of China" Office of Research, Opinion Analysis Department of State November 9, 2005.
34. Michael D. Swaine and Ashley J. Tellis' Contemporary Southeast Asia April 1, 2001 http://www.articlearchives.com/international-relations/national-security-foreign/769932–1.html)

CHAPTER THREE

The Domestic Political Context for China's Quest for Energy Security

Jean A. Garrison

Introduction

As record energy prices put the pinch on rich and poor states alike in 2008, they also led to fears of looming energy scarcity. China's increasing energy demand and ongoing insecurity of supply raised the specter of a dangerous security dilemma in which growing scarcity creates conditions for competition among states and fears of future "resource wars."[1] Such geopolitical analyses, which view energy as a strategic commodity through the lens of a classic zero-sum competition, traditionally predict that conflict over scarce resources is inevitable. This context places China's growing search for energy into a win-loss scenario that pits it against the United States and all other contenders.[2]

However, this is only one viewpoint and one which misses the broader context of the global energy market and China's search for energy security. The neoliberal perspective and the emphasis on economic interdependence point to the shared economic consequences if there is a disruption in energy supplies and the shared trans-boundary environmental consequences that emerge from reliance on fossil fuels. In the latter case, the common threat may set the stage for shared challenges in the need to diversify the energy mix, to shift to alternative energy supplies, and to improve energy efficiencies. Such a focus acknowledges the challenges facing energy security on the supply and demand side of the energy equation as it provides a means to avoid the self-fulfilling prophecy of the simplified geopolitical energy equation.[3]

These systemic level analyses point to a range of foreign policy choices available to states such as China in response to growing energy challenges. However, how and why China makes the choices it does means evaluating the domestic context that includes the imperative for continued rapid economic growth in order to secure economic prosperity and political stability. In light of the peak, or near peak, decline of China's own energy production capacity (and ever increasing demand), energy self-sufficiency is no longer an option for China. In oil, newly developed fields in western China and offshore are expected to only slightly offset production declines in its largest fields in the northeast, including Daqing.[4] Even in coal, China's long-term stable energy source, there are growing shortages and a need to import coal to meet the energy demand. Further, the damage caused to the nation's railway network due to massive snowstorms in winter 2008–2009 shows the growing domestic transportation bottlenecks that exist. These circumstances forced authorities to close many coal-fired plants, leading to blackouts in many cities. In response, the Chinese government has put its supply-side energy policy front and center in its diplomatic efforts, but also admitted that conservation and demand-side energy use policies are a key part of the national security debate regarding energy.

As we will see, China's energy security debate exists within a broader debate over sustainable development, national security, and environmental consequences. China is involved in a two-level game with external and internal factors each playing a role in the decisions it is making. Complicating the picture further is a decentralized policy apparatus which leads to competition over energy policy among China's central government, industry stakeholders, and provincial authorities. This chapter explores a broad range of China's energy policies as well as how the internal energy policy debate evolves in order to demonstrate the importance of domestic politics in the explanation of China's energy security "strategy." This chapter argues that China lacks the coherent energy strategy that geopolitical analyses assume, and instead has a policy made up of a loose collection of broader energy policy initiatives.

China's Energy Shortages and Effects on the National Security Debate

While China's long-sustained growth is an economic miracle, its corresponding growth in energy use and recurring shortages show an unsustainable energy policy. Domestic energy crises such as the widespread electricity shortages in twenty-four of China's thirty-one provinces across 2003–2004, which threatened its rapid growth path, have become common. These shortages led to a 15 percent spike in oil demand to 850,000 barrels per day (bpd) fueled by demand for diesel for power generation. Since then, periodic power shortages have kept this vulnerability front and center with Chinese policymakers.[5]

International Energy Agency (IEA) estimates postulate that China's energy demand will not abate any time soon. Through 2030 the IEA predicts that China's demand for oil will increase nearly 3 percent per year, with overall consumption doubling to 13.1 million barrels per day (bpd). Corresponding to this demand increase, China's decline in domestic oil production (down to an anticipated 2.4 million bpd by 2030) leaves the shortfall to be addressed by imports. This makes securing adequate energy sources a constant need.[6] Even the 2008–2009 financial crisis only temporarily decreased China's energy demand. In light of the economic downturn, petroleum consumption fell in the last quarter of 2008 and Chinese oil refiners cut back crude oil runs at a sharp pace. This change led the IEA to decrease its estimates for Chinese consumption by 10,000 bpd; predicting China's oil demand in 2009 would rise only 0.6 percent to 7.9 million bpd in 2009.[7] Still by spring 2009, oil prices were on the rise anticipating growing demand as China's economy showed signs of recovery.

Changing its energy-consumption patterns means adjusting away from a traditional economic growth model based on massive energy consumption, low efficiency, and heavy pollution in order to become less wasteful.[8] Today, Deng Xiaoping's economic growth model (or "growth-at-any-cost") vies with environmental concerns within the broad debate of sustainable development. The current economic slowdown in the world seems to show that China's record 9.6 percent average growth rates over the last twenty-five years cannot be sustained this year. China's manufacturing shrank for an eighth straight month in March 2009 and growth forecasts predicted that it could fall to 6.3 percent for the year. As collapsing global trade cut exports and growth across Asia, China's exports could drop by 10 percent in 2009.[9] The current lower global oil prices and softer domestic demand for raw materials will reduce imports in 2009 by about 7 percent, but imports are predicted to rebound 10 percent in 2010.[10] China's economy may grow as much as 10 percent by the final quarter of this year as the government's 4 trillion yuan stimulus package (US $585 billion) takes effect. China's spending plan will fund the building of railways, airports, power grids, bridges, and social housing.[11]

In the short term, China has forged a two-pronged domestic politics approach that addresses domestic consumption practices.[12] Beijing's efforts include attempts to develop cleaner energy and changing the way China uses existing energy sources. Optimizing the energy mix means expanding beyond readily available coal. The 2005 renewable-energy law set a goal to get 15 percent of China's energy from renewable sources by 2020, which would be up from the current 7 percent. Although there are financial incentives and a national renewable fund, discounted lending, and tax incentives to move renewable projects forward, the higher up-front costs can still make financing difficult.[13] Still China is heavily investing in renewable sources of energy and is actually increasing its goals for renewable energy generation. For example, in March 2009 China's central planning agency, the National Development and Reform Commission (NDRC), approved construction of two hydropower stations and two wind farms with a total capacity of 20 gigawatts.[14] In addition, China has diversified by investing in nuclear power and electric cars.[15] Energy-use changes are promoted through new energy laws and regulations, specific conservation plans, implementation of new technology, research and development, and policies favoring energy conservation, energy-efficiency standards, and labeling, for example.

In the eleventh five-year plan (2006–2010), the two quantitative development goals are to double the per capita GDP of the country by 2010 (compared with that of 2000) and to decrease the energy consumed per unit of GDP by 20 percent, targeting an annual savings rate of 4 percent. In 2008, China reached and exceeded its energy intensity target for the first time; largely due to decline in industrial manufacturing and the investments in nuclear and wind power generation noted above. This goal builds on previous improvements in energy intensity levels between 1990 and 2005 that decreased intensity overall by 47 percent per unit of GDP (despite an increase from 2003 to 2005). Zhou Dadi, from the NDRC, the bureaucracy responsible for setting development goals, believes that this can be done by scaling back the energy-consuming industrial projects that come online and by promoting new energy savings projects.[16] Mark D. Levine from the China Energy Group at Lawrence Berkeley National Laboratories argues that China makes great efforts in energy efficiency but that it needs technical assistance and knowledge transfer (capacity building) from countries such as the United States.[17] We should look more closely at China's export-led growth model and reliance on energy intensive industry, its power generation challenge, and the looming transportation challenge.

Delving into the Economic Equation and Addressing Energy Intensity

To address the sustainability of China's energy use practices in the long term, China must move its economy away from energy-intensive industries. To achieve such a goal, the Chinese people need structural adjustment in terms of what they produce and physically how they use energy.[18] China manufactures many of the energy-intensive products the globe uses, in 2006 this included 48 percent of global cement production, 35 percent of steel, and 28 percent of aluminum.[19] These industries form the base of China's energy demand given that they are very energy-intensive industries. They are characterized by huge outputs, fast growth, and low efficiency.[20]

Despite government attempts to stop the blind investment in energy-intensive sectors, it has been hard to stop investment in areas where there is high demand.[21] Part of this demand comes from the government, which spends disproportionately to build large infrastructure projects rather than focusing on energy conservation. Government investments in new buildings, highway construction, and railways promote market demands on cement, steel, aluminum, and other energy-intensive industrial products. Building and residential units account for 23 percent of Beijing's fixed investment at around $270 billion. After real estate, the next-largest destination for fixed-asset investment is in the transportation infrastructure, which stands at $140 billion, with half of the investment going to highways. The auto industry and China's growing car culture foster the building of new highways and work to block efforts to develop mass transit. In this environment, energy savings rely on improvements in efficiency standards and China's ability to leapfrog old industry and vehicle technology.[22] The recent stimulus package still focuses on these sectors to spur growth. China approved a massive new 4 trillion yuan (about U.S. $586 billion) two-year investment plan in November 2008 to curb economic downturn. It included a 210 billion yuan investment in environmental protection and energy conservation. Across 2008 China's energy consumption per unit of GDP dropped 4.59 percent in 2008 and 10.08 percent over the previous three years.[23]

Nicholas Lardy from the Peterson Institute of International Economics states that Beijing must adjust its export-led growth model by de-emphasizing manufacturing exports and expanding domestic consumption. He argues that such a change would reduce increases in energy consumption as well as help China sustain its growth, create new jobs, and slow the rising income gap as it reduces global economic imbalances.[24] While Chinese leaders rhetorically acknowledge the need to re-balance the country's growth model, to date only small (and inconsistent) steps have been taken to increase spending on the environment and energy-consumption side.[25] As part of its industrial policy, the government does tax exports of energy-intensive industries, such as its 15 percent tax on copper, nickel, and aluminum; 10 percent on steel; and 5 percent on petroleum, coal, and coke. Chinese officials also placed import tariffs on energy and resource products such as coal, petroleum, and minerals.[26] The central drivers for this acceleration in energy demand are China's increasing population, rapid urbanization in which urban dwellers use 2.5 times more energy than their rural counterparts, growth in its industry, the building and manufacturing sectors, and the greater wealth in a rising middle class that is driven by globalized markets. In addition, transportation is a looming problem; estimates are that cars in China will increase in number from 40 million today to 150 million by 2020.[27]

Addressing the Power-Generation Challenge

China's inefficient power-generation sector represents the fundamental energy and pollution trade-off that comes with China's coal use. As coal's use doubled during the Deng Xiaoping reform period, with it came air pollution problems, so that coal is responsible for 70 percent of the dust and smoke in the air, 90 percent of the sulfur dioxide, and a majority of the carbon.[28] Despite this, coal will remain the central source of China's power-generation sector through at least 2030 (see Figure 3.1).[29]

Coal demand will remain high because from national security and economic perspectives, coal continues to make sense for China in the short and mid-term. China relies on coal because of its large coal reserves and coal's historically cheap price (about $1 per million British thermal units in the mid-2000s[30]) compared to imported natural gas, about $6 or $7 per million British thermal units—especially when a carbon price is not factored into the mix. Other sources of power cannot meet China's energy demands in the near future; for example, nuclear power is projected to provide less than 10 percent of China's energy in 2030 despite recent government investments,

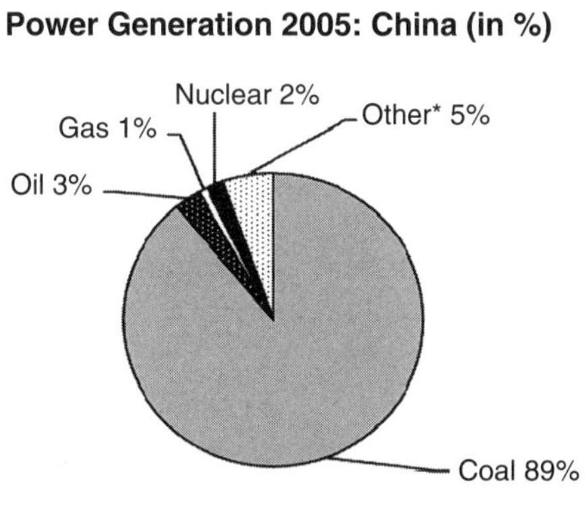

Figure 3.1 Other Energy: Hydropower 4.6%, Biomass and Waste 1.7%, Other Renewables 0.7%.

and natural gas less still. Coal power plants will make up the difference.[31] The challenge comes in the future makeup of that industry.

The central government seeks to consolidate its fragmented coal sector and to make coal use more efficient. However, it has several hurdles to overcome to make this goal. One problem is that China's rapidly expanding coal-fired capacity remains inefficient relative to the developed world—in 2007 China's coal-fired capacity increased by 110 gigawatts and was set to increase by 80 gigawatts in 2008. Based on IEA estimates, subcritical technologies (those only 30–36 percent efficient), which cost $500–600 per kilowatt, will remain the base of China's current fleet which is only about 32 percent efficient. Supercritical technologies that can reach 41 percent efficiency at a cost of $600–900 per kilowatt will be about half of current new orders and ultra-supercritical that can reach 43 percent efficiency level at a cost of $600–900 per kilowatt will have two 1000 megawatt plants in operation. The most efficient, integrated gas combined cycle (IGCC) technology can reach 45–55 percent efficiency at a cost of $1100–1400 per kilowatt. In 2008 there were twelve units waiting NDRC approval. However, IGCC technology faces high costs and needs more research, development, and deployment to be adopted more widely. If China's coal fleet adopts these changes, the average efficiency of coal-fired generation could improve to 39 percent by 2030. Increased efficiency, a function of technology, will mean that plants will generate more power using less coal while producing lower emissions.[32]

As part of its strategy the government seeks to consolidate mining operations, promote the best technology, and pursue efficient and safe mining operations, while addressing development and environmental priorities. The goal is to consolidate the coal industry into six to eight large companies with an output of about 100 m tons with another eight to ten companies with an output of 50 million by 2010. Simultaneously they seek to close 50 m kilowatt capacity in this eleventh five-year planning period, and they successfully closed 533 small thermal power generators in 2007.[33] Consumption has fallen largely due to a drop in industrial output. Across January–March 2009, China's total coal consumption fell 4 percent from a year earlier, to 674 million tons, while total national coal output rose 6.3 percent, to 602 million tons.[34] Because imported coal was cheaper, China's corresponding imports were up 37.4 percent.[35]

Addressing the Looming Transportation Challenge

The transportation equation brings new pressure in the medium and long term as the rising car culture fuels China's growing import dependence on oil. As of January 2009, China surpassed the United States as the world's largest car market. Strategies to change the transportation energy mix fit squarely into the discussion of China's coal usage. China's government has prioritized coal liquefaction processes (also known as coal-to-liquids, or CtL) to help decrease dependence on foreign oil. The price spikes and shortages of oil, which peaked in August 2008 and were on the rise again through 2009, made CtL a logical alternative as long as greenhouse gases (GHG) are not part of the assessment.[36] Despite the potential carbon spike, China looks set to become the world leader in CtL production, with eighty-eight CtL projects included in the eleventh five-year plan (2006–2010) and a further twenty to thirty in the works. If recent trends hold, oil substitutes may account for 10–15 percent of China's coal consumption by 2015 and provide the equivalent of up to 2 million bpd of oil products in an environment in which China currently consumes about 7 million bpd. CtL transport fuels can address China's energy security challenge.

Such efforts rely on the availability of funds to promote new technology and investment capital to expand and transform China's energy system. Gradually rules have loosened in order to encourage foreign investment in China's domestic energy sector. Companies such as Royal Dutch Shell Plc, South Africa-based Sasol Ltd, and General Electric (GE) have track records of working with Chinese companies to produce electricity and substitutes for crude oil derivatives from coal. For example, Sasol Ltd has plans to develop two CtL plants in cooperation with China's Shenhua Ningxia Coal Group and Shenhua Coal Group. Chinese commerce minister Bo Xilai states that foreign companies with clean coal technologies and who work with Chinese counterparts can get good returns on their investments.[37]

China faces a number of interconnected challenges based on its economic model and need to maintain high growth, which are at the heart of its energy policy. Complicating its ability to respond effectively is a decentralized central policy-making structure that fosters competing interests which makes the enforcement of a coherent energy policy difficult to provide.

China's Decentralized Policy-making Structure and the Energy Security Debate

Since Deng Xiaoping's reforms of the 1980s, which decentralized decision-making power and created various state-owned enterprises (SOEs) from previous government ministries, there has been an ongoing fragmentation in China's energy policy making. As authority within the central government fragmented, the provinces also gained greater authority and became directly responsible for maintaining economic growth. Kenneth Lieberthal and David Lampton describe China's system as one of "fragmented authoritarianism" with 1) competing bureaucracies and 2) the growing influence of the provinces.[38] In this system no single leader dominates policymaking, but key bureaucracies retain authority to coordinate certain aspects of China's foreign policy responses leading to a system of competing interests and different definitions of energy security.[39]

China's Fragmented Central Government

There have been various attempts to bring some coherence to the energy policy-making process in China since the elimination of the Ministry of Energy in the 1980s. In the early 2000s, the formation of leading small groups (LSGs) at the State Council and Politburo level were an attempt to provide better policy coordination of policy goals across bureaucracies. These groups attempt to build policy consensus across a diverse set of stakeholders inside and outside of government. Such coordinating bodies assume a greater role because of the diverse domestic and foreign aspects of many policy issues—energy among them—where it is difficult to reconcile competing interests. The goal was to use groups such as the National Energy Leading Group to elevate energy decisions to better manage the energy industry with the NDRC acting as the office director.[40] Even with this organization, however, many administrative functions were still handled by a variety of ministries, leading to a lack of planning for energy exploration, consumption, savings, and reserves. Thus coordination efforts faced their own bureaucratic resistance from influential stakeholders, such as the various energy and foreign policy ministries.

A broad range of bureaucracies want a say in the energy-environmental puzzle. A sample includes the state planning agency, or the NDRC that focuses its attention on broad development goals (and issues such as energy intensity and conservation); the Ministry of Commerce (MOC), which champions economic and trade issues; the Ministry of Foreign Affairs (MFA), which advocates sovereignty over natural resources (as well as diplomatic processes); the Ministry of Finance, which sets fines and has the power to incentivize behavior; and the Ministry of Environmental Protection (MEP), which holds regulatory powers in the environment, among others.[41] Because leaders at the highest levels generally set only key strategic guidelines or long-term policy goals, however, latitude is left tactically for agencies to make specific policy choices and plans to implement policy goals. In this context, there are competing stakeholders with vested interests ready to play bureaucratic politics. As such, China's energy policy has resulted from balancing interests and bargaining among a number of stakeholders rather than a coherent energy plan. For some, energy is a development concern; for others, environmental concerns are triggered; and for others still, access to technology and sovereignty issues emerge. Each perspective carries with it different policy prescriptions.

The NDRC has served as the lead agency in energy policy since the government re-organization of 2005. It remains China's lead in bilateral energy dialogues such as that with the United States; is the lead in the 5-Party Energy Talks involving Japan, the United States, Korea, and India; and sits at the table with the Ministry of Foreign Affairs in climate-change negotiations.[42] Officials in the NDRC Energy Bureau, however, faced the same difficulties as previous energy agencies had because they lacked the authority to coordinate policy among various stakeholders. In this instance, the administrative level of the Energy Bureau was lower than the ministry or vice-ministry level agencies and state-owned enterprises, such as Sinopec, that they tried to regulate.[43]

Discussions in 2007 surrounding the draft of China's first comprehensive energy law led to increasing voices to re-establish a Ministry of Energy to address redundancies in China's energy administration. A new ministry was seen by some as a means to standardize supervision over all aspects of China's energy policy and programs, including exploration, efficiency, security, and emergency responses as well as international cooperation.[44] During discussions in March 2008, key stakeholders who saw this as a threat to their position blocked the move to re-establish the Ministry of Energy. As a compromise a new coordination commission, the National Energy Commission (NEC), which would report to the NDRC, was proposed. The NEC would become responsible for drafting an energy development strategy, would consider energy security and development issues, and would monitor implementation. In its final form, the NEC was given ministerial rank and became somewhat separate from the National Energy Administration (NEA), which replaced the energy bureau in the NDRC. The NEC has been tasked to be the standing body to do the commission's day-to-day work, including setting policies and standards, developing energy industry programs, and promoting new and alternative energy and conservation. The NEA is supposed to integrate the NDRC's energy functions, the office of the NELG, and some other commissions. Its mandate is to manage China's energy industries, draft energy plans and policies, negotiate with international energy agencies, and approve foreign energy investments.

At the time of re-organization experts acknowledged that this new energy policy-making structure would succeed only by overcoming the parochial interests of powerful ministries who want to keep control. This new arrangement still struggles to fulfill its mandate because it does not have the tools to address the challenges. First, as of Fall 2008 the NEC remained unformed, making it an unfinished experiment in creating an authoritative department responsible for enacting a uniform energy strategy.[45] As such, no high-level coordinating body exists to shape broad energy policy. Second, the new NEA has not been given sufficient authority to coordinate the interests of the ministries, commissions, and state-owned companies. Energy expert Erica Downs argues that bureaucratic politics is obvious in the failed re-organization of the energy apparatus. The NDRC and SOEs opposed establishing a ministry, and so the NEC became the compromise. If a new ministry had formed, it would have deprived the NDRC of a large piece of its portfolio and tools of macrocontrol, and the SOEs feared it could limit their direct access to China's top leaders.[46]

Without a strong central government to serve as advocate, monitor, and enforcer of conservation practices, development at-any-cost interests prevail and status quo energy policies persist.

Provincial Challenges to Policy Implementation

The politics of implementation are exacerbated by the decentralization of Deng Xiaoping's reforms. Many times when the government tries to shut down energy-intensive industries, to force consolidation in industries such as coal or cement so that China reduces energy consumption, the affected enterprises are sheltered by provincial and local governments. Campaigns to consolidate coal production face resistance because over half of China's coal is still produced in ten thousand small local mines. China's power-generation sector remains dirty and inefficient, in part, due to the deliberate actions by local officials to keep open plants that provide local jobs and that keep cheap energy readily available. Although 89 percent of China's electricity comes from coal-fired plants, less than 15 percent of them have systems to remove SO_2 installed or running. As the central government attempts to consolidate energy suppliers into larger power plants where environmental technologies are employed, local governments have encouraged the proliferation of small plants under 50 megawatts (which in practice usually release three to eight times more particulates, consume 60 percent more coal, and add negatively to health and environmental concerns).[47] They use a loophole in the law that allows local officials to approve the building of small plants (less than 50 megawatts) that do not need NDRC approval or State Council approval. Ironically, these are precisely the ones the central government tries to shut down. In 2008, the Chinese government shut down small generators with a total capacity of 1,669 kw and 1,054 small coal mines.[48]

The pattern is similar for steel and cement—two of China's most energy intensive industries. The number of steel enterprises doubled between 2002 and 2006 as profits increased. There are seven thousand steel enterprises in China, with the largest three accounting for only 14 percent of total production in 2005 (the top three in the United States control over half of production). Of cement enterprises, although the central government asks that all small projects be shut down for energy efficiency purposes (and to slow economic development), those that have been closed were soon re-opened because of the strong demand for cement.[49] These companies and local officials often work together to resist any new standards and central government mandates because they increase costs. When threatened with environmental enforcement, industry complains to sympathetic local officials about a loss of competitiveness with provinces next door (which causes losses in jobs and tax revenue).[50]

The areas whose wealth is derived from foreign investment can be much more progressive and open to change. Communities with ties to the international community and financiers such as the World Bank or the Asian Development Bank and countries such as Japan have been the direct beneficiaries of attempts to increase energy conservation. For example, Beijing is in line for one US Department of Energy demonstration project focusing on developing best practices and energy savings standards precisely because the US government has close contacts with Beijing's planning agency that is receptive to these changes.[51] The real challenge is gaining traction outside the major east coast cities. Getting China's local government on board is essential to promoting broad energy efficiency programs (or any changes in energy use) because these are the officials in charge of implementing any such plans.[52]

Putting teeth in China's enforcement tool kit is the key. Up to this point, China's central government has mainly adopted administrative methods of enforcement to limit outdated production processes and to shut down inefficient small-scaled enterprises. These policies are clear in principles but short on enforceable measures. For example, financial support for energy efficiency is part of many policies, but funding allocation is separate from the policy itself and has been low.[53] In other words, estimates of specific targets for efficiency gains and $C0_2$ emissions have not been included, monitored, or reviewed. She argues that these are weak points in China's policy making in energy efficiency.[54] One report notes that a 7 billion yuan

($933 million) reward scheme encouraged companies to conserve energy and reduce emissions. This is part of a 23.5 billion yuan ($3.09 billion) program by the Ministry of Finance to promote energy efficiency and reduce pollution. Rewards go to enterprises that fulfill emission-reduction requirements to promote technological innovation. In 2007 3 billion yuan ($394 million) was set aside to improve data collection and environmental monitoring. Two billion yuan ($200 million) will be used to compensate and retrain workers from inefficient enterprises that were closed down. A Ministry of Finance official states that there has been a change in local practices to the extent that provinces such as Jiangsu, Shanxi, and Shandong have committed up to half of their revenue for energy conservation. Only enterprises and governments that make effective expenditures in energy conservation will be rewarded. A public campaign takes this message to the grassroots to build support for energy-conservation policies. As part of its new "scientific concept of development," the government also set mandatory targets and said it will monitor nationwide efforts to conserve energy and reduce emissions to enforce its targets. It threatens to block the promotion of officials and SOE heads who do not meet the targets.[55]

National environmental protection officials argue that violators will be shamed and subject to state supervision as part of the new energy conservation plan. Further, the government will not approve high polluting and energy consuming projects, and their access to bank loans will be affected by a "green-credit" policy that has China's new Ministry of the Environment (MEP) hand over lists of polluters to the central bank and regulatory commission.[56] Until very recently the old State Environmental Protection Agency did not have sufficient ministerial rank to enforce any conservation or environmental measures. It is an open question whether this reshuffling has strengthened the weak state of China's environmental bureaucracy. MEP officials may vow to get tough on local officials and companies who fail to meet energy-saving and pollution-reduction targets, but in practice they have faced an uphill battle in terms of access and resources.[57] On a practical level, past enforcement was hindered by cuts in the environmental bureaucracy's personnel from six hundred to three hundred, which came after the government re-organized in the mid-2000s. Similar cuts in related ministries have made it difficult to coordinate or enforce high-level environmental policy.[58] Before the re-organization, Pan Yue, the former vice minister of SEPA, argued that without a strategic environmental evaluation system, "China will not solve the problem of its too high resource and environmental price for economic growth. Without strategic environmental evaluation, more energy-consuming and heavy-polluting industries [will] spring up."[59]

The most important tasks of the new MEP are to enforce environmental standards and to oversee compliance of firms to those standards.[60]

Another tool available to the central government is to use the international system, and thus the two-level game nature of energy policy making, as an outside lever to push for local change. Bilateral negotiations such as the China-US energy-policy dialogues lead to agreements to cooperate on increasing energy efficiency in China's industrial sector, which creates mandates that the Chinese government can blame for local change. The agreement in September 2007 to jointly conduct audits to increase national, regional, and local energy efficiency at as many as twelve facilities may be controversial and need the "national interest" frame to overcome local resistance.[61] International actors also have used their influence to persuade Chinese colleagues to experiment with market-based mechanisms such as reforms in pricing of natural resources, tradable permits, and environmental service companies.[62] Framing energy security in the context of climate security is one of these opportunities. China's reliance on fossil fuels, the usage of which corresponds to China's carbon emissions, demonstrates the importance of climate security to energy security.

China's Energy Security and Climate Change Challenges

From a climate change perspective there are immediate and long-term consequences if energy use behavior does not change. At this point in time, China has not agreed on a post-Kyoto roadmap for emissions reductions or a specific carbon-mitigating energy-use plan. Mitigating carbon successfully requires a change in behavior in the power-generation and transport sectors, in particular, because demand for electricity and transportation accounts for 66 percent of the globe's total CO_2 emissions. Not surprisingly, in China power generation and industry are the main culprits. Despite its conservation and green energy goals, coal will continue to dominate China's energy mix through 2030. In the industrial sector steel and cement are the main drivers of emissions, and steel production is expected to double and cement to more than double by 2030.

China's carbon equation comes in the form of its continued construction of the equivalent of two 500-megawatt coal-fired power plants per week which leads to an increased capacity comparable to the entire UK power grid each year. To make inroads on this demand, the priority objective with respect to coal must be the successful large-scale demonstration of the technical, economic, and environmental performance of the technologies that make a large-scale integrated carbon capture and sequestration

(CCS) system.[63] However, finding the financing for big front-loaded investments in new technology in the context of higher risk investment presents obstacles to technology deployment. New IGCC plants cost up to $1 billion more than conventional plants, and carbon capture and sequestration (once available) is estimated to increase operational costs of electricity generation by 35–60 percent.[64] A comparison of China's coal-fired power fleet's carbon dioxide emissions to those of the global standard and newer technologies shows just how far China has to go—today the Chinese carbon dioxide fleet averages 1,140 grams per kilowatt hour while the global standard is 22 percent lower at 892 grams per kilowatt hour.[65]

Coal and industrial emissions were a central piece to the discussions in the George W. Bush-initiated and US-led Asia-Pacific Partnership on Clean Development and Climate (APP) multilateral partnership which defines energy security in development and climate terms. This organization brought together the leading energy users and carbon emitters—the United States, China, India, Japan, Korea, and Australia—to seek projects to stimulate joint ventures and investment in various sectors to create a lower-carbon economy.[66] The communiqué from the second ministerial meeting from October 2007 called the organization an innovative partnership seeking "to promote and create an enabling environment for the development, diffusion, deployment and transfer of existing and emerging cost-effective, cleaner technologies and practices, through concrete and substantial cooperation so as to achieve practical results."[67] Rhetorically, the partners work to integrate climate and development goals to find practical win-win opportunities for clean growth. In addition, they collaborate in a voluntary initiative across the public and private sector and implement policy change through a sectoral, bottom-up approach.[68]

However, there has been only limited success in this model of partnership. Funding has been sporadic, with the United States' APP funding coming online only in late 2007. The Chinese find it problematic that most joint projects focus on "soft" activities such as information sharing, capacity building, and standardization. Director General Gao Guangsheng, from the Office of National Climate Change Committee, notes that "there are almost no joint R&D projects between developed and developing Partnership countries." To him, the core issue is "the price of technology transfer and dissemination."[69] For China, there needs to be a financial mechanism to facilitate cooperation among the private sectors of partner countries. The prominent cancelation of the FutureGen project, which was to be the model multilateral clean coal project, illustrated how tough cooperation can be. This 275 megawatts-gasification (IGCC) syngas conversion, separation, and capture project was canceled in 2008 due to rising costs. It was to operate as the world's first coal-fueled, zero-emissions power plant to tackle climate change.[70]

Project deployment faces at least three broad challenges. First, China expects technology at a reduced rate or at cost. However, this is not an option in the modest budget set aside for projects in China or in the current budget environment within the US Congress. Underlying this need is the imperative for funding at appropriate stages that include development and deployment of projects. Projects need to go through these steps to test their commercial viability. Second, issues of intellectual property rights arise with any investment in China. Producers of technology need guarantees that their technology will not be stolen. Third, both sides have national security sensitivities to keep in mind. For example, China frequently asks for technology (that is, high-resolution satellites to map coal fires) that the United States considers dual use and will not make available to the Chinese. For its part, China remains sensitive about its geological information and sees mapping as a national security issue.[71]

Conclusion

China has a domestic imperative for continued growth and a constant need to expand its energy options. Its future clean economic development is dependent on the global integration of the energy system making it costly to become technologically isolated or institutionally isolated in energy or climate change negotiations. The US Secretary of State Hillary Clinton and China's Foreign Minister Yang Jiechi seemed to acknowledge this perspective in their initial talks in March 2009. The new Strategic and Economic Dialogue between China and the United States will have a heavy focus on climate and energy and the links between both of them. Theoretically it will be an important bilateral instrument to develop a common approach for the UN Climate Change conference in Copenhagen in November 2009.[72]

China's recent focus on assistance has been advanced coal technologies, but energy-efficient buildings, clean-vehicle technology, and advanced industrial technology also have great mitigation potential. Energy efficiency is considered appealing because it represents the "low hanging fruit" in that making these changes burns no fuel, emits no pollution, and costs from one-sixth to one-third the cost of generating power in China. It also avoids the need for additional generation facilities and infrastructure. As such, it can contribute to both short- and long-term energy goals. Bo Shen from the National Resources Defense Council in Beijing states that energy efficiency could meet between 29 and 56 percent of China's forecast 2014 electric load growth. The council is working with the NDRC and the newly established National Energy Administration to initiate a yearlong nationwide training program on energy efficiency to build human and technical capacity.[73]

The rise of energy security concerns as seen through a domestic development or climate lens can have important consequences for global energy stability and coordinated environmental responses. Essentially, China and others must substantially reduce consumption of fossil fuels (or clean up their use), and increase efficiency.[74] For China to truly embrace "clean energy" and, by definition, a lower-carbon economy that would include implementing policies to address climate change more directly, its concerns over the cost of moving toward higher-efficiency coal technology and CCS technology will have to be addressed.

Because China's goal is to address its real pollution and sustainable development problems and to be seen as a responsible stakeholder in the world system, it has incentive to cooperate. But it faces a two-level game and a domestic context that can be a hard sell. The focus on energy policy making and the resulting bureaucratic processes illustrates an eclectic crisis-driven policymaking process. China's leaders grapple with political, social, and economic changes brought about by rapid domestic growth that both limit and create opportunities in its foreign policy. In the energy sector, China faces the dilemma of reconciling powerful domestic groups and local governments with its broad national priorities. As such, the issues involved in the energy issue blur the distinction between foreign and domestic policy and create intermestic policy conditions that have both foreign and domestic policy aspects.

Over time China has adopted environmental standards, an energy and environmental bureaucracy has developed, and the economy has become more efficient. However, the United States can play a more constructive role in China's future energy transformation by leading by example and helping China meet its energy intensity targets, by encouraging clean-energy technology transfers, by focusing on constructing demonstration projects aimed at efficiency and carbon control, and by providing financial incentives.

Those in the United States and elsewhere who ignore China's domestic political drivers and define China's quest for energy security solely in terms of its growing equity positions around the world ignore the competing interests at play in China and possible areas of bilateral and multilateral collaboration. We must avoid the too-simple analysis of China's goals and intentions that emphasize growing energy vulnerabilities and define energy security narrowly in terms of geopolitical threats.

Notes

1 Michael Klare (2004) Blood and Oil: The Dangers and Consequences of America's Growing Dependency on Imported Petroleum (New York: Harry Holt and Company, LLC); Michael Klare (2008) Rising Powers, Shrinking Planet: The New Geopolitics of Energy (New York: Metropolitan Books).

2 Robert Ebel (2005) China's Energy Future: *The Middle Kingdom Seeks Its Place in the Sun* (Washington, DC: Center for Strategic International Studies).

3 Zhao, "China's Energy Procurement Strategy." See also Hongtu Zhao, "Energy and Conflict: Current Controversies." PowerPoint Presentation to the Conference organized by the Mandiaga European Foundation and the East West Institute, Paris, France, April 26, 2007; Clarissa Oon, "China Must Do More to Reign in Energy Use," Singapore Times, November 30, 2007, Open Source Center https://www.opensource.gov (accessed December 3, 2007); and David M. Lampton and Bo Kong, "China Comes in from the Cold." Johns Hopkins University School of Advanced Studies (Winter 2005), http://www.sais-jhu.edu/pubaffairs/publications/saisphere/winter05/lampton-kong.html (accessed January 18, 2008).

4 International Energy Agency (IEA). China's Worldwide Quest for Energy Security (Paris, OECD/IEA, 2000); Kent Calder, "Coping with Energy Insecurity," East Asia 23, no. 3 (Fall 2006), 3–54; Shahid Yusuf and Kaoru Nabeshima, China's Development Priorities (Washington, DC: World Bank, 2006), pp. 102–108. China's energy intensity remains high because of its reliance on coal. However, its efficiency is improving with improving technologies and incentives in place to promote energy efficiency.

5 Shai Oster and Ann Davis, "China Spurs Coal-Price Surge," The Wall Street Journal, February 12, 2008 http://online.wsj.com/article/SB120275985736359763.html?mod=hpp_us_pageone#printMode (accessed April 2, 2009).

6 International Energy Agency (IEA) World Energy Outlook 2007—China and India Insights (Paris: OECD/IEA, 2007), p. 376. See also Daojiong Zha, "China's Energy Security and Its International Relations," The China and Eurasia Forum Quarterly 3, no. 3 (November 2005).

7 "China's Oil Demand to be Positive in 2009," CommodyOnline, February 26, 2009 h ttp://www.commodityonline.com/news/China%E2%80%99s-oil-demand-to-be-positive-in-2009–15554-3–1.html (accessed April 6, 2009).

8 Fangchao Li, "Energy Use 'No Threat' to the World." China Daily, March 8, 2007, http://www.chinadaily.com.cn/china/2007–03/08/content_822288.htm (accessed January 14, 2008).

9 Kevin Hamlin, "China's Manufacturing Shrinks for 8th Straight Month," *Bloomberg*, April 1, 2009 http://www.bloomberg.com/apps/news?pid=20601080&sid=aK2dwnIrKL_E&refer=asia# (accessed April 3, 2009); Wang Bo, "OECD: China's Growth May Slow to 6.3 in 2009," China Daily, March 31, 2009 http://www.chinadaily.com.cn/bizchina/2009–03/31/content_7635497.htm (accessed April 3, 2009).

10 "Update: ADB Cuts China2009 GDP Forecast on Global Crisis," The Wall Street Journal, March 31, 2009 http://online.wsj.com/article/BT-CO-20090331–701881.html (accessed April 3, 2009).

11 Li Yanping, "China GDP Growth May Quicken to 10% by Year End, Nomura Says," *Bloomberg*, April 2, 2009 http://www.bloomberg.com/apps/news?pid=20601087&sid=aKVlsyz2eVaw&refer=home (accessed April 3, 2009).

12 Yishan Xia, "Partnerships Will Help Solve Energy Conflicts," China Daily, October 25, 2005, http://www.chinadaily.com.cn/english/doc/2005–10/28/content_488340.htm (accessed December 23, 2007); Dadi Zhou, "Five Steps to Prevent Future Energy Woes," China Daily, November 16, 2005, www.Chinadaily.com.cn (accessed December 20, 2007).

13 Joanna I. Lewis, Testimony before the U.S.-China Economic and Security Review Commission, August 13, 2008, http://www.uscc.gov/hearings/2008-hearings/written_testimonies/08_08_13_wrts/08_08_13_lewis_statement.pdf (accessed October 1, 2008), p. 3; Lampton and Kong, "China Comes in from the Cold."

14 Rujun Shen and Tom Miles, "China's Wind-Power Boom to Outpace Nuclear by 2020," Reuters, April 20, 2009 http://www.forbes.com/feeds/afx/2009/04/20/afx6309313.html (accessed May 5, 2009).

15 Ou Lu, "King Coal Losing His Power in Electricity Industry," China Daily, February 16, 2009 http://www.chinadaily.com.cn/bizchina/2009–02/16/content_7478767.htm (accessed April 6, 2009); Keith Bradsher, "China Vies to Be World's Leader in Electric Cars," The New York Times, April 1, 2009 (accessed April 6, 2009).

16 Economy, The River Runs Black, pp. 60–63; National Development and Reform Commission (NDRC). PRC, "China's National Climate Change Programme." June, 2007, http://www.pewclimate.org/docUploads/ChinaNationalClimateChangeProgramme%20June%2007.pdf(accessed March 2, 2008).

17 Mark D. Levine, Testimony before the U.S.-China Economic and Security Review Commission, August 13, 2008, pp. 3–9, http://www.uscc.gov/hearings/2008hearings/written_testimonies/08_08_13_wrts/08_08_13_levine_statement.pdf (accessed October 1, 2008).

18 See Purnendra Jain, "Japan to Shift Aid Focus from China to India," Asia Times Online, March 11, 2004, http://www.atimes.com/atimes/Japan/FC11Dh01.html (accessed February 20, 2008).
19 Yanjia Wang, "Energy Efficiency and CO_2 in China's Industry: Tapping the Potential" (first draft) March 20, 2006, p. 9, background paper for Annex I, Expert Group Seminar in Conjunction with the OECD Global Forum on Sustainable Development "Working Together to Respond to Climate Change," March 27–28, 2006, Paris, France.
20 Daniel Rosen and Trevor Houser, China Energy: A Guide for the Perplexed (Washington, DC: Peterson Institute for International Economics), May 2007, http://www.petersoninstitute.org/publications/papers/rosen0507.pdf (accessed December 15, 2007), pp. 5–9; Zhou, "Five Steps to Prevent Future Energy Woes."
21 Wang, "Energy Efficiency," pp. 10–17.
22 Rosen and Houser, "China Energy," pp. 12–16; Zhou, "Five Steps to Prevent Future Energy Woes."
23 Zhu Shaobin, "China's Economic Stimulus Plans Benefit Environment," Xinhua, March 10, 2009 http://news.xinhuanet.com/english/2009–03/10/content_10986048.htm (accessed April 2, 2009).
24 Nicholas R. Lardy, "China: Toward a Consumption Driven Growth Path," Peterson Institute of International Economics, Policy Briefs in International Economics, Number PB06–6 (October 2006), http://www.iie.com/publications/pb/pb06–6.pdf (accessed December 12, 2007).
25 Brookings Roundtable, "A Climate of Change." Erica Schliakjer, "China's Environmental Crisis—by Kenneth Lieberthal Part Two," Responsible China, February 9, 2009 http://responsiblechina.com/2009/02/05/part-two-and-prospects-for-the-future-by-kenneth-lieberthal/ (accessed April 6, 2009).
26 Lewis, Testimony before the U.S.-China Economic and Security Review Commission, p. 4.
27 Brookings Roundtable, "A Climate of Change." Erica Schliakjer, "China's Environmental Crisis—by Kenneth Lieberthal Part Two"; Peter Ogden , John Podesta, and John Deutch, "A New Strategy to Spur Energy Innovation." Washington, DC, Center for American Progress, January 2008, http://www.americanprogress.org/issues/2008/01/pdf/energy_innovation.pdf (accessed January 25, 2008); and Lampton and Kong, "China Comes in from the Cold."
28 Economy, The River Runs Black, pp. 72–76.
29 Kai Ma, "China is Shouldering Its Climate Change Burden," Financial Times, June 4, 2007, 13.

30 A British thermal unit (BTU) is the amount of heat required to increase the temperature of a pint of water (which weighs 16 ounces) by one degree Fahrenheit. Since BTUs are measurements of energy consumption, they can be converted directly to kilowatt hours (3,412 BTUs = 1 kilowatt hour) or joules (1 BTU = 1,055.06 joules).

31 See John Deutch, Peter Ogden, and John Podesta, "China's Energy Challenge." In China's March on the 21st Century edited by Kurt M. Campbell and Wiliow Darsie. A Report of the Aspen Strategy Group, Washington, DC, Aspen Institute, 2007, http://www.aspeninstitute.org, p. 55.

32 IEA, World Energy Outlook 2007.

33 See "China Coal Industry Policy 2007." English translation provided by Shanghai Zoom Intelligence Co., Ltd, www.zoomchina.com.cn (accessed March 5, 2008); and "Coal Fired Power on the Way Out, Says NDRC," China Daily, January 29, 2008, http://www.chinadaily.com.cn/ (accessed January 30, 2008).

34 "China Shenhua Energy's 1Q Profit up 17.2 Percent," Associated Press, April 28, 2009 http://www.forbes.com/feeds/ap/2009/04/28/ap6346758.html (accessed May 5, 2009).

35 "China's Coal Import up 37.4% in March," Xinhua, April 12, 2009 http://news.xinhuanet.com/english/2009–04/12/content_11174213.htm (accessed May 5, 2009).

36 Jason Furman, Jason E. Bordoff, Manasi Deshpande, and Pascal J. Noel (2007) *An Economic Strategy to Address Climate Change and Promote Energy Security* (Washington, DC: Brookings Institution), October, pp. 5–7.

37 "Foreign Coal Firms to Profit More," China Daily, September 24, 2007, http://www.chinadaily.com.cn/bizchina/2007–09/24/content_6129073.htm (accessed November 15, 2007).

38 See Kenneth Lieberthal and David M. Lampton, eds. (1992) Bureaucracy, Politics, and Decision Making in Post Mao China (Berkeley, University of California Press).

39 For a more comprehensive discussion of China's energy policy-making bureaucracy see chapter 2 in Jean Garrison, China and the Energy Equation in Asia: Determinants of Policy Choice (forthcoming 2009, First Forum Press—a division of Lynne Rienner Publishers).

40 "Wen Jiabao Convenes First Meeting of the State Leading Group on Work to Respond to Climate Change, Energy Conservation, and

Emissions Reduction," Xinhua (BBC Monitoring Asia Pacific), July 11, 2007, www.lexis/nexis.com (accessed November 15, 2007).

41 See Economy, The River Runs Black, pp. 178–185; and David M. Lampton, "China's Foreign and National Security Policy-Making Process: Is It Changing and Does It Matter?" In The Making of Chinese Foreign and Security Policy in the Era of Reform, edited by David M. Lampton, pp. 1–38 (Berkeley: University of California Press, 2001), pp. 10–20.

42 Barry Naughton, "The New Common Economic Program: China's 11th Five Year Plan and What it Means," China Leadership Monitor no. 16. Hoover Institution, Fall 2005, http://media.hoover.org/documents/clm16_bn.pdf (accessed December 21, 2007).

43 Government approval is necessary for deals over $30 million from China's central planning bureaucracy, the NDRC, and from the State Council for investments over $200 million (see Downs, China, p. 40).

44 Author discussion with various China and government experts in Fall 2007, Washington, DC; Lan, "Who'll Turn on the Lights."

45 "China Announces Overhaul of Energy Agencies, Management," Xinhua, March 11, 2008, www.xinhuanet.com (accessed March 31, 2008); Andrew C. Kadak, Testimony before the U.S.-China Economic and Security Review Commission, August 13, 2008, http://www.uscc.gov/hearings/-2008hearings/written_testimonies/08_08_13_wrts/08_08_13_mladineo_statement.pdf (accessed October 1, 2008); Downs, testimony before the U.S.-China Economic and Security Review Commission, pp. 1–2.

46 Downs, testimony before the U.S.-China Economic and Security Review Commission, p. 3.

47 Economy, The River Runs Black, pp. 72–76.

48 Wang Hairong, "Halfway Through: China's Energy-Saving Policy Analysis," Bewjing Review, March 19, 2009 http://www.bjreview.com.cn/nation/txt/2009–03/13/content_185077.htm (accessed April 1, 2009).

49 The previous examples came up in discussions with US government sources in November 2007.

50 Rosen and Houser, "China Energy," pp. 11–13; author discussions with various expert sources in Beijing May 2007.

51 Author discussions with US government personnel, Washington, DC, October–November 2007.

52 See Jain, "Japan to Shift Aid Focus."

53 Wang, "Energy Efficiency," pp. 1–2. See also Deutch et al.,"China's Energy Challenge," p. 54; and "China's Economic Puzzle," International

Herald Tribune, October 19, 2007, http://www.iht.com/articles/2007/10/19/opinion/edchina.php (accessed November 5, 2007).

54 Joanna I. Lewis, "China's Strategic Priorities in International Climate Change Negotiations," Washington Quarterly, Winter 2007–2008, no. 1, http://www.twq.com/08winter/docs/08winter_lewis.pdf, pp. 158–161.

55 "China Offers Rewards to Encourage Energy Conservation," China Daily, November 27, 2007, http://www.chinadaily.com.cn/china/2007–11/28/content_6283469.htm (accessed December 4, 2007).

56 Oon, "China Must Do More."

57 Economy, The River Runs Black, pp. 90–101, 178–185.

58 Ibid., pp. 104–107.

59 Pan, Yue, "Working Toward a Better Environment," China Daily, November 22, 2007, 10.

60 Edward A. Cunningham, IV. Testimony before the U.S.-China Economic and Security Review Commission, August 18, 2008, http://www.uscc.gov/hearings/2008hearings/written_testimonies/08_08_13_wrts/08_08_13_cunningham_statement.pdf (accessed October 1, 2008), p. 6.

61 "China and US Sign Energy Accord," China Daily, September 17, 2007, http://www.chinadaily.com.cn/china/2007–09/17/content_6110430.htm (accessed December 7, 2007). The MOU serves as a conduit for American companies to export environment-friendly, US-made equipment and services to China. The MOU signing is an example of the kind of partnerships available to increase energy efficiency and remove barriers to private investment in clean-energy technologies in China.

62 Economy, The River Runs Black, pp. 258–263.

63 Massachusetts Institute of Technology (MIT). The Future of Coal: Options for a Carbon-Constrained World (Massachusetts Institute of Technology Study, March 2007), http://web.mit.edu/coal/ (accessed December 3, 2007).

64 Ibid., pp. 145–146.

65 Robert Watson, "Financing the Transition to a Low Carbon Economy." Beyond Stern: Financing International Investment in Low Carbon Conference, Washington, DC: World Bank, 2007. One problem is that adopting CCS can also decrease plant efficiency, which raises the cost per kilowatt-hour. A November 2008 MIT study argues that a system using partial capture could get CO_2 emissions from coal-fired plants down to the emissions levels of natural gas plants. See David Ehrlich, "Carbon Capture Lite Could Cut Costs for 'Clean Coal'." CNNMoney.com.

(November 17, 2008) http://money.cnn.com/news/newsfeeds/gigaom/green/2008_11_17_carbon_capture_lite_could_cut_costs_for_clean_coal.html (accessed November 24, 2008).

66 For more information on the US Department of Energy's Carbon Sequestration Leadership Forum, see http://www.fe.doe.gov/programs/sequestration/cslf/. For information on the Asia-Pacific Partnership, see http://www.state.gov/r/pa/scp/2006/60852.htm.

67 Asia-Pacific Partnership (APP). "About the Asia-Pacific Partnership on Clean Development and Climate." http://www.asiapacificpartnership.org/About.htm (accessed February 2, 2008). My observations and discussions with US government sources reveal that Australia has been a central actor, providing around $150 million in Australian dollars for joint projects. The US overall contribution has been $45 million, with $5–8 million set aside for projects in China. Japan has been a more cautious actor and slow to provide funding. China is receptive to the joint projects, while India fears that its participation risks current funding from the World Bank and Asian Development Bank.

68 Griff Thompson, "Asia-Pacific Partnership on Clean Development and Climate." Presentation, 24th Mansfield Conference on Climate Security, Missoula, MT, September 25, 2008, PowerPoint presentation provided by author.

69 Gao Guangsheng. Speech at the 2nd Ministerial Meeting of the Asian Pacific Partnership, New Delhi, India, October 15, 2007.

70 See Office of Policy and International Affairs, US Department of Energy, "DOE-China Energy Cooperation." US Department of Energy, October 2007, http://www.fossil.energy.gov/programs/powersystems/futuregen/ (copy provided to the author). The necessary CCS technologies have been in use for years, but not with the intent to reduce CO_2 emissions. For example, enhanced oil recovery projects have been an important early carbon market that may serve as a model. The immediate need in the world is to speed the pace of these projects.

71 The author saw these issues raised in task-force meetings in 2007. The importance of these issues has been confirmed in the author's conversations with knowledgeable government personnel from October to November 2007 in Washington, DC.

72 "The U.S. and China Working Toward Clean Energy," The U.S. Department of State, February 22, 2009 http://www.state.gov/secretary/rm/2009a/02/119435.htm (accessed May 5, 2009).

73 Bo Shen, "International Cooperation to Promote Energy Efficiency as a Cost-Effective Energy Resource for Climate Change Mitigation."

PowerPoint presentation, 24th Mansfield Conference on Climate Security, Missoula, MT, September 25, 2008, provided by the author.

74 Michael Klare, "Global Warming: It's All About Energy," Foreign Policy in Focus, February 17, 2007, http://www.countercurrents.org/cc-klare170207.htm (accessed October 17, 2007).

PART II

Regional Case Studies

CHAPTER FOUR

China's Quest for Energy Security in the Middle East: Strategic Implications

Manochehr Dorraj and Carrie Liu Currier

Introduction

China has been experiencing an impressive rate of economic growth in the last three decades. Its annual rate of growth of approximately 9 percent over the last ten years makes it the fastest growing economy in the world. Since the 1970s, the size of China's economy has quadrupled and some estimate that its size may double over the next decade.[1] This development has culminated in expanding energy demand. To satisfy this increasing demand China has begun to look in earnest for new long-term energy supplies and sought to expand its relationship with major oil- and gas-producing nations in the Middle East and North Africa, where the largest oil and gas resources in the world (close to 60 percent of the total reserves) reside.

Whereas prior to the 1990s China's relationship with the Middle East was primarily confined to such political goals as isolating Taiwan, preventing the expansion of Soviet influence in the region, and supporting Arab radical regimes such as South Yemen, Libya, and the Palestinian authority, in the 1990s, China's policy transformed into a more pragmatic posture in which the primacy of economic interests took the center stage. This shift in policy has paid major dividends for China, culminating in an impressive expansion of trade relations and political ties with the region. Indeed, by 2006, China was importing close to half of its total energy imports from the Middle East.[2]

While China currently maintains trade and energy relations with numerous countries in the Middle East, in this chapter, we focus on China's expanding trade and political relations with the two largest energy producers and significant political players in the region, namely, Saudi Arabia and Iran. This chapter analyzes the geo-strategic issues surrounding China's quest for access to energy sources in the Middle East and how this might impact its relations with the United States and other global powers.

China-Middle East Petro-Politics

To satisfy its increasing energy demand, in the early 1990s, China began to look actively for new long-term energy supplies and sought to expand its relationship with major oil- and gas-producing nations in the Middle East and North Africa. Thus, whereas prior to the 1990s China's relationship with the Middle East was primarily with Arab radical regimes, in the 1990s China opted for a more pragmatic course and actively sought to expand trade and political ties with the other countries of the region.

China's initial oil imports came from small Persian Gulf states such as Yemen and Oman, because they produced light "sweet" crude that the Chinese refineries could easily handle. But as Chinese energy needs expanded, by the second half of the 1990s, China began to approach the larger OPEC producers such as Iraq, Iran, and Saudi Arabia. Two of these countries, Iran and Saudi Arabia have become the largest suppliers of oil and gas to China and they have also expanded their trade relations with Beijing exponentially. While China maintains energy relations with such diverse countries of the region as Qatar, Bahrain, Kuwait, United Arab Emirates (UAE), Syria, Egypt, Algeria, Libya, and Sudan, in this chapter we focus on the two largest energy producers and significant political actors in the region, namely, Iran and Saudi Arabia. These two states not only have the largest combined oil and gas reserves in the world, they also account for roughly two-thirds of Middle Eastern oil imports to China.[3] In addition, their different political postures, (one a close ally of the United States and the other a political adversary), pose distinct challenges to China's international diplomacy in general and its Middle East policy in particular. Through these two case studies, we will provide some evidence and insight into China's political behavior and assess the viability of China's strategy to secure long-term energy supplies and trade partners and expand its influence in the Middle East. We will also briefly discuss the larger global context in which China's drive for energy security in the region is unfolding and analyze their strategic ramifications.

China-Iran Relations

As the two great civilizations with a history of trade and political relations that goes back more than a thousand years, Iran and China identify with each other. The fact that both of these proud nations suffered the indignity of neo-colonial domination and share ideological commitment to Third World solidarity accentuates this sense of identification. It is not ideology however, that binds these two desperate regimes that respectively adhere to Marxism-Leninism and Islamic theocracy, rather it is the primacy of economic and political interests that drives the relationship. With the second largest oil and gas combined energy resources after Saudi Arabia, Iran has emerged as one of the major suppliers of energy to China. While China had been buying small amounts of Iranian oil since 1974, it was not until 1997 that China began to increase its imports of Iranian oil substantially. In that year China imported 700,000 bbl/day of Iranian oil, and by the year 2000, China was importing 2,700,000 bbl/day.[4]

Due to the damages incurred during the Iran-Iraq War (1980–1988) and the negative impact of the US-imposed economic sanctions on Iran since 1980, Iran's oil infrastructure, including exploration, refining capacity, and downstream production capabilities, have been deteriorating steadily. While Iran has sufficient hydrocarbon resources to satisfy China's expanding demands for energy well into the future, it lacks the necessary technology and investments to exploit them independently. The 1996 Clinton administration's Iran-Libya Sanctions Act imposed tough penalties on any foreign companies or individuals who were found to be investing more than $20 million or more in oil and gas development in Iran. This initiative further hampered Iran's ability to modernize its facilities and expand its production capabilities. This development proved to be a boon for China. Conscious of Iran's urgent need to explore its vast oil and gas reserves and rebuild its war-torn and decrepit energy infrastructure, China offered to rebuild it and engage in joint venture exploration and development of new oil and gas fields. In doing so, China hoped to lock into the Iranian energy market for the long haul.

After allaying Iranian representatives' worries about Chinese technological capabilities, Chinese efforts paid off. By 1997, the two countries signed an agreement for cooperation in oil and gas exploration. In 1988 a Sinopec subsidiary, Shengli Oil Company, had transferred to Iran a complete set of China-made oil equipment.[5] Iran was particularly appealing to the Chinese because its low rates of production of oil and gas compared to its vast reserves indicated that it was one of the few countries in the region with the resource potential to increase production substantially in the next decades and provide China with energy.[6]

After signing the Azadegan oil field contract (projected to be one of the largest oil fields in the world) with Japan in 2004, in a balancing act, Iran reached a $20 billion USD agreement with China to sell it 2.5 metric tons of liquefied natural gas over a period of twenty-five years starting in 2008, making it the world's largest purchaser of natural gas at that time.[7] A few months later, Sinopec and the NIOC signed another contract that would allow China to buy $250 million tons of Iranian liquefied natural gas for the next thirty years. This deal is estimated to be worth $70–100 billion. In addition, China's National Petroleum Corporation was also given the right to invest in the exploration of the Yadavaran oil field in exchange for the right to purchase 150,000 barrels per day at the market price once the oil field is operational. China has also become an active participant in Iran's development of Caspian Sea oil and gas resources and the modernization of its facilities in Neka and other regions. China is sympathetic to Iran's attempt to bring Caspian Sea oil and gas through pipelines to the Southern Iranian ports and ship it to Europe and Asia. However, the United States is opposed to these kinds of initiatives that may expand Iran's economic and strategic clout.[8]

In March of 2008 China began negotiating with Iran over the North Pars gas field exploration, a contract worth $20 billion USD. While in 1994, Iran was responsible for just 1 percent of China's total oil imports, China is now the largest importer of Iranian oil and gas in the world. Meanwhile Iran provides China with about 11 to 15 percent of its energy imports, making it the second Middle Eastern supplier of energy to China after Saudi Arabia. In addition, Iranian leadership is increasingly favorably inclined to expand its trade and energy relations with China. As the former Iranian Oil Minister, Mr. Bijan Namdar Zangeneh told *China Business Weekly* in November 2004, "Japan is our number one energy importer for historical reasons. But we would like to give preference to export to China."[9]

In addition to oil and gas, China is also a major supplier of military hardware and technology to Iran and, alongside Russia, has played a key role in the development of its nuclear program. China has also been involved in building the Iranian subway system in Tehran, and several other projects such as dams, fisheries, port facilities, automobile factories, television factories, and the creation of a broadband network throughout the country. Chinese businessmen have found Iran to be a lucrative market for their consumer goods, and trade between the two countries has expanded substantially. In 2007, China emerged as Iran's number one trading partner in the world, indicating its increasing importance to the Iranian economy.[10] As this discussion has shown, the relationship between these two countries is becoming increasingly important to both sides, politically and economically.

China-Saudi Relations

Ruled by a conservative absolute monarchy that is a close ally of the United States, historically, Saudi leadership has shunned close relations with Communist China. China's support of the radical regime in South Yemen and the guerrilla movement in Oman made the Saudi monarchy deeply suspicious of China's motives in the region. However, political developments such as the US normalization of relations with China in 1972, the collapse of Communism in Eastern Europe in 1989, and the emergence of a more pragmatic leadership in Beijing all led the Saudi leadership to establish full diplomatic relations with China in 1990. As the Chinese government began to shed its old political image as a hard-line Communist ideologue supporting radical movements in the Third World, and proved to be a viable consumer of energy, willing to pay hard cash for long-term oil and gas contracts, the Saudi elite began to rethink its traditional attitude toward China. In the 1990s, as China further opened its market and became more integrated into the global economy, the Kingdom began to see the merit of having an ally who is a viable trade partner and has a permanent seat on the UN Security Council.

So far as the Chinese leaders were concerned, Saudi Arabia, a country with the largest oil reserves in the world (262 billion barrels of oil reserves as opposed to Iran's 132.6 billions of barrels of oil reserves) and a production capacity of 8.5–12.5 millions of barrel per day (as opposed to Iran's 3.6–4.2 millions of barrels per day) is an even bigger prize than Iran. With such vast reserves and production capacity, the Saudis are known as "swing producers" whose level of production can have a great deal of influence on the price of oil. Therefore, for Beijing, a major consumer of oil and gas, it makes a great deal of economic sense to expand its energy and trade relations with Riyadh. The fact that the Saudi monarchy does not carry the kind of political baggage associated with the Iranian government, and is seen as a close ally of the United States and Western Europe, made business with the Saudis a less risky political proposition as well.

With the establishment of political ties in 1990, China's trade relationship with the Kingdom increased exponentially from $71 million in 1989, to $525 million in 1991, to $1.027 billion in 1994. By 1996, Saudi Arabia had become China's leading trade partner in the Middle East and accounted for more than 30 percent of China's total exports to the region.[11]

China's desire to expand relations with the Kingdom manifested itself in the 1999 visit of then-president Jiang Zemin to Riyadh. On that trip, the two sides signed an oil agreement, inaugurating a "strategic oil partnership."

In that agreement, Saudi Arabia pledged to open its oil and gas market to China, except for upstream oil exploration and production. China in turn agreed to open its downstream sector and allowed the Saudis to invest in refining products from crude for both marketing and sales. Following this agreement, Chinese imports of Saudi oil increased substantially. In 1995 for example, China ranked 25th on the list of countries importing oil from Saudi Arabia. However, by 2002, Riyadh had become Beijing's leading foreign supplier of crude oil.

China also managed to attract substantial Saudi investment in joint ventures to expand and update the Chinese refining capacity.[12] In 2001 for example, Sinopec paid $3.5 billion for a 25 percent share in a refinery to be opened in Fujian province in 2008. This deal granted Aramco, the Saudi National Oil Company, a license to operate 600 fuel stations in Fujian, while China received a 30-year contract for 30,000 barrels of oil per day import from Saudi Arabia.[13] This quickly led to another deal between the two governments that would allow Aramco to build another refinery in China's Qingdao province, with a production capacity of 400,000 barrels per day. These refineries would effectively expand China's capacity to process the heavier crude that is found in Saudi Arabia and other Middle Eastern nations. This deal also allowed the Saudis to replace South Korea and other Asian suppliers of petrochemicals for the Chinese textile industry. In 2004, Sinopec won one of the three concessions that the Saudis awarded to foreign companies to develop the Kingdoms gas resources.[14] And by 2007, China listed Saudi Arabia as its second largest source of oil imports (behind Angola), while Saudi Arabia's total exports to the Asian markets (chiefly China, Japan, South Korea, and India) were estimated to be approximately 50 percent of its total.[15]

In 2006, soon after ascending to the throne, King Abdullah bin Abdul-Aziz al-Saud traveled to China and India to express the Kingdom's desire for expansion of relations with both countries. Many observers called the event a "strategic shift" in Saudi foreign policy.[16] The expanding China-Saudi energy connection and China's ambition to procure long-term energy supplies from Saudi Arabia, Iran, and the Middle East at large portends the possibility that China and the United States may be heading toward conflict over preferential access to strategic energy sources in the Middle East. But this scenario is not an unavoidable outcome. Thus far China's skillful diplomacy— balancing its need for energy security and its strategically significant bilateral economic and political relations with the United States— has been successful to prevent the outbreak of major conflict between them. China's behavior also demonstrates that it is not interested in political instability in the Middle East. On this issue, the interests of the United States and China coincide, thus these tensions and China's political posture in the region deserve a closer look.

China, US, Saudi Arabia, Iran Relations: Geo-Strategic Dimensions

If China's economic growth continues unabated in the future, its demand for energy will increase exponentially and its dependence on Middle Eastern energy sources will continue to grow in the next two decades. According to some projections, China is expected to outstrip Japan and Germany as the second largest economy by 2022. At this rate, global demand for petroleum would increase to 118 million barrels per day by the year 2025. More specifically, China and India would be responsible for 43 percent of the increase in this demand.[17]

The rising dependence of China on Middle Eastern oil supplies has ramifications for its relations with the region and for its relationship with the United States. For example will the United States, as a close ally and until recently as Saudi Arabia's biggest energy customer with 17 percent of Saudi exports, sit on the sidelines and do nothing while Beijing's influence in the Kingdom expands? On some accounts, the United States may not have many options with the onset of the 2008 recession. While China rebounded quickly, the recovery in the United States has proven to be much slower, slashing the oil consumption in the United States by 10 percent from 2005. Consequently, "Saudi Arabia exported more oil to China than to the United States last year."[18] Whether this is a long-term or a short-term transition is debatable. What is unquestionable, however, is a transition in the geopolitics of oil in general and in the Middle East in particular. China plays a large role in this transition and is regarded as the future of the market growth potential for Saudi Arabia over the United States. In fact Saudi Arabia now trails Canada, Mexico, and Venezuela as the top energy supplier to the United States. Hence, Aramco "no longer provides oil to American oil refineries for $1 less than to Asia. The Saudis no longer see the need to subsidize their oil exports to the United States. While the Saudi oil exports to the United States fell from 1.5 million barrels to 989,000 barrels a day in 2009, the lowest level in 22 years, its sales to China surged over one million barrels a day last year, nearly doubling from the previous year. The Kingdom has become an important supplier for China, and now accounts for a quarter of China's oil imports."[19] However, declining US dependence on Saudi oil could be problematic for the Kingdom since it still relies on the United States somewhat for its security. China may also be adversely affected by this development as the US navy works to safeguard the security of energy exports in the Persian Gulf. Although Saudi Arabia is just one part of the equation, the question remaining is how will the United States react to the rising power of China in the strategically significant region of the Middle East at large?

To ensure the success of its trade and foreign policy in the Middle East, China pursues a three-pronged strategy toward the region. First, the Chinese Communist Party (CCP) functions as a type of "economic actor" by using diplomacy to advance the country's economic interests. Second, in order to facilitate this, China has adopted a policy of "offend no one," refraining from intervention in the internal affairs of countries, and not taking sides in regional conflicts. Third, Beijing uses its soft power to "cultivate goodwill" and maintain friendly relations with regional powers in order to better serve its own economic and political interests.[20] These goals however, may not be easily achieved when challenges such as China's expanding ties with Iran put it at odds with the United States. It also remains to be seen if China will eventually feel compelled to take sides if the regional political landscape is further polarized. A final strategy employed by China is to build regional cooperation and security pacts to counter the hegemonic policies of the United States in the region, such as the Shanghai Cooperation Organization (SCO). The SCO is a collective security and cooperation pact founded in 2001 that includes such countries as Russia, China, Kazakhastan, Kyrgyzstan, and Tajikistan as members, and where Iran has been enlisted as an observer since 2005.

With respect to the strategic role Saudi Arabia plays in the region, the unfolding of the September 11, 2001 terrorist attacks on US soil, in which 15 of the 19 terrorists were identified as Saudi citizens, was a major turning point in the US-Saudi relationship. As the media and some members of Congress became increasingly critical of the close ties between Washington and Riyadh, the ever cautious Kingdom sought to distance itself from the United States and began to look in earnest to expand its export markets and build new global and regional alliances. Flush with cash, possessing a seat on the UN Security Council, lacking a history of colonial dominance in the region, and not having a particularly close alliance with Israel, China became increasingly an attractive alternative to the United States in the eyes of the Saudi leadership. In short, China provides Saudi Arabia a unique opportunity: a mutually beneficial economic relationship without the political baggage and pressure often associated with the United States.

Given the increasing erosion of the United States' political legitimacy in the Middle East in the post-2003 era, marked by US military involvement in Iraq and Afghanistan, the Kingdom's close relationship with the United States comes at a political cost: an increasing delegitimation of the monarchy. In light of these new political realities, as one observer has noted, in the post-9/11 era, US-Saudi relations have become more "*transactional*" rather than political. Both sides are trying to gain financially without damaging the relationship politically.[21] A sign of Riyadh's new autonomy from Washington was already evident in 2003 and 2004, when American companies lost key oil contracts to French, Chinese, and Russian companies.[22] Another sign of the Saudi leadership's attempt to demonstrate its autonomy from Washington manifested when King Abdullah invited Iranian President Ahmadinejad to join him in the annual Gulf Cooperation Council (GCC) gathering in Doha, Qatar in December of 2007. This invitation was issued despite numerous exhortations of the Bush administration to Iran's neighbors to join Washington and Israel in isolating the Islamic Republic as "the foremost terrorist state." This was a first GCC visit for an Iranian president and is one of many indicators that the political and economic relationships between the two countries have expanded in recent years. However, several tensions and rivalries between Saudi Arabia and Iran remain—as indicated by Saudi military participation in crushing the Shi'ite rebellion in Yemen in 2009–2010, whereas the Iranian government sympathized with the plight of Yemeni Shi'ites (Huthies). In addition the two sides are at odds over their respective support for the Shi'ite (Iran) and the Sunni (Saudi Arabia) groups in Iraq, and the Saudis also have concerns over Iran's nuclear ambitions.

It is important to note that relationships among the various actors do not constitute a zero-sum game, and conflict is an undesirable outcome. For example, closer Sino-Saudi ties do not necessarily connote confrontation between the US and Saudi governments or a major deterioration in Sino-US relations. Currently, the mutual economic benefits in bilateral relations for all actors outweigh the cost of conflict and confrontation. Indeed, China's increasing dependence on Middle East energy resources portends its increasing interest in the stability of future energy supplies and the secure flow of oil and gas from the region. Thus, it is vested in the region's political stability. Since political instability in the region often induces higher oil and gas prices and possible disruption of supplies, neither China nor the United States would like to see conflict. As major importers, the US and China's interests in the security of supplies and safeguarding their investments in the region are dependent on maintaining political stability in the region. Therefore, China is largely interested in maintaining the status quo rather than working to actively transform the political climate in the region.

Though the situation is slightly different in its dynamics, a similar pattern of behavior in China's relations with the Islamic Republic of Iran can be discerned. As discussed earlier, in pursuit of its national interests, China has expanded its trade and political relations with Iran considerably in the last two decades. However, as a member of the UN Security Council, it has not hesitated to vote in favor of three sets of sanctions on Iran over its nuclear ambitions. In fact, one can even make the case that such sanctions may indirectly benefit China economically, as sanctions further restrict the access of Western companies to Iran's market, and increase Iran's dependence on China's capital investments, products, and partnership. However, China's support of such sanctions is more complex than that, and unconditional acceptance of sanctions introduced by the US and Western allies that may cripple the Iranian economy would damage its long-term financial interests in Iran, which is undesired.[23] China's limited support of sanctions is not evidence that it has turned its back on the Islamic Republic. China has proven to be assertive in protecting what it regards as its core national interest, continued economic development and the integrity of sovereignty, and is willing to challenge the United States on policies it considers to be a manifestation of "hegemonic unilateralism."

China's energy-driven penetration of the Middle East also provides states such as Iran an alternative diplomatic ally and trade partner. For example, in the aftermath of the disputed elections of June 12, 2009 that reinstated Mr. Ahmadinejad for a second term as Iranian president, China denounced the opposition (Green Movement) as the stooges of American Imperialism. Although this perspective may change, initially the Chinese were not forthcoming to overtures of the Obama administration to enlist its support for a new set of sanctions on Iran. This reveals China's willingness to assume a more assertive political posture versus the United States when its national interest is at stake. Therefore, the ties that bind the two countries are primarily economic and political considerations rather than ideological ones.

For Iran, China provides a reliable long-term energy export market and a crucial trade partner whose membership on the UN Security Council and the board of the International Atomic Energy Agency (IAEA) has helped water down sanctions against the Islamic Republic. For instance, China has repeatedly opposed the use of a military option to punish Iran for its nuclear program. China also continues to be a supplier of major weapons and armaments to Iran, thus an important player in its national security.[24] As the Bush administration escalated its campaign to isolate the Iranian government, China provided Iran with an "Eastern Strategy," an alternative to US hegemonic policies and hostile posture. In a sign of souring Sino-US relations during the first year of the Obama administration, thus far China has refused to join the Western coalition and Russia to impose a fourth set of sanctions on Iran over its nuclear program. In fact, on February 11, 2010, in defiance of the Obama administration's announcement of its desire to impose new sanctions on Iran, CNPC, the parent company of Petro China, announced that China had finalized a deal with Iranian officials to develop phase two of South Pars natural gas field as early as March 2010; a deal valued at $4.7 billion.[25] Unable to convince China to come on board and vote for new sanctions on Iran as of yet, the US government has attempted to convince Saudi Arabia and the United Arab Emirates, the two regional allies of the United States with large volumes of trade with China, to use their leverage and pressure China to join the Western coalition against Iran. Thus far China has refused to budge, although it is not inconceivable that Iran's nuclear pursuits may result in a fourth round of sanctions at a later date that may include Chinese participation.[26]

For China, Iran is a major long-term energy supplier and a lucrative market for Chinese goods and services. Lacking the political baggage of Washington, China is well- positioned to enhance its influence and position in Iran's energy market and beyond. China also sees Iran as a useful political asset in its attempt to decrease US influence in the Middle East and Central Asia, two regions that are major suppliers of China's energy. This became evident in 2005 when Iran was invited to participate in the Shanghai Cooperation Organization. Although Iran currently only has observer status, in 2010 it was announced that Iran, Pakistan, and India will soon likely join the organization as full members. Should Iran join the SCO, it may become more difficult for the United States and its allies to either impose sanctions or take military action against Iran.[27]

This competition China has with the United States, however, is balanced against the reality of Sino-US bilateral economic and political relations, which looms much larger than its relationship with Iran in the Chinese leadership's political calculus. Some of the important factors include China's substantial trade surplus with the United States. As the nation with the largest foreign currency reserves in the world, China's more than trillion-dollar investment in US long-term treasury bonds helps to finance the large deficit in the United States and maintains the value of the US dollar. China also knows that its enlistment in global financial and international institutions is still reliant on having an amicable relationship with the United States. Therefore, in a larger global context, China is not willing to risk its significant bilateral relations with the United States by allying itself too closely with the Iranian government, should the tensions between Tehran and Washington escalate substantially in future.

China and the Rise of the "Second World"

Some scholars contend that in the post-Cold War era the scramble for global energy resources in the developing world among Russia, China, and the United States have now replaced the Cold War ideological rivalries. This new competition is now a major factor defining the power politics and the geo-strategic map of the world.[28] Other scholars speak of the emergence of a "Post-American World" in which wealth and power is shifting away from the United States and dispersing in multiple centers in which multipolarity and non-polarity co-exist.[29] Others contend that as the age of Empire gives way to "the age of convergence," Asian countries, most notable among them China, are moving to the "gravitational center" of this new configuration of power.[30] Yet, others argue that China's energy-driven penetration of the Middle East must be appreciated in what is tantamount to a paradigm shift in global politics. There is an emerging "Second World" that has now replaced the old Communist bloc. While ideologically divergent, these Second World countries agree in their opposition to what they perceive to be Washington's militarism, unilateralism, and pre-emptive hegemonic policies as manifested under the Bush administration. They also attempt to create an alternative to the "Washington Consensus." Leading this Second World are such energy consumers as China and India and such energy producers as Russia, Brazil, Iran, Saudi Arabia, and Venezuela. These countries are willing and able to challenge US hegemony on a wide range of issues in global affairs.[31]

With respect to the Middle East, countries like Saudi Arabia have already seen the writing on the wall and are diversifying their sources of foreign investment in the post- 2001 era. As Khanna has observed, "America's share of the foreign direct investment into the Kingdom decisively shaped the country's foreign policy, but today the monarchy is far wiser, luring Europe and Asia to bring their investment shares toward a third each. Saudi Arabia has engaged Europe in an evolving Persian Gulf free trade area, while it has invested close to $1 billion in Chinese oil refineries."[32]

Thanks to its skillful diplomacy, economic leverage, and an absence of the political baggage of colonialism in other regions, China has managed to simultaneously maintain "positive ties with the world's crucial pairs of regional rivals: Venezuela and Brazil, Saudi Arabia and Iran, Kazakhstan and Uzbekistan, India and Pakistan."[33] It is in this larger global context of declining American political capital and economic power and the emergence of the Second World, that we must understand Chinese foreign policy behavior in the Middle East, and indeed, the larger world.

Conclusion

Some scholars consider the rise of China to be "one of the greatest dramas of the twenty- first century."[34] Others go further and assert that if the twentieth century was the American century, then the twenty-first belongs to China, predicting that China's economy will outstrip the United States' GDP by 2020, and that the Yuan will surpass the value of dollar by 2030.[35]

While the Chinese government and many Chinese academics proclaim that China is in pursuit of global harmony (as opposed to hegemony), insisting that its rise is peaceful and its goal is to see the fruition of a "harmonious Middle East" where all nations co-exist peacefully and abide by international law,[36] the view among Western academics is decidedly divergent. Some scholars such as Ikenberry do not regard the rise of China as one that would necessarily entail great military conflict with the United States, whereas others such as Mearshimer are not as sanguine about a peaceful rise scenario. Ikenberry notes that China is well aware that the road to global power runs through the Western order and its multilateral economic institutions.[37] As such, China has no interest in radically transforming the present world order; it is a beneficiary of it. Moreover, the nuclear revolution has made war among great powers extremely costly and thus unlikely, eliminating the major tool that the rising powers have used to overturn international systems defended by declining hegemonic states. Today, the Western order, in short, is hard to overthrow and easy to join.[38] Mearshimer on the other hand, sees the rise of China as a phenomenon that is pregnant with conflicts with the United States and its allies that neither side would be able to manage peacefully. As Mearshimer states, "if China continues its impressive economic growth over the next few decades, the United States and China are likely to engage in an intense security completion with considerable potential for war."[39]

While China is keen to take advantage of the opportunities provided by US-Iran political conflict and the desire of the Saudi monarchy to avoid an over-reliance on the United States for trade and its security needs, given the political cost of close ties, it does so realizing that its bilateral relations with the United States loom much larger for China's long-term global ambitions than its relations with smaller nations such as Iran or Saudi Arabia. As our examination of China's economic and political relations with Iran and Saudi Arabia demonstrates, Chinese desire to secure long-term energy supplies and expand its trade and political ties with the Middle East is tempered by its willingness to remain a responsible international stakeholder. Indeed, as China becomes more dependent on Middle East energy sources to fuel its growing economy, it becomes more vested in security of energy supplies, hence, the political stability of the region. Only such stability can foster continued Chinese access to the crucial sources of energy. In fact, since China does not have a littoral navy, it must rely on the US navy for the security of oil shipping lanes in the Persian Gulf. This reality also indicates the convergence of US-China interests in maintaining the security of regional energy supplies and their vested interest in regional political stability. While China has proven to be more assertive in defending its core national interest in the region as of late, nevertheless, it is not a transformative agent. It is arguably still a status quo power preoccupied with safeguarding its economic interests.

More specifically, our case study of China's behavior toward Iran and Saudi Arabia demonstrates the effectiveness of China's three-pronged pragmatic strategy toward the region discussed earlier. The following observations confirm this. First, the fact that China has managed to maintain viable political and economic relations with such ideologically diverse countries as Saudi Arabia (a conservative absolute monarchy and a US ally) and Iran (an Islamic theocracy with contentious, and at times, acrimonious relations with the United States) is a testimony to the Chinese non-ideological and pragmatic approach to foreign policy. In this regard, China's upholding of such principles as non-intervention, respect for sovereignty, and maintaining political neutrality (which stood in sharp contrast to the Bush administration's policies of militarism, interventionism, and imperial overstretch), has served China's interests well in the region so far. Second, as discussed above, China's assessment of the extent and limitations of its power unfolds within an evolving political dynamic marked by diminishing American economic and political power. The political fallout from the Bush administration's invasion of Iraq, the as of yet undetermined outcome of the Obama administration's military escalation in Afghanistan, the decline of the dollar, and the onset of global recession are but a few manifestations of this new reality. These developments have created a political vacuum for China to step in and take initiatives to further expand its influence and power in the region. Third, the rise of "the Second World" provides China with opportunities for global alliances to counter US hegemonic policies. But as a status quo power, ever mindful of the gravity of its economic and political relations with the United States, Chinese leaders so far have demonstrated a remarkable discipline to balance the pursuit of their national interest with managing their competition with the United States within the bonds and norms of international law. Chinese leaders have shown that they are willing to protect their national interest, yet they are also capable of holding back when the aggressive pursuit of those interests may bring them to a decisive confrontation and conflict with the United States. Their relationship with the Islamic Republic is a case in point. Given the larger significance of Sino-US relations in Beijing's global strategy, should the relations between Iran and the United States become more antagonistic in future, China is likely to distance itself from the Islamic Republic. This can be seen clearly in Beijing's willingness to vote in favor of three UN-sponsored resolutions imposing sanctions on Iran for its nuclear ambitions. Indeed, the imposition of US-led UN Security Council sanctions on Iran has inadvertently served to solidify China-Iran relations. The imposition of sanctions discourages Western banks and companies from doing business with Iran, thus expanding China's access to the Iranian market in general and the energy sector in particular. For example, the withdrawal of Royal Dutch Shell, Repsol of Spain, and the French Total energy companies from Iran's vast gas fields under US pressures in May and July of 2008 has left Iran more dependent on China's energy companies and their investments.[40] Yet, China is willing to go along with sanctions as long as it does not damage its strategic interests in Iran, as evidenced in its refusal to go along with the new set of sanctions proposed by the Obama administration.

The observations and analysis presented in this chapter confirm that Chinese foreign policy behavior in the Middle East is a fluid (rather than static) phenomenon. It is constantly adapting and adjusting to a rapidly changing global and regional environment. In other words, as the power structure in the world shifts, the economic and political leverage of China as a rising power provides those states alienated by US foreign policy choices an alternative partner. In turn, such nations as Iran and Saudi Arabia, with a history of colonialism and foreign intervention in their domestic affairs, may also see in their partnership with China the possibility of a new configuration of power in which they are no longer marginalized members on the periphery, but are regional players with significant assets and power to set the agenda that affects their political destiny.

Notes

1 Zheng Bijian (2005) "China's Peaceful Rise to Great Power Status," *Foreign Affairs*, Vol. 84, No. 5 (September/ October), p. 1.

2 Energy Information Administration (2005) "China Country Analysis Brief," August. www.eia.doe.gov/emeu/cabs/China.html, accessed February 5, 2009.

3 Jin Liangxiang (2005) "Energy First: China and the Middle East," *Middle East Quarterly*, Vol. X11, No. 2 (Summer), p. 1.

4 Mohamed Bin Huwaidin (2002) *China's Relations with Arabia and the Gulf, 1949–1999* (New York: Routledge-Curzon), pp. 165–172.

5 John W. Garver (2006) *China and Iran: Ancient Partners in a Post-Imperial World* (Seattle and London: University of Washington Press), pp. 266–268.

6 Flynt Leverret (2007) "The Geopolitics of Oil and America's International Standing," Testimony to the Committee on Energy and Natural Resources, United States Senate , January 10, 7, p. 7.

7 Garver, Opcit., p. 269.

8 Ibid., pp. 270–275. See also Jin Liangxiang (2005) "Energy First: China and the Middle East," *Middle East Quarterly*, Vol. X11, No. 2 (Summer), pp. 1–2.

9 Roger Howard (2007) *Iran Oil: The New Middle East Challenge to America* (London: I.B. Tauris), p. 95.

10 Manochehr Dorraj and Carrie Liu Currier (2008) "Lubricated With Oil: Iran-China Relations in a Changing World," *Middle East Policy*, Vol. 15, No. 2 (Summer), pp. 66–80.

11 Huwaidin. Opcit., pp. 228–236.

12 Flynt Leverett and Jeffrey Bader (2005–2006) "Managing China-US Energy Competition in the Middle East," *The Washington Quarterly*, Winter, pp. 191–192.

13 Henry Lee and Dan A. Shalmon (2007) "Searching For Oil: China's Initiatives in the Middle East," *Environment*, June. See also (2006) "China, Saudi Arabia Forge Closer Relationship," *China Daily*, January 24.

14 Leverett and Bader, Opcit., p. 192.

15 Country Analysis Briefs-Saudi Arabia. Energy Information Administration. February, 2007. http://www.eia.doe.gov/emeu/cabs/Saudi_Arabia/Full.html. Accessed January 10, 2009.

16 Harsh, V. Pant (2006) "Saudi Arabia Woos China and India," *Middle East Quarterly*, Vol. 13, No. 4 (Fall), p. 45.

17 "World Oil Markets" (2006) *Energy Information Administration Informational Outlook 2006*, pp. 25–33.
18 Jad Mouawad (2010) "China's Growth Shifts the Geopolitics of Oil," *The New York Times*, March 19, p. B 1.
19 Ibid., pp. B2–B3.
20 Mao Yufeng (2007) "China's Interest and Strategy in the Middle East and the Arab World," In J. Eisenman, E. Heginbotham, and D. Mitchell (eds), *China and the Developing World: Beijing's Strategy for the Twenty-First Century* (Armok, New York: M.E. Sharpe), p. 113.
21 Rachel Bronson (2006), *Thicker Than Oil: America's Uneasy Partnership With Saudi Arabia* (New York: Oxford University Press), pp. 250–251. See also Thomas W. Lippman (2004) *Inside the Mirage: America's Fragile Partnership With Saudi Arabia* (Boulder, CO: Westview Press), p. 340.
22 Bronson, ibid., p. 251.
23 China has been very reluctant to support sanctions against Iran, often trying to water-down the extent of sanctions or delaying implementation of them. This is consistent with a key element of Chinese foreign policy dealing with non-intervention and the value of sovereignty. However, Iran's continued defiance of the international community over the development of its nuclear program has put China in a difficult situation where it must weigh its image as a responsible stakeholder against its economic pursuits in Iran. In this case, limited support of certain sanctions has been a compromise between the two—without creating too much of a strain on its image with either the international community or Iran.
24 Carrie Liu Currier and Manochehr Dorraj (2010) "In Arms We Trust: Strategic and Economic Factors Motivating China-Iran Relations," *Chinese Journal of Political Science*, Vol. 15(1), . 49–69.
25 Xinhua Economic News Service, February, 11, 2010.
26 Elisabeth Bumiller (2010) "U.S. Defense Chief Visits Saudi Arabia to Bolster Effort Against Iran," *New York Times*, March 11.
27 Flynt Leverett, "Iran, China and the Shanghai Cooperation Organization" http://www.racefor iran.com/iran-China-and –the –shanghi-cooperation-organization. Accessed March 20, 2010.
28 Michael T. Klare (2009) *Rising Powers Shrinking Planet: Oil and the "New International Energy Order"* (New York: Metropolitan Books).
29 Fareed Zakaria (2008) *The Post- American World* (New York: W.W. Norton).
30 Jeffrey D. Sachs (2008) *Common Wealth: Economics for a Crowded Planet* (New York: Penguin Press).

31 Parag Khanna (2008) "Waving Goodbye to Hegemony," *The New York Times Magazine*, January, pp. 1–16. See also Parag Khanna (2008) *The Second World: How Emerging Powers Are Redefining Global Competition in the Twenty-First Century* (New York: Random House).

32 "Waving Goodbye to Hegemony." Ibid., p. 5.

33 Ibid.

34 John Ikenberry (2008) "The Rise of China and the Future of the West," *Foreign Affairs*, Vol. 87 (January/February), pp. 23–57.

35 Ted C. Fishman (2006) *China, Inc.: How the Rise of the Next Superpower Challenges America and the World* (New York: Scribner Publishers).

36 Shi Yongminh (2006) "Rational Order," *Beijing Review*, December 21. See also Zheng, Opcit.

37 Ikenberry, Opcit.

38 Ibid.

39 John L. Mearshimer (2006) "China's Unpeaceful Rise," *Current History*, Vol. 105, No. 690 (April), pp. 160–162.

40 David Jolly (2008) "Amid Political Uncertainty, Total Cancels Investments in Iran," *The New York Times*, July 11.

CHAPTER FIVE

China, Russia, and Central Asia: Triangular Energy Politics

Gregory Gleason[*]

Introduction

Nowhere has the dramatic rise of China and its unprecedented economic growth in the last two decades been more apparent than in its neighboring states in Central Asia and its major northern neighbor, Russia. China's expanding political influence on the global stage has been intermediated by its access to the energy resources of these neighboring countries. For this reason, upward forces on energy commodity prices can be expected to further contribute to the politicization of commercial competition among the world's leading energy producers and energy consumers, intensifying political pressure in particular on the newly emergent energy suppliers in Central Asia. Newly accessible oil and gas reserves in Azerbaijan, Kazakhstan, Turkmenistan, and Uzbekistan involve shipments through third-party countries before reaching Western markets. Fewer constraints confront shipment to the East. At the same time, Russia and China have both conflicting and complementary stakes in consuming, transporting, processing, and marketing Caspian energy resources. As a consequence, the triangular relationship among China, Russia, and Central Asian countries involves complicated commercial and political objectives that have contributed to producing what all the Central Asian states refer to as their "multi-vector" foreign policies. This chapter analyzes these multi-vector policies in terms of the region's production, transport, and trade of energy resources.

In geometry, three points define a plane and generally constitute the conditions for stability. In diplomacy, however, a triangular relationship describes a dynamic political interaction which may not take place in a single plane and which may not constitute conditions of stability. In a triangular diplomatic relationship, even small differences among the interests of the parties can lead to a situation in which two sides compete against the third. As a consequence, the stability of a triangular diplomatic relationship often depends upon the way that foreign policy relations come into alignment. The triangular foreign policy relationships among the three most important actors in the central regions of Asia may be conceived of as a triangular diplomatic relationship organized in relation to the energy trade. China, the largest actor, is one aspect of the relationship. Russia, the largest energy producer is a second. The countries of the Caucasus and Central Asian states—thought of as comprising a "greater Central Asian Basin"—may be regarded as a third major actor. This triangular relationship is structured around three distinguishing features: (1) the Caucasus and Central Asian states' energy producing capacities, middle-man position in trade relations, and political vulnerabilities given their smaller size; (2) Russia's ample natural resource endowment but limitations on economic capacity; (3) and China's expanding energy demands emerging from its rising economic prowess.

China's energy policy is integrated into the country's unique and deeply positioned foreign policy. Its energy policy is comprehensive in the sense that it is closely connected to the country's other policy principles, goals, and practices. China's energy policy involves both "push and pull" factors, implying greater and continuing engagement in the world economy yet on a very carefully defined and balanced basis. In contrast, Russia's energy policy is substantially different. Russia's great natural resource endowment is the country's most valuable foreign policy advantage. Russia's resurgence in economic and political matters during the past decade has been almost exclusively fueled by energy exports. Russia's planners are aware of the country's long-term vulnerability in a world in which excessive dependence upon a primary commodity exporting strategy threatens to relegate a country to a second-rate status as a supplier of natural resources rather than an innovator or beneficiary of technological progress. In yet another contrast, the energy policies of the Caucasus countries and the Central Asian states are the expression of newly emergent foreign policy agendas. Principle and purpose compete with gain and influence in all the Caucasus and Central Asian countries when determining government policy.

The triangular relationship among China, Russia, and the Central Asian states is expected to be one of the most influential relationships in the twenty-first century. Great possibilities and opportunities as well as great risks and threats lie ahead for this triangular relationship. The potential gains of prosperity brought from harnessing energy sources are in sharp contrast with the dangers of invidious commercial competition, the political risks of energy disruption and the long-term social and environmental effects of boom and bust cycles of energy exploitation.[1]

The way that China, Russia, and the Central Asian and Caucasus policies will play out depends less on balance among forces than on competition among very unequal partners with greatly varying interests. This chapter analyzes the national energy policies of China with Russia and the Central Asian states in terms of their importance for international relations.

China's Energy Policies

China is a vast country with many subtleties and features but its foreign policy is rather pragmatic. China's diplomatic influence dramatically increased with the shift during the 1990s to a more realistic foreign policy aimed at stabilizing relations with immediate neighbors and solidifying the commercial relations with its major consumer, the United States.[2] From a certain perspective, China's foreign policy can be seen as realism with Chinese characteristics. China's leaders appear to make calculations based on modestly defined and scrupulously narrow ideas of national interest. Foreign policy has not become a battleground of partisan, commercial, or ideological interests. Rather, foreign policy is defined as a prerogative of the state and is largely based in upholding the principles of sovereignty. The state is sufficiently consolidated to have the means to define and pursue its interests.

From the point of view of Russia and the Central Asian states, these features of China's foreign policy and energy policies make it distinct from the more holistic and demanding assumptions of the western Anglo-Saxon models of business and politics. China's core principles are simple. China maintains a rather unique sense of self and does not easily give into international pressures. China is devoted to notions of sovereignty and non-interference. China is opposed to control by others, and so it opposes hegemony and world domination. China also promotes the idea of peaceful co-existence and it maintains a sympathetic relationship with developing countries in opposing colonialism. Finally, China maintains a flexible and pragmatic view toward economic development and international organizations in which it takes a role.

Important concepts which are unique in modern Chinese thought include people's war and comprehensive national power. The new security concept that was announced in the late 1990s asserts that in the post-Cold War period, nations are able to increase their security through diplomatic and economic interaction, and the Cold-War mentality of antagonistic confrontations is outdated. Around 2002 and 2003, this security policy seemed to merge with the foreign policy doctrine known as China's "peaceful rise," which was later amended to be China's "peaceful development."

China's oil production, transportation, and distribution are managed through hybrid public-private enterprises that are controlled by the state but act in some respects as private sector entities. China's petroleum industry has undergone structural changes that began roughly a decade ago, when the national oil sector was re-organized into two large companies, China National Petroleum Corporation (CNPC) and the China Petroleum & Chemical Corporation (Sinopec), but where the state remains the controlling shareholder. Another big change, related to demand, is that China became a net-importer of hydrocarbons as of 1993.

China's largest oil field is CNPC's Daqing field in northeastern China. The field accounts for more than 900,000 bbl/d (million barrels a day), or one quarter of China's total crude oil production. Meanwhile, offshore sources account for about 15 percent of China's production. Anticipating an increase in demand, the Chinese government has encouraged greater offshore activity. China energetically began seeking to gain access through acquiring interests in exploration and production abroad. CNPC has acquired exploration and production interests in many countries, including Kazakhstan, Sudan, and others. For example, CNPC in October 2005 purchased PetroKazakhstan. This was followed in December 2005 by completion of the 600-mile Sino-Kazakh oil pipeline designed to deliver roughly 200,000 bbl/d of crude oil. In June 2006, Sinopec acquired a 97 percent stake in Udmurtneft, a mid-sized unit of BP's Russia vehicle TNKBP, for $3.5 billion.

The Kazakhstan–China oil pipeline is China's first direct oil import pipeline allowing oil imports from Central Asia. It runs from Kazakhstan's Caspian shore to China's far northwestern province of Xinjiang. The pipeline is owned by the China National Petroleum Corporation (CNPC) and the Kazakh oil company KazMunaiGaz. The 2,228-km (1,384 mi) long pipeline runs from Atyrau in Kazakhstan to Alashankou in China's Xinjiang. In April 2009 CNPC bought out a controlling share of KazMunaiGaz, Kazakhstan's fourth largest oil producer with a controlling interest in Kazakhstan's Karachaganak oil field. CNPC works under guidance from the SASAC, China's Assets Supervision and Administration Commission.

With natural gas use on the rise in China, and uncertainties surrounding the potential of piped Russian natural gas, liquefied natural gas (LNG) has increasingly been considered by Chinese companies as a preferred source of energy. In a joint venture with BP and local firms, CNOOC (China National Offshore Oil Corporation) built China's first LNG import terminal in Guangdong province, which received its first 60,000 ton shipment of LNG in May 2006. The facility has a capacity to handle 3.7 million tons per year (Mmt/y) of LNG, with a planned second phase that would double capacity in the future. CNOOC also awarded a 25-year, 3.3 Mmt/y LNG supply agreement to Australia's North West Shelf consortium to supply the new import terminal.

Russia has tried to tap into the increasing LNG interest in China and the rest of Asia, by developing this industry. In February 2009, Russian President Dmitry Medvedev opened Russia's first LNG plant built by Sakhalin Energy Investment Company Limited (Sakhalin Energy). The LNG plant is the heart of the Sakhalin II Project, one of the largest integrated oil and gas projects in the world. The Project includes three offshore platforms, an onshore processing facility, 300 km of offshore pipelines and 1,600 km of onshore pipelines, an oil export facility, and the LNG plant. This Sakhalin II facility was designed to lead Russia in becoming a leading energy exporter to the highly competitive energy markets of the Asia-Pacific region.

Russian National Energy Policies

Following the collapse of the Soviet Union in 1991, Russia's economic policy gravitated toward commodity exports, enabling the breakup of the Soviet gas and oil industry into private firms and planning the privatization of the electric power sector. After the 1998 Russian financial crisis that led to sovereign default and a precipitous fall in the value of the Russian ruble, Russian gas and oil producers became much more competitive on the international energy market. By 2000, political power from the Yeltsin era political elite had transitioned to a new era of centrally managed, more state-oriented and more nationalistically inclined commerce and politics. A cadre of former Soviet government officials assumed political control, tying their influence to the most available source of revenue, oil, and natural gas. Russia's oil and natural gas exports assumed a priority. In 2004, rising hydrocarbon revenues were sequestered in a government stabilization fund. The fuel sector grew to almost one quarter of the country's nominal GDP. As energy exports grew, the Russian government became more focused on state control of the oil and gas companies, gradually edging out foreign-owned competitors or sequestering them to technology transfer and managing contractors rather than owners. Russia's electricity reforms were initiated in July 2008 when the Russian electricity monopoly RAO UES was dissolved and production was unbundled from transmission facilities.

Today Russia holds the world's largest natural gas reserves, the second largest coal reserves, and the eighth largest oil reserves. Russia is also the world's largest exporter of natural gas, the second largest oil exporter, and the third largest energy consumer. As one of the world's major oil producers, Russia sometimes produces even more than Saudi Arabia. Russia's output rebounded during the early 2000s, but the effects of high government taxation and a mature field base threaten an overall decline in production in the years ahead. Russia's future oil outlook is complemented by its natural gas prospects, particularly the "threat" of shale gas. But that picture is complicated by the fact that Gazprom, Russia's state-controlled gas producer, is facing imminent production declines without embarking on major new field investments. Therefore, Russia's natural gas industry will face investment challenges in bringing online new, more challenging and expensive fields.

Russia's resurgent influence over energy resources as an instrument of foreign policy has stimulated fears among Europeans over dependence on Russian energy sources. European vulnerability to natural gas supply disruption was underscored by the cutoff of Russian natural gas deliveries to Ukraine in early 2006. US Vice President Dick Cheney, speaking at a conference in Vilnius, accused the Kremlin of using the manipulation of gas and oil supplies as "tools of intimidation and blackmail."[3] However, Russia's greatest future comparative advantage in translating energy supplies into political influence may be its access not to the energy markets of Western Europe—which are forecasted as having modest future growth—but to the sharply growing energy markets of south Asia and China.

The Russian Ministry of Foreign Affairs came to regard energy politics as the principal instrument for countering American and European influence in Central Asia while also building a bulwark against Chinese encroachment. Harnessing Russia's comparative advantage in energy and power would indeed seem to be a way to make good business out of strategic purpose. However, the energy infrastructure in Central Asia, the Caucasus, and South Asia has potential political instability. While most attention has been focused on gas and oil pipelines and transit routes, in fact electric power transmission is the dominating factor in the state-to-state relationships in the region. For a number of reasons, electric transmission is less influenced by market fluctuations and is more dependent upon state-to-state policies.[4] It is well known that in general there is a critical disjunction between electric power production and use in the region. Given the configuration of the electric generation and distribution system in the greater Central Asian region, production capacity and emerging demand are out of sync. Electricity markets are not organized in abstract expressions of supply and demand but are organized in terms of expensive fixed physical infrastructures for production, transmission, and distribution of electricity that require a significant amount of capital investment, maintenance, and regulation.

The goal of creating a region-wide West Asian electric grid that links electric grids in Russia with electric grids in China and India was a major goal of the Russian government and the leading electric company, the Unified Electric Systems (UES), the Russian state-owned electric provider before UES underwent deregulation and divided into unbundled providers and transmission. The establishment of a West-Asian regional electric market was envisaged as creating vast new electric markets for Russian electric producers interested in making use of Russia's leading comparative advantage in foreign affairs, energy trade in general, and natural gas energy sources in particular. The establishment of a West-Asian regional electric market was also expected to offer great new energy resources for development in India and China. An enlarged electric wholesale market would reach from European consumers to consumers in the very different weather conditions of East China and Southern India. The market would also bring connections to Pakistan, Central Asian states, and reconstruction in Afghanistan. The potential for expanding production revenues and creating new opportunities for supply in regions that are starved for energy is a major motive behind the Russian diplomacy throughout the region.

Russia is not alone in this goal. The US government put a significant amount of work into developing a coordinated regional response to the challenges of Central Asian energy production and distribution. USAID (US Agency for International Development) provided technical assistance to aid in promoting the development of a regional electricity market in Central Asia. In late 2005 USTDA (US Trade and Development Agency) initiated three power sector projects, one providing technical assistance on hydropower investment in Tajikistan, a feasibility study on the rehabilitation of the Kairakkum and Varzob cascade hydroelectric plants in Tajikistan, and a feasibility study on the southern Kyrgyzstan Transmission upgrade project. The benefits to integration into a Greater Asian Regional Energy system for all the countries of the region are clear. First and most apparent and motivating for all the regional players is the prospect of the economic benefit of integration. Higher revenues for power producers and greater access to cheaper energy for consumers constitute the benefit that is luring everyone. The economic objectives have led all the major players in the region—Russia, China, India, Pakistan—toward strategic policies that are motivated by the prospect for these economic gains. The diplomacy of the region is primarily to enhance an economic drive for expansion motivating

Russia's "North-South" policies, China's "Go-West" policies, and even the rapprochement between Pakistan and India. But even if large-scale wholesale electricity markets are beneficial to everyone, the regulatory framework of the market has enormous influence on who wins, at what scale, and under what circumstances.

Energy Production Dynamics in Central Asia

The Central Asian countries and the neighboring Caucasus countries on the other side of the Caspian Basin have widely different energy profiles and prospects for energy trade in the future.[5] Forecasting future energy trade, there are two basic components in the calculations: (1) current capacity; and (2) factors that influence change in current capacity with respect to future demand. Current capacity refers to the aggregate calculation of production, processing, transportation, marketing, and substitution factors. The aggregate calculation includes the influence of substitution factors because some forms of energy are substitutable while others are less so.

The current energy capacity of the Central Asian and Caucasus states with importance for the region's import and export relationships is represented in Table 5.1. A number of conclusions are immediately apparent from the overall profile. Russia is a major producer, user, and exporter of oil, gas, and coal and has an important impact on energy in the region.[6] Kazakhstan is a major producer and exporter of oil and coal, but an importer of gas. Turkmenistan is a major gas exporter. Uzbekistan is a major exporter of oil and natural gas and is relatively self-sufficient in coal. Meanwhile, Azerbaijan is a major oil exporter but has played a limited role in natural gas production and trade, but has announced plans to significantly increase production.[7]

Going beyond the features represented in this general profile, however, involves considerable calculation that hinges upon market dynamics that are world-market dependent or technology-dependent, thus beyond the influence of the regional actors. Two decades ago the sharp increase in China's demand for oil and gas was unexpected. Accordingly, the transport facilities were not constructed in advance of the unmet demand and the upward pressure on prices.[8] Russia inherited from the Soviet period a physical plant which was not well configured for the repositioning required by international markets. Russia's gas industry is a good example. Gazprom, the heir to the Soviet-era natural gas production and distribution network and the largest tax payer in Russia, is a commercial company held and managed by the Russian government. The reasoning behind this hybrid public-private entity is that it is designed to run on a commercial basis, turn a profit, and operate under government control in order to serve public interests. Long-deferred

Table 5.1 Central Asian/Caucasus Energy Profiles

	Azerbaijan	Kazakhstan	Russia	Turkmenistan	Uzbekistan
Petroleum (1000 Barrel/day–2008					
Crude Oil					
Production	870	1,345	9,357	170	50
Consumption	121	244	2,916	103	143
Net Exports/Imports	749	1,191	6,890	77	−64
Refinery Capacity	399	345	5,428	237	222
Natural Gas (Billion Cubic Feet–2007					
Production	345	985	23,064	2,432	2,302
Consumption	345	1,080	16,746	688	1,807
Drynatural gas					
Net Exports/Imports	0	−95	6,318	1,745	495
Coal (Million Short Tons)					
Production	0	95	346	0	4
Consumption	0	74	244	0	4
Electricity (Billion Kilowatt hours–2007)					
Net Generation	22	68	941	13	47
Net Consumption	19	62	820	10	42

Source: Compiled from Energy Information Administration, Country Energy Profiles, Updates as of November 18, 2009. http://tonto.eia.doe.gov

maintenance and inadequate investment have produced a situation which Gazprom is struggling to overcome through a mixture of foreign investment and government subsidies. Gazprom seeks to attract foreign investment in order to finance the modernization of its facilities, but in order to do this it needs to ensure foreign investors of the company's financial reliability. At the same time Gazprom seeks to retain subsidies and government protection, but can only do so at the expense of its commercial orientation and at the risk of losing investor confidence. As it works out, every step closer to the government appears to be a step away from the investors; every step toward the investors appears to be a step away from the government. Thus Gazprom finds itself in a quandary.

Market signals in the energy business are very hard for government officials to read when they are making political calculations. Particularly in the globalized and fluid world of energy relationships, the extrapolation of current dynamics of supply and demand can lead to distorted judgments and unrealistic expectations. A decade ago energy forecasters anticipated that advances in technology would lead to vast expansion in the market for natural gas. With natural gas reserves greater than twice that of any other country and as much as a third of the entire globe, a gas development strategy was seen as the ideal instrument to lead Russia's return from the post-Soviet recession. The Russian political leadership pressured Gazprom to embark on an ambitious strategy to corner the gas market. The goal of the strategy was to reel in commercial gain for Gazprom, which would have the effect of casting a much broader Russian geopolitical net.

Another part of Russia's strategy involved shifting to capture emerging markets for LNG by constructing liquefaction facilities to prepare natural gas, principally methane, for transportation as a liquid. Investor interest in LNG facilities grew during the 1990s as concerns over "peak oil" led to anticipations that oil would be gradually replaced by the natural gas as a more environmentally friendly fuel and LNG would be more market responsive than piped natural gas. Russia embarked on construction of a major facility—Sakhalin II—in order to liquefy and ship Far Eastern natural gas through a newly constructed liquefaction facility to Asia Pacific Rim customers. In negotiating the construction, the Russian government pressured the conclusion of a deal which involved outside partners but which notably left more than 50 percent of the shares in the hands of Gazprom. Construction of Russia's first LNG plant on Sakhalin Island started in August 2003 and was completed at the inauguration of the plant in February 2009. The deal involved long-term contracts with an expectation that approximately 65 percent of the output would be destined for buyers in Japan. The remainder would go to other Asian and Pacific Rim partners, including the United States. Overall, Russia worked to solidify its European markets by making those consumers reliant upon Russia's supplies and to free up supplies for marketing to newly emergent Asian markets. But this strategy ran into a number of unanticipated changes.

One complication to Russia's gas strategy is represented by what may be a technological breakthrough that could undermine the main thrust of Russia's reliance on natural gas as the locomotive to drive the Russian "resurgence." Only a few years ago American energy planners were anticipating a shift to foreign gas resources and new LNG facilities. But the advent of new gas extraction methods from areas previously thought to be inaccessible through drilling and fracturing methods have reversed anticipations about the role of gas in American energy markets and, possibly, global energy markets. Natural gas production from hydrocarbon rich shale formations, known as "shale gas," is the most rapidly expanding trends in onshore domestic oil and gas exploration and production.[9] Shale gas extraction started gradually but quickly emerged as a technology that could significantly shift markets, potentially leading to sufficient production in the United States to meet or exceed domestic market demand.[10] As the following timeline of events shows, this is a newer area of exploration and it is affecting the energy industry within China, the United States, and Russia. In April 2009 the US Department of Energy made available an overview of the burgeoning shale gas industry. In November 2009 the White House announced a partnership with China to explore shale gas extraction in China.[11] In January 2010 at the Davos Forum, British Petroleum CEO Tony Hayward referred to the sudden emergence of this new extraction technology as a "complete game changer," saying it would "change the energy outlook in the US for the next 100 years."[12] These developments have important implications for the future of LNG in energy markets.

If the above analysis is accurate, there are two basic components in calculations of future national energy policy, namely a state's current capacity and its assessment of the risks and opportunities involved in altering policy to benefit from future changes. It is therefore useful to consider the formation and conduct of national policy in each of the region's major energy trading partners.

The Central Asian States

The Central Asian countries are highly interdependent with respect to energy resources, transportation infrastructure, and markets. The greatest source of wealth in the region is natural resources, particularly gas and oil. Many of the oil resources are located on the Caspian Sea littoral or in remote western Kazakhstan, and the potential for increasing oil and gas production in the region is great. Oil industry analysts expect that the region could be exporting as much as two million barrels a day by the end of 2010. But because all the region's oil-producing countries are landlocked, routes to the market invariably involve shipment through third-party countries. As a consequence, the complexities of the region's geography and the differing national interests of the countries make access to markets a matter of mutual agreement, or at least mutual negotiation.

Kazakhstan

Kazakhstan's objectives and capabilities defined what may be called its pro-globalization strategy. Kazakhstan emerged from the USSR with a deliberate goal of establishing a democratic system and a market-oriented economy. Kazakhstan's nuclear status, its oil and mineral wealth, its enthusiasm for structural reform, and its mixed Kazakh and Russian populations were defining influences on the domestic political context of foreign policy making during the first years of independence.

During the first years of Nursultan Nazarbayev's tenure as Kazakhstan's president, diplomatic efforts were consistently associated with the concept of "Eurasian-ness," the idea of the close linkages among the peoples of the Central Eurasian landmass. Based on the idea of "Eurasian integration," Kazakhstan's foreign policy followed a careful line, balancing interests based upon many factors. Balancing interests implied not turning away from Russia while at the same time not permitting Russia to dominate decision making for Kazakhstan. For Kazakhstan this meant maintaining a balanced distance from Russia, remaining neither too close nor too distant. Maintaining good relations with the West and international organizations was an ideal instrument for achieving what Kazakh policy makers eventually began to refer to as Kazakhstan's "multi-vector" foreign policy. A primary motive for Kazakhstan's globalization policy was the goal of preventing the re-emergence of Russian domination in the region.

As early as 1991 the Kazakhstan government began negotiating with international oil firms to develop Kazakhstan's "Tengiz" oil fields. The Kazakhstan government joined the large multinational oil firm Chevron to form a joint venture, "Tengizchevroil." The agreement committed Chevron to spend about $20 billion over twenty years to develop the Tengiz field's six billion barrels of proven reserves. The agreement anticipated that eventually Kazakhstan would be exporting as much as 700,000 barrels a day from the field. Other firms, including Birlesmis Muhendisler Burosu, British Gas, and Agip also committed investment in the country's oil fields. Beginning in 1992, the Russian government privatized management of the state-owned energy sector and major private oil companies emerged from the re-organization. The new Russian firms and the Russian government cooperated to restrict the access of the Caspian states to the Russian pipeline system and its connections to Western markets. Russia first sought to impose high taxes and surcharges on the movement of gas and oil and then, in order to block economic development that might run contrary to the interests of Russian energy firms, sought to blockade its southern neighbors by cutting off access to foreign markets entirely.

The Caspian countries began developing ways to bring energy supplies to market without having to pass through Russian territory. Russia lobbied for a continued reliance on the Soviet-era pipeline system, the so-called northern option. European and North American countries were partial to the idea of shipment across the Caucasus and on to world markets through the Bosporos, the "western option." The Economic Cooperation Organization (ECO) urged "southern options," involving four possible routes, Baku–Ceyhan (Turkey); Kazakhstan–Turkmenistan–Afghanistan–Pakistan to the Indian Ocean; Turkmenistan–Iran–Turkey toward Europe; and the supply of Uzbek and Turkmen gas to Pakistan through Afghanistan.

The western and southern alternatives left Kazakhstan with a limited number of options. However, the Chinese government was anxious to develop its relatively underdeveloped western province of Xinjiang, and invested in oil development and refinery during the 1980s and early 1990s. In September 1997 the Kazakhstan government and CNPC agreed to invest in the construction of a pipeline. The pipeline will carry Kazakhstan crude from the oil-producing regions of western Kazakhstan eastward across to China. In addition, CNPC is participating in a joint venture in the Uzbek oil fields in Mangistau Oblast and is also participating in Aktobemunaigas. Thus China has become an important part of Kazakhstan's new energy strategy.

Turkmenistan

Turkmenistan is a major oil and gas producer and a major gas exporter.[13] Natural gas was first developed and extracted during the Soviet period, but it was only when Turkmenistan became an independent state in 1991 that the natural gas sector emerged as the locomotive of the country's economic and political development. During the 1990s Turkmenistan was exclusively dependent upon the Russian natural gas transport system. When Turkmenistan's President Niyazov disagreed over the price of their natural gas, he pulled out of the arrangement, resulting in a disastrous downturn in Turkmen revenue during the late 1990s. After Vladimir Putin came to power, the new Russian government became keen on drawing Turkmenistan back into Russia's sphere of influence, agreeing to higher prices for Turkmen gas on a long-term basis. The president's statement came in the wake of competing demands for greater gas production. Commercial relations with Russian Transneft were restored as Turkmenistan began using the pipeline traveling through Russia to reach Western customers, transporting 60 billion cubic meters per year at its peak.

In October 2008, the results of Turkmenistan's gas audit were announced by an internationally recognized and independent engineering company,

Gaffney Cline & Associates. The announcement stated that Turkmenistan's newly discovered Yolotan-Osman gas field was one of the biggest in the world, containing between 4 and 14 trillion cubic meters of gas.[14] In early 2009, Turkmenistan president G. Berdymukhamedov set the country's production target for oil at 10.9 million metric tons and the natural gas target at 75 billion cubic meters (bcm).[15] The drop in gas prices in 2008 shifted Russia's position and weakened the demand for Turkmen gas. When an accident resulted in the closure of the main gas pipeline to Russia in April 2009, disagreements emerged. Transport through the pipeline was not resumed as late as February 2010.

Turkmenistan's strategy has focused on diversifying routes rather than relying on Russian access to European markets. For example, Turkmenistan is in the final stages of construction of a major gas pipeline from the Yolotan field to China, traversing Uzbekistan and Kazakhstan. The pipeline is still under construction but is using transfers through existing pipelines and was officially inaugurated in December 2009 in Kazakhstan. The pipeline is designed to eventually transport 40 bcm/y to China. Thus China promises to be an important emerging market for Turkmenistan, in order for it to diversity its routes and continue its path of economic development.

Conclusion

A multi-vector policy is a complex stratagem. In practice, multi-vector foreign policies are essentially risk-averse lines of action, emphasizing multiple partners, multiple dimensions, and multiple issues, and relying largely on diplomatic hedging against unreliability, threat, and hard-to-calculate advantage. Multi-vector foreign policies assign low importance to ideological considerations and high importance to instrumental alliances and calculated advantage. What a multi-vector policy means in the context of these relationships is that any of the Central Asian states will have a policy of one vector toward Russia, one vector toward China, one vector toward Europe, and so on. There is logic to the "balancing symmetry" that is inherent in the calculation of interests in Central Asia. Russia is a factor in every balance. Russia is too big and too close to ignore, too aggressive to contest. At the same time, Russia is not easy to interact with simply as an equal partner. Central Asian policy officials use the concept of "multi-vector foreign policy" to explain and justify their diplomatic and security relationships with other countries within the Central Asian region, with other countries outside the region, and with international organizations.

The idea of a "multi-vector" foreign policy merits more than mere academic consideration because it has very real policy implications. In algebraic calculations, of course, equal and opposing vectors cancel one another. In geometry, equal and opposing forces will add to zero. But in the world of diplomacy, opposing vectors may continue to retain their values. The idea of multi-vector relations, technocratic and clinical in its euphemistic expression of diplomatic relationships, is in actuality moved by a profound respect for historically based realism.

As a cross-roads region, Central Asia forms a bridge, interconnecting the Asian and Eurasian landmasses and providing a territory where outside powers have extraordinary influence in business, government, and international security. Prediction is too strong a concept to apply to any forward-looking practices of trade and diplomacy in the contemporary world of multipolar energy politics. The demise of the Soviet Union, the unwillingness or incapacity of the United States to pursue successful unipolar policies, and the remarkably rapid rise of China to a position of prominence in commercial as well as political respects have changed the world. It is no longer possible to predict the future on the basis of the past alone. We are witnessing what is obviously a dynamic period of global change in which major assertions of influence may not be determinative and yet even minor, well-positioned efforts at influence may be effectual. All the same, if prediction is not possible, planning is nevertheless unavoidable. The best basis for looking forward may be calculated anticipation rather than an attempted resort to the conventional wisdoms of the past.

As China's remarkable economic growth and its need for new sources of energy to sustain its development continues, it has returned to a region where it has historical and trade ties that go back more than a thousand years. The new energy grid linking China, Russia, and Central Asia is now replacing the ancient Silk Road. What distinguishes this new Silk Road is that the economic and political stakes are higher and the nature of the triangular relationship is more complex. But China's skillful diplomacy has proven to be adept in adjusting to the shifting regional political tide, allowing it to navigate successfully in the turbulent regional waters that have drowned many amateur upstarts. China has traversed this path before and knows the way. Flush with cash, and utilizing political instruments such as the Shanghai Cooperation Organization, China is poised to expand its energy relations and political ties with Russia and the Central Asian states for years to come.

Notes

* The author is grateful for the assistance of Susannah Pratt of the George C. Marshall European Center for Security Studies.

1 On the risks and opportunities inherent in the politics of the energy trade, see Brenda Shaffer, *Energy Politics* (Philadelphia: University of Pennsylvania Press, 2009).

2 For an analysis of Chinese trends toward a practical foreign policy, see Bates Gill, *Rising Star: China's New Security Diplomacy* (Washington, DC: Brookings Institution Press, 2007).

3 Stefan Wagstyl, "Cheney Rebukes Putin on Energy 'Blackmail.' " *Financial Times* (May 4, 2006).

4 Electric power supply has special characteristics: it is necessary, it is vulnerable, and it is interrelated. It is necessary in the sense that electricity plays a critically important role in an economy. Access to power at reasonable rates is a major component of industrial growth, technological change, and quality of life. Electric power is vulnerable in the respect that shortages or service interruption can impose unacceptably large social and economic costs. If demand exceeds supply at any one time, brownouts and blackouts can occur. Because electricity cannot be economically stored in large quantities, production must be continuously matched to consumption. Typical markets match supply and demand through equilibrating forces that vary around the equilibrium point as oversupply pushes prices down and undersupply pushes prices up. But electric markets tolerate very little variance in deviation between supply and demand. If one producer is unable to satisfy demand the entire market may be affected as service interruptions radiate throughout the entire distribution grid.

5 It is traditional to distinguish between the countries of the Caucasus (Armenia, Azerbaijan, and Georgia) and the countries of Central Asia (Kazakhstan, Kyrgyzstan, Tajikistan, Turkmenistan, and Uzbekistan). These two groups of countries differ in important respects regarding culture and foreign connections. However, regarding energy trade, it is often useful to regard the region as the "Caucasus and Central Asia" or the "greater Caspian Basin." Multilateral funding organizations and commercial enterprises often use this larger geographic concept. See The Asian Development Bank's "Strategy for Regional Cooperation in the Energy Sector of CAREC Countries." ADB strategy was endorsed by the Seventh Ministerial Conference on Central Asia Regional Economic Cooperation (November 19–21, 2008) in Baku, Azerbaijan. See http://www.carecinstitute.org/uploads/docs/CAREC-Regional-Cooperation-Strategy-in-Energy.pdf

6 See Amy Myers Jaffe, "Russia and Caspian Energy in the Global Energy Balance: Executive Summary." Energy Forum, James A. Baker Institute for Policy (May 2009) http://www.rice.edu/nationalmedia/multimedia/2009–05-07-RussEnergyExecSum.pdf

Also see Martha Brill Olcott and Nikolai Petrov, "Russia, Central Asia, and the Caspian: How Important is the Energy Trade-off?" Energy Forum, James A. Baker Institute for Policy (May 2009) http://www.bakerinstitute.org/programs/energy-forum/publications/energy-studies/russia-and-the-caspian-states-in-the-global-energy-balance

7 Ilham Aliev, the Azerbaijan president, told the Davos Forum in January 2010 that the Azerbaijan government intends to triple gas production in the near term. See World Economic Forum, January 28, 2010. http://www.weforum.org/en/knowledge/KN_SESS_SUMM_29946?url=/en/knowledge/KN_SESS_SUMM_29946

8 Natural gas prices have been historically associated with oil prices; despite the fact gas market fundamentals are not dependent upon oil market fundamentals. While natural gas consumption is related to oil demand in terms of consumption patterns, natural gas is only tangentially related to oil in production, processing, and transport. Natural gas prices, as calculated in inflation-adjusted terms, broke from the linkage to oil prices in the mid-1980s. In 1985 natural gas prices fell precipitously and for over a decade remained low. Natural gas prices rebounded in 2000 with a sharp increase and dropped back considerably until spiking in mid-2005 and then dropping back again until reversing again by more than doubling in mid-2008 before dropping back again.

9 "Modern Shale Gas Development in the United States: A Primer." Report Prepared for US Department of Energy Office of Fossil Energy and National Energy Technology Laboratory (April 2009) http://www.netl.doe.gov/technologies/oil-gas/publications/EPreports/Shale_Gas_Primer_2009.pdf

10 See the "2010 Outlook for Eurasian Energy" by Richard Morningstar, Special Envoy for Eurasian Energy, January 28, 2010 at the Center for American Progress, Washington DC. http://www.state.gov/s/eee/rmk/136141.htm

11 See the Whitehouse announcement of the US-China Shale Gas Resource Initiative. http://www.energy.gov/news2009/documents2009/US-China_Fact_Sheet_Shale_Gas.pdf

12 Gerard Wynn and Ben Hirschler, DAVOS-Shale gas is US energy "game changer" -BP CEO Reuters (January 28, 2010). http://www.reuters.com/article/idUSLDE60R1MV20100128

13 See the BP Statistical Review available at www.bp.com. Figures are also available at the Energy Information Administration of the US Department of Energy at www.eia.doe.gov

14 Guy Chazan, "Turkmenistan Gas Field Is One of World's Largest," *The Wall Street Journal* (October 16, 2008). In 2002 the Asian Development

Bank began assisting Turkmenistan in helping to arrange independent gas assessments and financed the American firm DeGoyler and MacNaughton in 2005 to provide an independent audit. While the audit results were not made public, Turkmenistan government sources soon began referring to the conclusion that the Dovletabat gas field alone contained approximately 4.5 trillion cubic meters and that the country's total reserves exceeded 6 trillion cubic meters. But because the audit was not made public, many observers simply rejected assessments from Turkmenistan government officials as wishful thinking.

15 Reported on January 17, 2009 on the Uzbek government website www.turkmenistan.gov.tm

CHAPTER SIX

China's Energy Relations with Africa

ZHAO Hong

Introduction

Historically, China and Africa have had friendly relations. Their official ties date back to the founding of the People's Republic of China (PRC) in 1949. At that time, China cultivated friendships with a number of African countries and provided moral, financial, and political support for their fight for independence in spite of its own economic and political difficulties. However, formal establishment of a diplomatic relationship did not follow until the Bandung conference of 1955 in Indonesia. The Bandung conference brought together Asian and African states, most of which were newly independent. The conference's stated aims were to promote Afro-Asian economic and cultural cooperation and to oppose colonialism or neocolonialism. Since then, relations between the two continents on both bilateral and multilateral levels have blossomed. It was after this conference that Egypt became the first North African country to establish a formal relationship with China in 1956. Today, approximately 45 African countries have formal diplomatic relations with China.

China was a major actor in Africa in the 1960s and 1970s, when, as part of its ideological rivalry with the Soviet Union, it supported national liberation movements (notably those that were prepared to eschew Soviet aid) and some friendly post-independence regimes in the area in spite of its own economic and political difficulties. As one scholar has observed, "Between 1955 and 1977, while many African countries were fighting for independence and self-determination, China sold $142 million worth of military equipment to Africans. Moreover, China opened its universities to over 15,000 African students for free education and has consistently supported Africa's development and responded to emergencies."[1]

In contemporary times, globalization and partly global political dynamics have encouraged China to be more proactive in its relationship with Africa. As part of its new African strategy, China created the Forum on China-Africa Cooperation (FOCAC) in 2000. In November 2006, the FOCAC Summit was held in Beijing, and the theme was friendship, peace, development, and cooperation. At this summit meeting, China announced that over the period of 2007–2009, it will establish a $3 billion USD preferential loan package and a $2 billion USD preferential buyer's credit for Africans; it will double aid to Africa, cancel all debts owed by African countries that were due in 2005, and establish a $5 billion USD China-Africa Development Fund to provide start-up capital to Chinese companies investing in Africa. As China's influence in Africa increased, its activities there were widely seen by Western and some African countries as negative and a "threat." Many were left wondering how can we look at the expansion of China's economic activities in Africa and is it really a threat? This chapter will review the bilateral economic relations between China and Africa, and analyze China's energy venture in Africa. In addition it will look at the possibility of China clashing with the United States and other Western countries over African oil interests to better understand China's interests in the region.

Bilateral Trade

Increased political activity between China and Africa has enabled bilateral economic ties to progress quickly, especially since China adopted its open-door policies and market reforms. In 1995, the trade volume was about $3 billion USD and exponentially rose to $74 billion USD in 2007 (Table 6.1). In 2008, trade between the two countries reached a record $109 billion, up 45 percent from a year earlier, and China had a trade deficit of $5 billion, compared with a surplus of $940 million in 2007.[2] China's top five trading partners in Africa are Angola, South Africa, Sudan, Nigeria, and Egypt—accounting for more than 60 percent of China's total trade with the continent in 2008. China has surpassed France to become the second largest trade partner with Africa behind the United States. According to an estimate by the Chinese Academy of Social Sciences, trade with China has contributed 20 percent to the continent's growth.

Investment

In addition to trade, China has significantly stepped up its foreign direct investment (FDI) in African countries. China's investment in Africa has

Table 6.1 China's Trade Balance with Africa (US$ billion)

	2006			2007			2008		
	Total	Export	Import	Total	Export	Import	Total	Export	Import
Africa	55.4	26.7	28.8	73.7	37.3	36.4	107.2	51.2	56.0
Top 10 countries									
Angola	11.8	0.9	10.9	14.1	1.2	12.9	25.3	2.9	22.4
SouthAfrica	9.9	5.8	4.1	14.0	7.4	6.6	17.9	8.6	9.2
Sudan	3.4	1.4	1.9	5.7	1.5	4.2	8.2	1.9	6.3
Nigeria	3.1	2.9	0.3	4.3	3.8	0.5	7.3	6.8	0.5
Egypt	3.2	3.0	0.2	4.7	4.4	0.2	6.3	5.9	0.4
Congo	3.0	0.2	2.8	3.3	0.4	2.8	–	–	–
Libya	2.4	0.7	1.7	2.4	0.9	1.5	4.2	1.6	2.6
Algeria	2.1	2.0	0.1	3.9	2.7	1.2	4.6	3.8	0.9
Morocco	1.9	1.6	0.3	2.6	2.2	0.4	2.8	2.3	0.5
Guinea	0.3	0.2	0.1	0.4	0.3	0.1	0.4	0.3	0.03

Source: China Statistic Yearbook, 2009

Table 6.2 China's FDI in Africa (non-financial sectors) (US$ million)

	2003	2004	2005	2006	2007	2008	Accumulation by the year 2008
Africa	74.8	317.4	391.7	519.9	1574.3	5490.6	7803.8
African top 10 countries							
SouthAfrica	8.9	17.8	47.5	40.7	454.1	4807.9	3048.6
Nigeria	24.4	45.5	53.3	67.8	390.4	162.6	795.9
Sudan		146.7	91.1	508	65.4	−63.1	528.3
Zambia	5.5	2.2	10.1	87.4	119.3	214.0	651.3
Algeria	2.5	11.2	84.9	98.9	145.9	42.3	508.8
Egypt	2.1	5.7	13.3	8.9	25	14.6	131.4
Mauritius	10.3	0.4	2	16.6	156	34.4	230.1
Tanzania		1.6	1	12.5	−3.8	18.2	190.2
Ethiopia	1	0.4	5	24	13.3	9.7	126.5
Congo	0.06	12	5.1	36.7	57.3	24	134.1

Source: The China Commerce Yearbook, 2009

been growing rapidly as well, especially after 2006. From 2003 to 2008, China's FDI (in non-financial sectors) increased from $74.8 million USD to $5490.6 million, with accumulation being $7803.8 million (Table 6.2). These investment projects covered areas including trade, resource exploration, transportation infrastructures, and agriculture. Up to now, China has signed a Bilateral Investment Promotion and Protection Agreement with 29 African countries, and has signed and an Avoidance of Double Taxation Agreements with a few of these countries. These agreements will further encourage Chinese enterprises to invest in Africa. To encourage Chinese enterprises to expand their investments in Africa, the Chinese government has established the China-Africa Fund with an initial sum of $1 billion USD. By the end of 2008, the fund had invested about $400 million USD in over 20 projects, increasing Chinese investments in Africa to approximately $2 billion USD.[3]

China has also emphasized technological cooperation with African countries. According to the Chinese Ministry of Commerce, in 2007, Chinese enterprises signed contracts and labor service agreements with African countries worth $29 billion USD. By the end of 2007, the accumulated value of these contracts and labor services reached $100 billion. Currently, the number of engineers and workers engaged in these projects amounts to 114,000.[4] These projects and labor services were involved in various areas, including housing construction, petrochemicals, mining, water resources, transportation, infrastructure, and so on.

Although Sino-African economic relations have been making great progress in recent years, the significance of this relationship cannot be over-emphasized. China's activities are still limited and they face some challenges. China is still a newcomer in the Western-dominated market of Africa. For example, according to the International Monetary Fund (IMF), the total value of China-Africa bilateral trade in 2006 ($49 billion) accounted for 8.5 percent of Africa's total foreign trade ($568 billion), while in the same year, the United States accounted for 15 percent ($86 billion), and the EU accounted for 38 percent ($214 billion) of Africa's trade.[5] In 2008 the value of China-Africa bilateral trade had increased to $96.2 billion ($52.9 billion in imports, $43.3 billion in exports), compared to the value of US trade at $132.3 billion ($110.5 billion in imports, $21.9 billion in exports).[6] In terms of oil trade and investment, in 2007, the United States purchased 31 percent of Africa's oil, Europe 31 percent, and China 12 percent. However, Chinese investment in the oil industry in Africa was still less than 1/16th of that invested by Western oil companies.[7] China's national oil companies (NOCs) currently are minor actors among the foreign investors in Africa's largest energy producers, such as Libya, Nigeria, Algeria, and Angola. China's NOCs lag behind the international oil companies (IOCs) significantly in terms of their African assets' value and production. The commercial value of China's NOCs investments in African oil is just 8 percent of the combined commercial value of the IOCs investments in African oil and 3 percent of all companies invested in African oil.[8] In 2006, the total African output of the Chinese NOCs (267,000 barrels of oil equivalent per day) was only one-third of that produced by ExxonMobil (4.1 million boe/d)—the largest foreign producer in Africa.[9]

China's aid to Africa is also easily dwarfed by that given by developed countries. Between 2000 and 2006, US economic aid to sub-Saharan Africa increased from $2.1 billion to $5.4 billion USD. In 2006, European countries gave $21.9 billion to Africa, and the United Kingdom alone gave $5.2 billion to Africa, both were sizable contributions in comparison to the aid offered by China.[10] In recent years, Japan has also increased its aid to Africa to compete with China. In May 2008 Japan's former Prime Minister Fukuda Yasuo announced at the Fourth Tokyo International Conference on African Development that Japan would double its overseas development assistance (ODA) to Africa in the next five years, bringing annual aid from the current $900 million to $1.8 billion by 2012.[11] Although there has been an increase in aid from China to Africa, it is apparent that the more developed countries still have a larger presence in the region.

China's Oil Venture in Africa

Chinese state-owned companies began their first wave of "going out" to explore the possibility of acquiring foreign assets in 1993 when China became a net oil importer. Since the late 1990s, China's policies toward Africa have been closely linked to the objectives of its major state-owned companies, such as China National Petroleum Corporation (CNPC), in their attempt to access African oil and gas. China's direct investments (non-financial sectors) in Africa's energy sector increased from $75 million USD in 2003 to $1,574 million in 2007, totaling $4,462 million.[12] In recent years, China's oil imports from Africa have been increasing at an annual rate of 30 percent, slightly higher than that of the rest of the world (26 percent). Among African oil-producing countries, China imports oil mainly from Angola, Sudan, Republic of Congo, and Equatorial Guinea, with Angola the leading supplier of oil from Africa. In 2006, Angola accounted for 50 percent of China's oil imports from the continent and narrowly overtook Saudi Arabia to become China's top crude oil supplier.[13] However, China has also benefited from its ties with Sudan. As much as 52 percent of China's equity oil comes from Sudan, and 65 percent of Sudan's oil exports go to China.[14] Moreover the number of Chinese workers, including those working in oil fields, in Sudan has tripled since the early 1990s, reaching 24,000 in 2006.[15] Chinese non-oil investments are significant as well, including hydro-electric facilities, a new airport for Khartoum, and several textile plants. China also operates the vast bulk of Sudan's oil production and has a 50 percent stake in the nation's only major refinery in Khartoum.[16] Thus Africa represents an important energy partner for the Chinese and it is working to develop its presence in the region.

The Allure of African Oil

The Persian Gulf and Asia-Pacific regions were China's main source of oil imports in the 1990s. In 1995, these two regions supplied almost 87 percent of China's oil imports (Persian Gulf 46 percent, Asia Pacific 41 percent). But since the late 1990s, the importance of these two regions in China's oil imports has diminished. In 2006, the Asia Pacific's portion declined to 8 percent, while the Persian Gulf's portion hovered at 45 percent. One factor contributing to this decline is that the Asia Pacific region does not have the supply to meet China's increasing oil import demand. Indonesia, the region's second largest oil producer (behind China) and once China's largest supplier (31 percent in 1995), is now a net oil importer.[17] As is the case with most countries, the Persian Gulf will remain an important source of crude oil for China. Yet, the 9.11 terrorist attacks on the United States, the predominantly American-driven "war on terror," and the military interventions in Afghanistan and Iraq have all heightened China's sense of insecurity and vulnerability. Beijing is concerned that the United States' reaction to the 9.11 terrorist attacks has further destabilized the unstable oil-producing regions of the Middle East and Central Asia.

In Southeast Asia, China perceives the current oil production order and partnerships there as entrenched. Over the past five decades, US, Japanese, and European companies have already forged relationships with key producing countries. Southeast Asia had been under the exclusive control of Western powers during the colonial period. The oil-producing territories of Indonesia, Brunei, Sarawak, and Burma (Myanmar) had been controlled by the Dutch and British. Western control gave Western oil companies a head start in exploration, development, transport, refining, and petrochemicals as well as the natural gas industries, and helped to entrench Western interests there. Thus it is difficult for Chinese oil companies to compete effectively in those markets, and Chinese oil companies have felt compelled to find alternative sources of oil and diversify their oil imports.

China's interest in Africa is not surprising, since Africa is believed to be one of the main growing sources of future global oil supply. The *Wall Street Journal* predicted that by 2010 "West Africa will be the world's number one oil source outside of OPEC."[18] Africa's oil surplus has grown over the past decade, and the light, sweet crude of West Africa is well suited to China's refineries.[19] More importantly, unlike the Middle East and Southeast Asia, African oil upstream markets have opened to foreign investors. However, Europe and the United States have yet to monopolize some of these new oil producers, such as Sudan and Angola.

The US influence and control over oil in this region has been either weak or counterbalanced by political factors. Some African countries, such as Libya and Sudan, had been barred from US energy investment and trade. In Libya's case, its support for terrorism and its pursuit of weapons of mass destruction has prevented US companies from investing. In Sudan's case, egregious human rights violations have deterred investors. This provides China with a unique opportunity to obtain a significant position in one of the few remaining underdeveloped oil regions in the world without competition from Western companies. China's own foreign policy of respecting sovereignty allows it to invest in states where Western countries and companies have trouble accepting the domestic politics and practices of the ruling regimes. Thus China can invest without the moral and political baggage that restricts Western states.

Other factors compelling Chinese oil companies to scour the world for investment opportunities in untapped energy reserves are the limited opportunities to raise domestic upstream production combined with thin margins on downstream activities.[20] To establish an upstream business there are only two options: one is to explore somewhere risky, where the possibility of finding untapped sources of energy is more likely, the other one is to expand through mergers and acquisitions. Following China National Offshore Oil Corporation (CNOOC's) aborted bid to acquire Unocal, Chinese firms see bigger risk in bidding for US and European energy firms than in drilling for oil in Sudan, Syria, or Iran, where Western oil companies are either prohibited from investing or hesitant to do so fearing the political risks there. Moreover, Chinese oil companies are state-owned and can thus accept a higher risk premium compared to IOCs. A good example is CNPC whose 2006 profits alone totaled $24 billion USD.[21] Since CNPC is not required to pay dividends to the state, it is able to overcome various investment hampers or take on higher risk levels than BP or Chevron, whose shareholders would rather take their money and re-invest it elsewhere if the company cannot deliver double-digit returns.[22]

Finally, the success of Chinese oil companies going into Africa should be attributed to concessions from some African countries. With a dramatic fall in foreign direct investment (FDI) after the end of the Cold War, the introduction of Chinese FDI was welcomed. There is genuine enthusiasm on the part of African governments to grant concessions to Chinese entrepreneurs investing in their respective countries and opening new business opportunities in some neglected sectors of their economy, such as the oil and gas industry. In this context, China's project in Sudan is a good example.

Sudan's oil industry began to develop in the 1970s when the American company Chevron began its oil exploration in 1974 in the Muglad Basin. When civil war broke out for the second time in 1984, Chevron abandoned over one billion dollars of private investments and sold its interests to a Canadian firm, which formed the Greater Nile Petroleum Operating Company (GNPOC). In 1995 Sudan's president Omar al-Bashir visited China and expressed hope that Chinese oil companies could invest and explore oil resources in Sudan, assisting in the development of its modern oil industry. Since China had recently become a net oil importer, it was anxious to explore new markets. CNPC responded by conducting its preliminary study of Sudan and concluded that the fields in question were similar, in terms of geological formation, to China's Bohai Bay region. In 1997, CNPC decided to join the oil exploration project in Sudan, and bought a 40 percent share from GNPOC. The goal of the newly formed company was to develop

Sudan's oil field in the south-central part of the country and build a 1,500-km pipeline to a coastal port facility at Marsa al-Bashair, near Port Sudan.

To support CNPC's business in Sudan, the Chinese government signed a framework agreement with Sudan's government in September 1995, agreeing to provide a preferential credit line of 1.15 billion Renminbi (RMB) for oil exploration projects in Sudan.[23] After discussing with representatives from the Financial Ministry and Central Bank of Sudan, it was agreed that preferential line of credit would be provided to Chinese companies while the project would come under the supervision of the Sudan Bank.[24] Sudan agreed to give China generous concession terms, such as no restrictions on profit reparations and exemptions of all domestic taxes on exported oil. These terms continue to remain among the most generous in the world. Thus from a purely commercial basis, investment opportunities in Sudan were almost too good to turn down, especially given China's perception that most energy producing regions were tied to US, European, and Japanese interests, and might be less receptive to Chinese overtures.

China's Energy Strategy in Africa

China's overseas investment and oil expansion overseas have raised some concerns that Beijing is maneuvering to lock up global energy assets for the long haul. In the United States and Europe, some NGOs (Non-government Organizations) are critical of China's general investment and lending policies in Africa. Thus China has been trying to re-adjust its policies and approaches to ensure that the bilateral economic ties with Africa are mutually beneficial and flourish in the long run.

Changing the Forms of Diplomatic Aid

The Chinese government began giving financial support to African countries in the 1970s. At the outset, the objectives of support were largely ideological in nature. With the advent of its economic reforms in 1978, the Chinese government stepped up its diplomatic aid to Africa and such assistance began to serve multiple purposes, including economic and oil objectives. In the last few years, the assistance has become both more sophisticated, in terms of instruments utilized, and more geographically diverse. In the 1980s, the Chinese government provided much of its economic aid in the form of building large non-commercially oriented projects, such as sports stadiums, hospitals, schools, and government office buildings in Gambia and Sierra Leone, among other countries. In the 1990s, support began to shift to grants. Today, the proportion of non-commercial aid has been decreasing, with commercially oriented loans accounting for the vast majority of Chinese government-sponsored African aid.

China's Export-Import Bank, which was established in 1994 as a state policy-bank, is the sole state-owned entity the Chinese government uses to dispense official economic aid worldwide, including to Africa. According to the World Bank in 2007, as of 2005, the Chinese Export-Import Bank had made an accumulated commitment of $800 million USD in loans for 55 projects in nearly 22 African countries. As of mid-2006, the total amount of Export-Import Bank loans to Africa reached over $12.5 billion USD in infrastructural development alone.[25] These projects are mainly concentrated in oil-rich countries, such as Angola, Mozambique, Nigeria, Sudan, and Zimbabwe. In the summer of 2006, a $2 billion infrastructure loan was announced during Premier Wen Jiabao's visit to Angola as part of a seven-nation African tour.[26] When visiting Africa in early 2006, Chinese President Hu Jintao promised to provide preferential credit of $3 billion USD and preferential credit of $2 billion, and announced that China's support to African countries would be doubled by the year 2009.[27] China is also using debt relief to assist African nations. Since 2000, Beijing has taken significant steps to cancel the debt of 31 African countries. That year, China wrote off $1.2 billion USD in African debt; in 2003, it forgave another $750 million.[28]

In the past, developing bilateral relations with African countries had been a priority in China's grand diplomatic strategy, and most of the aid was given through bilateral channels. As China becomes a greater player in Africa, it has begun cooperation with more multilateral organizations. For example, China has joined the "Donor Coordination Groups" which are based in Kenya and Tanzania. China also started cooperation with New Partnership for Africa's Development (NEPAD) in 2003, discussing development priorities in Africa. China's role in the UN, its contributions to the African Development Bank, and its recent conference with African leaders in Shanghai are testimony to its evolving recognition that a strategy based on international cooperation may be more important than one that relies on special arrangements.

Incorporating Oil into a Broader Business Regime

Realizing that it did not have the historical linkages with key oil-exporting countries as enjoyed by US and European multilateral companies, China tried to approach Africa not simply as a supplier of its energy needs, but as part of a greater interdependent business relationship. By the end of 2005,

China had invested in 27 major oil and natural-gas projects in 14 African countries, including Angola, Sudan, and Nigeria. China plans to further increase its investment in Africa's oil through its state-owned oil companies. In 2006, CNOOC paid $2.7 billion USD to obtain a minority interest in a Nigerian oil field and $4 billion to build refineries in the same country; while Sinopec paid $2.2 billion for two oil fields in Angola.[29] China has been also investing in related infrastructure. In Nigeria, China Civil Engineering Construction Corporation signed a $8 billion contract in October 2006 to build a 1,315 km railway line which will connect the commercial cities of Lagos and Kano with the oil cities of Jos and Port Harcourt.

China believes that modern international oil cooperation is largely based on a "win-win" principle which is needed for sustainable development and the enlargement of energy cooperation. In implementing its "going out" strategy in Africa, for instance, CNPC focused on mutual benefits with energy producing countries. In the Sudan project, nearly 50 percent of the revenue went to Sudan's government. CNPC and its branches in Sudan have employed over 4,000 Sudanese and over 7,000 contract workers, greatly relaxing the employment pressure in that country.[30] Meanwhile, CNPC stresses training for its Sudanese employees. Since 1998, CNPC has spent $ 1.5 million, sending 35 Sudanese students to study at various universities in Beijing.[31]

In developing its relationships with African countries, China has deliberately avoided a singular focus on oil supplies and attempted to enlarge the range of economic exchanges. China's goal is to create a level of economic interdependence that will lead to greater trade, including the purchase of oil and gas supplies. For example, by the end of 2006 China had established over 800 non-financial enterprises in Africa, with the accumulated value of investment reaching $11.7 billion USD. The investment projects covered trade, textiles, power generation, road construction, tourism, and communication. Strategically, these endeavors were meant to reinforce Beijing's efforts at establishing itself in Africa as a desirable long-term customer for the continent's energy exports.

China is presently negotiating for the establishment of a regional economic free trade area with the Southeast African Customs Union. China joined the African Development Bank and Western African Development Bank, and has built its more expansive engagement in Africa within the Forum on China and Africa Cooperation (FOCAC) framework. The third FOCAC summit in Beijing in November 2006 stands out from the previous two (2000 in Beijing and 2003 in Addis Ababa) for its exuberance, scale, and ambition. Meanwhile, China has established mechanisms, such as bilateral committees between China and African countries and political consultation between foreign ministries of the two sides, to conduct dialogue and consultation in a flexible and pragmatic manner. All of these steps indicate Beijing has launched a more comprehensive and ambitious program to court Africa as a whole and integrate it into the world market.

Adjusting the Approach to Africa

Until November 2006, China actively worked to block US initiatives at the UN Security Council aimed at forcing Khartoum into allowing a more robust peacekeeping mission in its Darfur region. China has been careful not to endorse UN involvement in the domestic affairs of the host government without consent, fearing that someday such a standard could be used against its own interests. China argued that its activities in Sudan were commercial in nature, and doubted foreign intervention could bring democracy and justice to that troubled nation, because "history has shown that oil-importing countries have little power to effect change in many of the world's oil states."[32] As the Sino-African relationship develops further, however, China has begun to alter this policy.

In the last decade, China's investment interest has been repeatedly jeopardized and harmed in Sudan as well as some other African countries. As one observer puts it, "China is finding it more difficult to follow its non-interference policy in Sudan, while also ensuring the stability of its investments in the country's oil industry."[33] Indeed, Beijing does not believe that Khartoum's actions will lead to a resolution of the crisis, and this could potentially undermine China's investments and oil interests in Sudan. Beijing now believes that the only way to maintain stability in the region is for outside powers to force a negotiated settlement.

China started to adjust its approach in October 2006 when it voted in favor of a bigger UN peacekeeping presence in Khartoum to buttress a weak African Union force on the ground.[34] On his visit to Khartoum in February 2007, Chinese President Hu Jintao told al-Bashir, "Darfur is a part of Sudan and you have to resolve this problem."[35] By May 2007, China announced the dispatch of 275 military engineers to help strengthen the international presence. China subsequently appointed Liu Gui Jin (former Chinese ambassador to South Africa and Zimbabwe) as China's special representative for African affairs, indicating that China was loosening its "non-interference" policy in certain circumstances.

However, there is little reason to believe that China will shift toward an isolationist policy advocated by the United States. In 2009, China held several meetings with Sudanese officials, pushing for closer relations and a more "flexible" approach to Darfur. In each meeting, China used every opportunity to reassure Khartoum that it has not fallen out of favor with Beijing.[36] In fact, China's approach to solve the long-lasting conflict in Darfur has been to provide comprehensive development assistance, while finding every tactical means to persuade al-Bashir's government to comply with Western requests.

Will China's Energy Venture in Africa Fuel Rivalry with the United States?

China's increasing oil investment in Africa has aroused the concern of some American officials. In the past few years, another perceived threat has arisen: the possibility that China will pre-empt US firms in the development of future oil fields and compete with the United States for the loyalty of local governments. Although not all US officials would put China in the "threat" category with respect to African oil, there is concern over growing Chinese presence in the region among some in the Congress and the Department of Defense (DOD).

For example, Representative Christopher Smith of New Jersey told the House Committee on International Relations in July 2005 that "China is playing an increasingly influential role on the continent of Africa, and there is concern that the Chinese intend to aid and abet African dictators, gain a stranglehold on precious African natural resources, and undo much of the progress that has been made on democracy and governance in the last 15 years in African nations."[37] Another example is the view reflected in the DOD's 2005 report on Chinese military capabilities and how China's role in African oil could affect US interests and policy. The report notes that "China's growing reliance on imported energy, especially oil and natural gas, 'is playing a role in shaping China's strategy and policy.' Such concerns factor heavily in Beijing's relations with a number of major oil producers, including Angola and Sudan. Beijing's belief that it requires such special relationships in order to assure its energy access could shape its defense strategy and use of force in the future."[38] This suggests the DOD believes that any such efforts on China's part could pose a challenge (direct or indirect) to US security interests.

But this does not necessarily follow that China's quest for oil is bound to lead to clashes over energy with the United States. In fact, the United States and China are not really in conflict on many energy issues. Nevertheless, China's search for oil is positioning itself as a rival to the United States for influence in Africa. If not managed prudently and properly, this rivalry might generate bilateral friction between the two great powers.

US Policy on African Oil

Like China, the United States has exhibited extraordinary interest in African oil. In light of Africa's unique ability to increase its output in the years ahead, "Africa is expected to be one of the fastest-growing sources of oil and natural gas for the American market."[39] It is predicted that within the next decade, the United States will rely on Africa for 20 to 30 percent of its oil imports. Moreover, the US government is seeking to enhance its access to African oil in order to reduce its dependence on the ever-turbulent Middle East. In recent years, the US oil imports from Africa increased from 16 percent in 2000 to 20 percent in 2005; while China's imports increased from 24 percent to 30 percent in the same period (see Table 6.3). In 2006, the United States imported 2.23 million barrels per day (bpd) from Africa, slightly higher than that from the Middle East (2.22 million bpd).[40] These examples show that private-sector investment in the energy sector was steadily rising, with annual bilateral trade reaching $60.6 billion USD in 2005, up 36.7 percent from 2004.[41]

For the most part, the US policy regarding African oil is aimed at improving the investment climate for American firms and strengthening the internal security capabilities of friendly governments. For instance, to enhance US access to African oil, the Bush government sought to expedite the removal of several obstacles to participation by US oil companies in Libya and Sudan. In February 2004, following a declaration by Libya that it would abandon its weapons of mass destruction and comply with the Nuclear Non-Proliferation Treaty, the White House eased sanctions on Libya and announced that "U.S. companies will be able to buy or invest in Libyan oil and products." Sudan could experience similar relief, if a peace agreement between the northern government in Khartoum and the Sudanese People's Liberation Front takes hold and conditions improve in Darfur.[42]

The US defense establishment devoted relatively meager resources to Africa (in comparison with US military expenditures geared to Europe, Asia, and the Middle East). As a result of a growing American reliance on African oil and the uncertain security climate in the region (partly due to China's growing influence there), the US Department of Defense is paying closer attention to Africa. The largest portion of US aid to Africa is being directed to Angola and Nigeria, the leading African oil suppliers to the United States. Total US security aid to these two countries in the Fiscal Years

Table 6.3 US and China's Oil Imports from Africa (million tons)

	1997		1998		1999		2000		2001		2002		2003		2004		2005	
	US	China	US	China	US	China	US	China	US	China	US	China	US	China	US	China	US	China
Algeria	13.92	…	14.13	…	12.61	…	11.1	…	13.56	…	12.9	…	18.63	0.13	22.11	0.68	23.35	0.82
Egypt	1.81	0.29	0.57	0.20	1.15	0.11	0.52	0.12	0.34	…	0.52	…	0.43	0.8	0.69	…	0.71	0.8
Angola	20.86	3.84	22.85	1.11	17.6	2.88	15.0	8.64	16.0	3.80	16.2	5.71	18.12	10.1	15.5	16.21	23.07	17.46
Equatorial Guinea	0.26	0.20	0.1	0.24	0.2	0.81	0.38	0.92	1.02	2.15	2.22	1.78	3.26	1.46	3.8	3.45	3.4	3.84
Congo	2.3	0.98	2.6	0.38	2.2	0.38	2.53	1.45	2.33	0.64	1.34	1.05	1.53	3.39	0.7	4.78	1.55	5.53
Gabon	11.24	0.38	10.1	…	8.19	0.65	7.02	0.46	6.82	0.15	7.0	…	6.37	…	7.0	…	6.22	…
Cameroon	0.22	…	0.20	…	0.25	0.25	0.34	0.43	0.32	0.82	0.62	0.35	0.60	…	1.14	…	0.4	…
Libya		0.07		0.14		0.13		0.13		0.25		…		0.13	1	1.34	2.74	2.26
Nigeria	34.04	…	34	0.12	32	1.37	43.86	1.19	43.2	0.77	30.3	0.49	42.32	0.12	55.77	1.49	56.9	1.31
Sudan		0		…		0.27		3.31		4.97		6.43		6.26		5.77		6.62
Chad		…		…		…		…		…		…	0.21	…	3.29	0.83	4.76	0.55
Africa	63.8	5.91	84.6	2.19	74.0	7.25	80.6	16.96	83.6	13.55	71.1	15.80	91.8	22.18	111.0	35.30	123.1	38.47
Total%	14.2	17	18.0	8	15.5	20	15.9	24	15.7	22	13.8	23	16.7	24	18.8	29	20.1	30

Note: % in each country's total annual imports.
Sources: US Energy Information Administration; Zha Daojiong, "China's Oil Interest in Africa: International Political Problems," *Journal of International Political Studies*, No. 4, 2006.

2004–2006 amounted to approximately $180 million, a substantial increase over the previous three-year period.[43] US military engagement in Africa has expanded significantly, especially in the Horn of Africa, the Sahara/Sahelian zone, and the Gulf of Guinea maritime zone. Most of the US operations there are directed against terrorism, but the longer-term oil interests also loom large, especially in relation to China.[44]

Reducing the China-US Oil Rivalry in Africa

It is possible for China and the United States to have serious conflict and confrontation over energy resources in Africa. China's increasing oil investment and expanding trade relations with Sudan obviously clash with the United States and its allies' sanction on Sudan, because "Chinese investments and trade will increase the host government's coffers, giving it the ability to buy more arms."[45] Foreign policy analysts in Washington warned that "Beijing's strategy of 'locking up' the world's remaining oil supplies through long-term purchase agreements and aggressive diplomacy could lead Washington and Beijing into a struggle which is described as the 'geopolitics of oil.'"[46]

Undoubtedly, China has been paying the costs and even running a risk in its oil-related diplomacy in Africa. China has been criticized for doing business with "rogue states" and labeled as "new colonialist," intent on plundering the resources of Africa. The benefits of having relatively uncontested access to oil supplies may be worth the short-term political costs, but these costs will rise as China becomes more involved in the international market and these developments in turn affect China's credibility in other forums.

One of the arguments for China's oil investment in Africa is that acquiring oil through direct investment can provide domestic consumers with a more secure and less expensive supply of oil than the international market. The idea that equity oil enhances energy security is prevalent among some Chinese officials. However, it seems that the case of Sudan cannot efficiently support the belief that equity production by China's oil companies abroad can guarantee China a supply of oil that is more reliable and less expensive than the international market. In the case of Sudan, the Khartoum government had expressed that concession terms given to CNPC in the late 1990s were overgenerous, and there is growing talk of renegotiating the existing contracts. Meanwhile the government in the South expressed that it has no interest in dealing with the Chinese companies.[47] In addition, the Khartoum government has initiated negotiation with an Indian Oil and Natural Gas Corporation with the intent to sell a portion of its stake in the Greater Nile Petroleum Operating Company. Furthermore, the Chinese government has unofficially agreed to sell two new blocks, one to the Romanian company, Rompetrol, and the other to the Algerian national oil and gas company, Sonatrach. It seems that the Sudan government is looking to balance its policies among foreign investors, and China's position of exclusivity is perhaps deteriorating.

Based on this new reality, China cannot take for granted that Sudan and other African countries will repay China with lucrative energy contracts for not condemning the conduct of the Khartoum regime. China has invested a lot of capital with the expectation that over a long period it will get its money back, in addition to a generous rate of return. In case these concessions are renegotiated or expropriated by the Sudanese government or its successors, China may find that the net present value of its returns may be far lower than anticipated. China has already realized this and doubts whether equity production by China's oil companies, as small as they are, can greatly increase the country's energy security. If not, why endure the damage to China's image and risk the potential conflict with the United States? It was this thinking that has led China to adjust its approach to Sudan.

China's strategy is "one of humanitarian and development aid plus influence without interference, in contrast to the West's coercive approach of sanctions plus military intervention."[48] Through high-level diplomacy, such as Chinese President Hu Jintao's visit to Sudan in February 2007 and dispatch of special envoys, and multilateral platforms such as the United Nations and the China-Africa summit, China has been making tactical moves to press the Sudanese government to comply with the international community's requests.

To prevent the potential conflict from becoming a self-fulfilling prophecy, it is important for China and the United States to intensify mutual understanding and expand their cooperative relations. Politically, China needs to do more than send peacekeeping troops to Sudan, and be more proactive in responding to US complaints rather than repeating "non-interference in domestic affairs" as its guiding principle of foreign affairs. Economically, Chinese companies could lead the way by giving business opportunities to their US partners in markets where Chinese companies have better political access. More importantly, China's decision makers need to keep in mind that energy security is a global issue, and in an era of globalization, unilateralist policies no longer work well in addressing energy security.

In the future, a strategy based on international cooperation may look more attractive than one based on special arrangements with a few "rogue states."

So far as the United States is concerned, first, it is essential to see that both sides share the same view on many controversial issues and for them to understand China's position and predicament. As the American president's special envoy to Sudan said, "Our policy and Chinese policy (on Darfur/Sudan) are closer than I realized they were, and I think the Chinese are going to play an increasingly important role in helping us to resolve this. I think the visit was a very successful one because we found many more areas of common agreement, both about our objectives and our strategies for achieving those objectives."[49] It is clear the two sides have become deeply intertwined economically and have a joint interest in managing their political relationship in a way that assures continued bilateral economic and oil interests in Africa.

China's political influence in Darfur should not be overestimated. While Beijing's investment in Sudan provides economic leverage for the regime, it also makes Beijing a hostage. Beijing's role is limited, as it will lose its credibility and influence if it overreaches politically, as "the effective influence that Beijing can exert over the Darfur crisis lies in its delicate balance between practicing an influence-without-interference strategy and maintaining the hard-won trust of the Sudanese government."[50]

Second, it is evident that China's energy investment in Africa is not a threat but something to be encouraged, because it has enlarged the availability of oil and gas in the world market. For instance, China's investments and technical assistance in Sudan have helped turn this country into an energy exporter, thus providing more oil on the global market. This abundance of oil is beneficial to energy importing countries such as the United States, as it keeps prices low. As shown in Table 6.4, from 1996–2009, the output of crude oil in Sudan greatly increased from 0.2 million tons to 23.7 million tons (against China's flat domestic output), thus significantly contributing to the availability of oil in the world market.

Third, the United States can play its role by trying to lead China in the right path, for instance, enlisting China's membership in the International Atomic Agency (IEA),[51] so as to turn China's unilateral energy policy into a multilateral one. In other words, it is essential for China to be further integrated into global energy markets, have an opportunity to participate in the decisions on the "rules" governing that market, be able to share information on world energy market, and be ensured that its oil interests will be protected in the event of turbulence and political turmoil.

Table 6.4 Sudan's Output of Crude Oil (million tons)

Year	1996	1997	1998	1999	2000	2001	2002	2003	2004	2005	2006	2007	2008
Sudan	0.2	0.4	0.6	3.1	8.6	10.7	11.9	13.1	14.9	15.0	16.3	23.1	23.7
China's domestic output	158.5	160.1	160.2	160.2	162.6	164.8	166.9	169.6	174.1	180.8	183.7	186.7	189.7

Source: BP Statistics Review of World Energy, June 2009.

Conclusion

As China's engagement in Africa expands economically and politically, it is continuing its emphasis on Africa as part of its energy strategy. At the November summit in 2006, China announced that over the period of 2007–2009, it would establish a $3 billion USD preferential loan package and a $2 billion preferential buyer's credit for Africans. It would double aid to Africa, cancel all debts owed by African countries that were due in 2005, and establish a $5 billion China-Africa Development Fund to provide start-up capital to Chinese companies investing in Africa. Meanwhile, China has established institutional mechanisms, such as bilateral committees between China and African countries, and political consultation between foreign ministries of the two sides to conduct dialogue and consultation in a flexible and pragmatic manner. In addition, cultural exchanges have also been active and fruitful between the two sides. China's Confucius Institutes have sprung up all over Africa since its first introduction in the University of Nairobi, Kenya, in December 2005.

However, as mentioned above, China's activities in Africa still have met with some unexpected difficulties. Although China's investment in Africa has been diversified in recent years, encompassing many sectors, China's business strategy in Africa has gone far beyond oil and other energy resources, and China's investment has still been labeled by some Western media as "new colonialist." Meanwhile several Western media reports and concerns have not only tarnished China's positive image in Africa, but also made China's business interests vulnerable to international pressure. For example, China's biggest investment deal in Africa valued at $9 billion USD faltered early in 2009 as Western donors created pressure to renegotiate a minerals-for-infrastructure contract in the Democratic Republic of Congo. Under this deal, a consortium of state-owned Chinese companies agreed to build roads, railways, hospitals, and universities in return for the right to develop a copper and cobalt mine. However led by the Paris Club of creditors and the IMF, pressures to alter the deal have come from Western donors that will not offer relief on the historic debt of $11 billion USD to the cash-strapped government of President Joseph Kabila, if it accepts Chinese financing on commercial terms.[52]

China undoubtedly has its own interests in Africa, but its engagement there takes into account the interests of African countries and their desire to promote economic development. China has provided African countries with some urgently needed aid, such as concession loans and infrastructure construction (building bridges, roads, dams, and power plants), but China did not get the appropriate credit for its activities. China needs to reconsider its unconditional support of African regimes and help African countries find a new development model that is suitable for their particular historical and social reality.

China's economic reform and development can be an example to Africa. China's financial system has played an effective role in developing the underdeveloped areas of Africa. Moreover, China's advancement and progress in the last two decades that has turned it into one of the fastest growing economies in the world can be emulated by many African countries. As a forerunner of economic reform China can also transfer its expertise in creative development to African countries. Many African countries hope that China will take the lead in building a new and more equitable international economic order from which all nations, including African countries, can benefit. This would bolster China's image as a constructive and positive partner rather than as a colonial power out to plunder resources.

In short, by improving its activities and image, China can largely change Western perceptions of its behavior in Africa, thus greatly reducing potential conflicts with the United States. Both China and the United States are becoming increasingly dependent on imported energy. As such, they are finding more common interests with regard to oil affairs in Africa. Both hope to see political and social stability in Africa and a stable supply of oil at a fair price in international oil markets. Therefore they have the foundation and desire to turn oil in particular and energy resources in general into a source for confidence building and cooperation.

Notes

1 Michael Klare and Daniel Volman, "America, China & the Scramble for Africa's Oil," *Review of African Political Economy* No.108:297–309, ROAPE Publications Ltd., 2006.
2 *China-Africa Trade Up 45% in 2008 to $107*, China Daily, 2009–2-11.
3 *China Signs US$260m Airport Deal with Mauritius*, China Daily, February 19, 2009.
4 The China Commerce Yearbook, 2008, p. 684.
5 *IMF, Direction of Trade Statistics*, Yearbook, 2007.
6 *IMF, Direction of Trade Statistics*, Yearbook, 2009.
7 China Daily, February 11, 2009.
8 Erica S. Downs, *The Fact and Fiction of Sino-African Energy Relations.* China Security, Vol. 3, Summer 2007.
9 Erica S. Downs, *The Fact and Fiction of Sino-African Energy Relations.* China Security, Vol. 3, Summer 2007.

10 Homi Kharas, *A Reality Check on African Aid*, The Brookings Institute, February 20, 2008.

11 Ramesh Jaura, *Japan Seeks to Outbid China in Quest for African Support, Inter Press Service, May 29, 2008.*

12 The China Commerce Yearbook, 2008.

13 "Why is China Chasing African Oil?", *Reuters News*, November 3, 2006.

14 "China's CNPC Targets Overseas Integration Deals," *Petroleum Intelligence Weekly*, January 23, 2006.

15 "Friend or Forager?"', *Financial Times*, February 23, 2006.

16 Henry Lee and Dan A. Shalmon, "Searching for Oil: China's Oil Initiatives in the Middle East," *Faculty Research Working Papers Series*, March 2007. Available at: http://ksgnotes.harvard.edu./research/wpaper.nsf/rwp/PWPOT-017/$File/rwp-07.017.lee.pdf

17 In Indonesia, the outputs of oil and gas have sharply dropped due to the aging of oil and gas fields. The decline in crude oil production combined with increasing domestic demands turned this country into a net oil importer in 2004. (ADB, Energy Outlook for Asia and Pacific, 2009, www.adb.org/Documents/Book/Energy-outlook/default.asp)

18 Jeffrey Ball, "Angola Possesses a Prize as Exxon, Rivals Stalk Oil," *Wall Street Journal*, December 5, 2005.

19 Maryelle Demongeot and Judy Hua, "Analysis-No let up seen yet for China sweet crude imports," *Reuters News*, November 12, 2004, Factiva.

20 For fear of passing inflation to an increasingly automobile-oriented and vocal middle class, as well as to low-income farmers and taxi drivers, China has to tightly control the gasoline and diesel prices.

21 Winnie Lee, "CNPC Earned $23.85 Billion Profit in 2006, up 5.7%," *Platts Oilgram News*, January 24, 2007.

22 Daniel H. Rosen, "China Energy," Peterson Institute for International Economics, May 2007.

23 Lin Mei, "Reform and Practice of Foreign Aid," *International Economic Cooperation*, 1997 (11).

24 In 1994, China began to reform and changed the forms of its foreign aid, combining foreign aid with investments, trade and other bilateral cooperation projects (including energy cooperation).

25 Bates Gill, Chin-hao Huan, and J. Stephen Morrison, "China's Expanding Role in Africa." CSIS (Center for Strategic and International Studies) Report, January 2007. Available at: www.csis.org

26 Benoit France, "China Makes Headway in Angola with Multiple Trade Ties," *Dow Jones International News*, November 30, 2006.

27 *Financial Times*, December 28, 2006.
28 Harry G. Broadman, *Africa's Silk Road: China's and India's New Economic Frontier*, Washington D.C., World Bank, 2007, p. 275.
29 "China in Africa: Never Too Late to Scramble," *The Economist*, October 26, 2006; "China and Angola Strengthen Bilateral Relationship," *Power and Interest News Report*, June 23, 2006.
30 "CNPC in Sudan." http://www.cnpc.com.cn/cnpc/ywycp/cnpczqq/非洲.tm
31 "CNPC in Sudan." http://www.cnpc.com.cn/cnpc/ywycp/cnpczqq/非洲.tm
32 Zha Daojion, "An Opening for U.S.-China Cooperation," *Far Eastern Economic Review*, May 2006.
33 Adam Wolfe, "China Adjusts its Approach in Africa," *The Power and Interest News Report*, February 5, 2007. Available at http://www.pinr.com/report.php?ac=view_report&report_id=613
34 Michael Richardson, "China-Sudan Ties: Beijing Walks a Tightrope," *The Straits Times*, May 23, 2007.
35 Adam Wolfe, "China Claims Success on Darfur," *The Power and Interest News Report*, April 24, 2007. Available at http://www.pinr.com/report.php?ac=view_report&report_id=643&languag
36 When visiting Khartoum in February 2007, Hu Jintao provided al-Balshir with an interest-free 100 million yuan loan to build a new presidential palace, and wrote off another 70 million yuan in debt.
37 Michael Klare and Daniel Volman, "The African 'Oil Rush' and US National Security," *Third World Quarterly*, Vol. 27, No. 4, 2006.
38 US DOD, Office of the Secretary of Defense, "The Power of the People's Republic of China." Annual Report to Congress, Washington, DC: DOD, 2005, p. 10.
39 Michael Klare and Daniel Volman, "The African 'Oil Rush' and US National Security," *Third World Quarterly*, Vol. 27, No. 4, 2006.
40 "Africa Took the Place of Middle East as the Largest Oil Supplier for America," http://www.china5e.com/news/oil/200702/200702240073.html
41 Bates Gill, Chin-hao Huan, and J. Stephen Morrison, "China's Expanding Role in Africa." CSIS (Center for Strategic and International Studies) Report, January 2007. Available at: www.csis.org
42 Michael Klare and Daniel Volman, "The African 'Oil Rush' and US National Security," *Third World Quarterly*, Vol. 27, No. 4, 2006.
43 Michael Klare and Daniel Volman, "The African 'Oil Rush' and US National Security," *Third World Quarterly*, Vol. 27, No. 4, 2006.

44 Paul Rogers, "The United States, China and Africa: Eyes on the Prize," *Japan Focus*, March 21, 2007.

45 Henry Lee and Dan A. Shalmon, "Searching for Oil: China's Oil Initiatives in the Middle East," *Faculty Research Working Papers Series*, March 2007.

46 "China's Energy Policy is No Threat," *Business Times Singapore*, May 24, 2007.

47 The two sides in Sudan signed a peace treaty in 2005—the Comprehensive Peace Agreement. Under its terms, the South has a six-year period of autonomous self-rule. The South has formed its own oil company—Nilepet, and disputes are already emerging about which side has the rights to grant concessions for future oil exploration (Henry Lee and Dan A. Shalmon, "Searching for Oil: China's Oil Initiatives in the Middle East," *Faculty Research Working Papers Series*, March 2007. Available at: http://ksgnotes.harvard.edu./research/wpaper.nsf/rwp/PWPOT-017/$File/rwp-07.017.lee.pdf)

48 Jason Qian and Anne Wu, "Playing the Blame Game in Africa," *International Herald Tribune*, July 23, 2007.

49 Andrew Natsios, US president's special envoy to Sudan, speaking at a press briefing before departing Beijing on January 12, 2007.

50 Jason Qian and Anne Wu, "Playing the Blame Game in Africa," *International Herald Tribune*, July 23, 2007.

51 In the near future, China is unlikely to join the IEA, which requires membership in the OECD (Organization for Economic Cooperation and Development) and the maintenance of emergency oil stocks equivalent to at least 90 days of net oil imports.

52 Barney Jopson. Congo pressed over China deal. http://www.ftchinese.com/story.php?storyid=001024803 February 10, 2009.

CHAPTER SEVEN

China, Latin America, and the United States: The Political Economy of Energy Policy in the Americas

Gregg B. Johnson and Jesse T. Wasson

Introduction

In September of 2005 and June of 2008, respectively, the United States Senate Committee on Foreign Relations and House Foreign Affairs Subcommittee on the Western Hemisphere held hearings to examine the People's Republic of China's (PRC) increased presence in Latin America. Although the meetings covered a number of issues, elected officials were especially concerned with Chinese energy interests in the region and understandably so given the timing of the discussions.[1] Crude oil prices had already doubled from $30 a barrel in 2003 to $60 in August of 2005 as Hurricane Katrina pounded the Gulf Coast of the United States. To make matters worse, in March of that same year Venezuelan President Hugo Chávez had once again threatened to cut off oil supplies to the United States. By the time of the House hearing in June of 2008, oil was surging toward $150 a barrel with regimes of questionable democratic authenticity such as Russia and Venezuela flexing newly found political muscle fueled by record high energy prices. Unbeknownst to all was an impending collapse of the US financial system, a world-wide recession, and an almost $100 skid in oil prices.

Despite oil's current price instability, its seemingly unrelenting rise from 2003–2007 caused the United States and governments world-wide to seriously reassess their energy security. China's impressive economic growth and enormous population undoubtedly contributed to the swelling costs of crude oil, iron ore, and other commodities during these years, and naturally, this raised questions surrounding her long-term impact as an emerging giant in global resource consumption. From where would China acquire the vast amount of energy needed to sustain its phenomenal growth and political stability? Certainly domestic sources and those closest to home are the most cost-effective; however, securing access to more distant markets is quickly becoming prudent policy as China's energy demands are expected to more than double in the next twenty years. With its abundance of both fossil fuels and other commodities needed to fuel China's continued economic expansion, Latin America is an appealing trading partner, though China faces a unique problem when dealing with this region. Namely, unlike South East Asia and Africa, it is a region historically dominated by the world's lone superpower, the United States.

Since the advent of the Monroe Doctrine in the early nineteenth century, the United States has routinely exercised overwhelming influence in Latin America, affecting the region's economic and political development. No matter how quaint a notion this may seem in the modern international system, the ideological significance of the Monroe Doctrine should not be underestimated. With the United States distracted by two wars, economic crisis at home, and seemingly unwilling or unable to engage its neighbors to the South as it has in the past, many scholars and policy makers wonder whether China's dealings with energy-rich Latin American states are opportunistic, strategic, or rather simply a benign consequence of her economic development.[2] The Congressional hearings cited earlier may simply preview larger debates on the horizon over the economic and political ramifications of Chinese relations with Latin America.

This chapter attempts to evaluate the relative merit of these arguments, while also providing new information and insights. In the sections that follow, we discuss how China's energy demands have intersected with Latin America as a whole before examining relations on a state-by-state basis. Later we analyze the political, logistical, and economic factors affecting China's role in the region, in addition to constraints brought on by globalization and the larger geopolitical environment. To conclude, policy recommendations are offered on how the United States, China, and Latin America can all ensure peaceful returns from these new relationships.

China and Latin America

China's hosting of the 2008 Summer Olympics symbolized the arrival of a new world power; however, for observers of international affairs her presence has been known for some time now. With a population currently over 1.3 billion and a territory close to the size of the United States, China possesses vast amounts of labor and land. These natural endowments, combined with market reforms instituted by Deng Xiaoping and continued by his successors, helped the Chinese economy grow remarkably in the past three decades. Powering one of the largest economies in the world, however, also requires numerous energy inputs. So much that the US Government's Energy Information Administration (EIA) estimates that China will likely surpass the United States as the planet's biggest energy consumer by 2030 due to a projected annual growth in usage of over 4 percent. Some organizations have predicted that China will overtake the United States even sooner.

Regardless of the pace and magnitude of China's ascension, she is already and will continue to be a major force in world energy markets. To maintain social stability China's policy makers have focused on keeping unemployment under control, which they claim necessitates maintaining a growth rate of around 8 percent per year. Fueling such aggressive expansion requires seeking out new markets and sources of energy outside China's traditional East Asian zone of influence. Latin America presents an excellent opportunity for China to perhaps "kill three birds with one stone" by: (1) securing access to commodities markets, particularly energy concerns, (2) providing the region with new export markets, and (3) pushing manufacturing competitors in Latin America into bankruptcy.

Chinese President Hu Jintao's tour of Latin America in 2004 was widely reported as signifying a new era in Sino-Latino relations. It culminated with a promise of $100 billion in new Chinese investment over the next ten years and came on the heels of already increasing commercial and diplomatic ties. That same year China convinced a number of major Latin American countries to no longer treat her as a non-market economy, thus, mitigating punitive damages from anti-dumping investigations. A year later the PRC signed a Free Trade Agreement with Chile and is currently working on pacts with Peru and Costa Rica. From 1993 to 2003, trade between China and Latin America grew by approximately 600 percent. By 2007 total trade had exploded to over $100 billion, dwarfing the $12 billion in trade to start the millennium. On the capital account, almost half of total Chinese foreign direct investment (FDI) outflows in 2006 and one-third of her total FDI stock by 2006, over $8 billion and $19 billion respectively, was hosted in Latin America.[3] China is also active in international organizations, recently becoming a non-borrowing member of the Inter-American Development Bank (IDB) and achieving observer status at the Organization of American States (OAS).

For the Chinese government, Latin America is seen as a region that offers a number of lucrative economic opportunities. In November 2008, the

Chinese government issued its very first policy paper on Latin America, stating among other things that the region is being viewed from a "strategic plane" and that China would like to "expand" and "deepen" resource and energy cooperation.[4] Although the document also explains that the two should strive for "equality" and "mutual benefit" in trade, the likely scenario would reflect dependency theorists' fears, with Latin America exporting raw materials, primarily oil, food, and minerals to China, while China exports manufactured goods to Latin America.

Turning to energy, Latin America is estimated to possess over 13 percent of the world's proven oil reserves, yet it exports less than half that amount.[5] The region also contains approximately 4.6 percent of the world's natural gas and 2 percent of its coal.[6] The economic evidence presented above seems to suggest neo-dependency might already be taking place. Moreover, as can be seen in Table 7.1 China's imports of Latin American oil have surged as of late, increasing from 2.3 percent of total oil imports in 2005 to 5.9 percent in 2008. Understanding the true extent of Chinese involvement in Latin American energy resources, however, requires more than a cursory regional analysis. Therefore, bilateral relations are the focus of the next section, beginning with Latin America's largest energy exporter.

Table 7.1 China's Oil Imports from Latin America

	2005	2006	2007	2008
	Percent of China's Total Imports			
Argentina	052	0.9	0.7	0.32
Bolivia	0	0	0	0.03
Brazil	0.77	1.06	0.99	1.17
Chile	0	0	0	0
Colombia	0	0.06	0.41	0.48
Cuba	0	0.02	0.02	0
Ecuador	0.04	0.09	0.12	0.51
Guatemala	0.03	0.03	0	0
Mexico	0	0	0	0
Peru	0	0.57	0.55	0.09
Venezuela	0.97	2.69	2.53	3.3
Total	2.32	5.41	5.32	5.88

Source: Amjadi, Schuler, and Jammes, 2006

Venezuela

In terms of energy security in the Americas, China's burgeoning relationship with Venezuela poses the greatest *potential* threat to the regional status quo. Currently, about 11 to 12 percent of US oil imports come from Venezuela, close to 60 percent of the country's total oil exports. The geographic proximity of the two states, technical expertise of America energy firms, and the capability of the United States to refine Venezuela's heavy crude has over the years fostered interdependence. Nevertheless, President Chávez sees the United States as an imperialistic and parasitic force in Latin America and wishes to reduce, if not completely eliminate, his country's dependence on the US market—a point made abundantly clear in numerous public tirades and in the de facto expulsion of ExxonMobil and Conoco Phillips in 2007. Yet breaking ties with the United States entails finding new energy partners to help access, refine, and deliver his state's estimated 80 billion barrels in proven oil reserves, the largest in the Western Hemisphere.[7] In China, Chávez believes he has found an ally that can fill these roles, with the ancillary benefit of aiding an American rival.

Chinese energy ventures in Venezuela have drawn a great deal of attention thanks in part to Chávez's boisterous reactions and subsequent jabs at the United States, likely to the dismay of Chinese officials[8]. Early energy deals between the two states involved increasing the production of Venezuela's Orimulsion—a dirty, low-grade, and plentiful fuel that can be used to generate electricity inexpensively. In 2001, a $330 million joint venture between China National Petroleum Corporation (CNPC) and Petroleos de Venezuela (PDVSA)—both enormous, state-owned firms—created Orifules Sinoven, S.A. to expand production of the fuel, and in 2003 CNPC began construction of an Orimulsion power plant in Guangdong province.[9] In addition, despite Venezuela having only modest coal resources, China stated in 2004 it would help develop mines in the Orinoco River Basin.[10]

Following repeated trips to Beijing by Chávez, in January 2005 Chinese Vice President Zeng Qinghong travelled to Caracas for the signing of 19 cooperation agreements of which energy deals were a significant component.[11] China pledged $350 million to develop the infrastructure of 15 declining oil fields and $60 million for natural gas, railways, and refineries. It was also reported that China extended a $700 million credit line to Venezuela for Chávez's low-income housing program. In return for Chinese investment, CNPC was granted access to oil and gas development projects.

Furthermore, Venezuela agreed to export 100,000 barrels of oil per day with promises to substantially increase that amount in the coming years.[12]

More recently, China and Venezuela have struck deals that could advance Chávez's desire to wean the nation off the American export market. In 2006, PDVSA signed a $1.3 billion agreement with China to buy 18 oil tankers from China Shipbuilding Industry Corporation and in September 2008 the two announced they would work to build three refineries in China capable of processing heavy crude.[13] To speed delivery and lower costs, Chávez has said to be pursuing building an oil pipeline, either across Colombia or underwater to Panama, so that Venezuelan oil can reach the Pacific Coast. China and Venezuela have also created a $6 billion joint development fund for infrastructure and energy through their respective development banks, with the majority of the money coming from China.[14] Lastly, in September 2009 Chávez publicized the procurement of $16 billion in new Chinese investment for oil projects in the Orinoco River Basin.[15] This will likely help fill the void created when Chávez seized control of ExxonMobil and Conoco Phillips interests there, prompting the two companies to leave.

The combination of China's rapidly increasing need for oil and massive currency reserves has put the country in a unique position vis-à-vis Venezuela, given Chávez's desire to decrease his country's dependence on America. Table 7.1 shows Venezuelan oil exports went from comprising less than 1 percent of total Chinese oil imports in 2005 to over 3 percent in 2008. Of greatest concern to the United States is the disadvantageous position it is in relative to China when it comes to doing business. Chinese government-owned oil companies can barter with Chávez for contracts, offering cash and credit up front to circumvent market prices and divert oil away from other buyers. In contrast, the US government and private US companies are prohibited from doing so legally. The worst case scenario is at some point in the future China will have a cost-effective refining and delivery capacity that will allow Chávez to reduce or completely cut off oil exports to the United States.[16]

Brazil

Brazil, South America's second largest holder of proven oil reserves and expected net oil exporter by the end of 2009, has attracted Chinese interest as well.[17] Much like China's approach to Venezuela, Brazilian President Lula De Silva's 2004 visit to Beijing was reciprocated during Hu Jintao's tour of Latin America, a trip that carried along with it $10 billion in energy investments for Brazil.[18] That same year the China Petroleum and Chemical

Corporation (Sinopec), China's second largest state-owned oil company, signed cooperation accords with Brazil's state-owned oil company Petróleo Brasileiro S.A (Petrobras). The two sides agreed to collaborate in all aspects of the industry, from exploration and extraction to refining and delivery.[19] Sinopec also signed a memorandum of understanding with Petrobras, worth a purported $1.3 billion, to construct a 730-mile natural gas pipeline.[20] Work on the pipeline, which connects Brazil's northeast and southeast networks, began in 2006 and should be completed by 2010.[21] Lastly, the Chinese government and Petrobas have held discussions on increasing ethanol exports to China.[22] Brazil is the world's largest ethanol exporter and Chinese demand for the fuel has increased after curtailing its own production efforts due to concerns over food prices. Moreover, Brazil's sugar-based ethanol is a far more efficient fuel than Chinese ethanol made from grain.

Although Brazil's oil exports to China account for a much smaller fraction than Venezuela's, they still represent the second highest total in the region, about 1 percent of total Chinese oil imports the last few years (see Table 7.1). If Petrobras continues to improve the state's refining and extraction capabilities, this number could increase in the coming years. The company does have a $174 billion expansion plan which includes augmenting the state's heavy crude refining capacity. In September 2009, Petrobras and PDVSA completed negotiations on the construction of a $12 billion joint oil facility in northeastern Brazil.[23] The refinery is reported to be capable of processing heavy crude, but is not expected to be fully operational for some time.

Accessing deep sea oil has also become especially critical for Brazil as it recently discovered a vast oil and gas field in the Santos Basin approximately 16,000 feet below the ocean floor. The total area could contain as much as a 56 billion barrel equivalent of oil and natural gas.[24] Moreover, oil in this location is of the lighter variety, and thus, much more profitable than the heavy crude found elsewhere. To this end in May 2009 Petrobras secured $10 billion in funding for projects in the region from the China Development Bank and Sinopec in exchange for 200,000 barrels of oil a day over the next ten years.[25] Around the same time the U.S. Export-Import Bank granted Petrobras $2 billion in additional loans, expected to reach as much as $20 billion by the end of the year.[26] This move, while not the first act of American re-engagement in the region under the Obama administration, is significant in that it demonstrates direct competition with China for influence over the Brazilian oil industry. Just how successful each state will ultimately be in its attempt remains to be seen, but in the meantime, Brazil seems content in playing these two thirsty giants off one another to its own benefit.

Argentina, Peru, Colombia, Ecuador, and Bolivia

Hu Jintao's pledge to invest as much as $20 billion in Argentina, once again, came during his 2004 Latin American expedition and following a visit by Argentine President Nestor Kirchner to Beijing a few months earlier. More than half the funds, some $14 billion, are reportedly for infrastructure improvements, while $5 billion are dedicated to energy exploration.[27] Argentina is the third largest producer of oil in South America and a net exporter in part because of its reliance on natural gas for domestic consumption. Declining production in recent years has limited the amount of Argentine oil available for the Chinese market, less than 1 percent of total Chinese imports in 2007 and declining ever since (see Table 7.1). China, however, hopes its investments in exploration, such as its joint venture between petroleum firm China Sonangol International Holding (CSIH) and Argentina's state-owned Energia Argentina, S.A. (Enarsa) to probe offshore opportunities, can revitalize the industry.[28] A point reinforced perhaps by a rumored August 2009 offer of $17 billion from CNPC and the Chinese National Offshore Oil Corporation (CNOOC) to buy an 84 percent stake in YPF, Argentina's largest private oil firm held by the Spanish company Repsol, YPF.[29]

China has not exclusively targeted the region's largest energy exporters. Her dealings have also included emerging players in oil and natural gas, such as Peru, Colombia, Ecuador, and Bolivia. Although these states currently export much less oil to China than Venezuela, Brazil, and Argentina (see Table 7.1), their proximity to the Pacific coast and relatively underdeveloped production capacity makes them prime candidates for Chinese investment. Furthermore, they are uniquely appealing destinations in that their energy industries are partially privatized, and thus, may allow China a level of control unattainable elsewhere in the region. In 2004 CNPC acquired a 45 percent stake in PlusPetrol Norte, an Argentine company that controls more than half of Peru's oil industry.[30] This purchase amplified previous Chinese holdings, like the operation of northern oil fields by CNPC subsidiary Sapet.[31] Peru is also close to completing a massive liquefied natural gas project (LNG) south of Lima that may prove valuable to China if its future energy portfolio consists of more natural gas.[32]

In 2005 Andes Petroleum, another CNPC subsidiary, purchased $1.42 billion in Ecuadorian oil fields previously held by the Canadian firm EnCana.[33] The acquisition also gave CNPC a 36 percent share in the 310 mile Oleoducto de Crudos Pesados (OCP) oil pipeline which runs from Lago Agrio to the Balao terminal on the Pacific coast.[34] As a testament to its unfilled potential, Ecuador is estimated to have the third largest proven oil reserves in South America, but is only the fifth largest producer.[35] China has entered the Colombian oil market as well. Colombia, estimated to have only the fifth largest reserves, offers oil that is sweeter and lighter compared to that found elsewhere in the region. Sinopec, along with an Indian firm, bought a 50 percent ($850 million) stake in Ominex de Colombia, a subsidiary of the American Ominex Resources, in 2006.[36] Bolivia too has had talks with China on investing in the country's vast natural gas reserves—second only to Venezuela in the region.

Much Ado About Nothing?

With this flurry of Chinese activity it is no wonder some American policy makers are starting to get nervous. The suddenness and scope of Sino-Latino economic linkages detailed above portray China as rapidly encroaching, wooing political and business leadership while strategically selecting and securing energy resources. By providing Latin American states with capital, market diversification, and attention (an undervalued element of soft power), China may be opportunistically filling the gaping hegemonic hole left by the US. Leftist regimes like Venezuela, Bolivia, and to some extent Ecuador, further complicate matters as they seek alternative investment partners and outlets for their energy to reduce, if not actually eliminate, Washington's influence.

China's seemingly insatiable energy needs, coupled with foreign-currency reserves estimated to be over $1.5 trillion and state-owned energy firms, gives the Chinese government the motivation, resources, and conduit to sacrifice short-term profit for long-term gains in the international system. In other words, Chinese energy firms are not necessarily individual profit maximizers, but instead, instruments of the government that, when advantageous, can operate according to the laws of politics, not economics. This is not to say Chinese firms always act as zombies without regard for their own economic well being. In fact, CNOOC's failed attempt to purchase the Californian oil company Unocal in 2005 could be interpreted as a situation where good business supplanted political expediency. Exactly to what extent Chinese leadership involves itself in the dealings of CNOOC and alike is unknown; however, it is reasonable to assume that on average these companies are far more vulnerable to political exploitation than privately held companies in the United States or elsewhere. China's focus on trade, investment, energy extraction, and transportation does suggest some level of coordination when it comes to her relations with Latin America.

Given that the United States imports nearly 20 percent of its oil from Latin America (excluding Mexico) at any given time (see Table 7.2), the preceding evidence could indicate an emerging threat to America's energy security. Specifically, a far-sighted Chinese strategy that slowly diverts Latin American resources away from the United States and toward China can simultaneously weaken the former and strengthen the latter. At least this is what a superficial interpretation of China's actions may lead one to conclude. A deeper examination of Sino-Latin American energy relations, however, reveals a story that is much more pedestrian and pragmatic than ominous.[37] There are serious logistical, economic, and political obstacles preventing a significant Chinese presence in the region that, when combined with globalization and geopolitics, paint a much different picture than outlined earlier.

To begin, the statistics so often used to illustrate China's economic incursion into Latin America must be put into context and scrutinized.

Table 7.2 United States' Oil Imports from Latin America

	2005	2006	2007	2008
	Percent of USA's Total Imports			
Argentina	0.84	0.45	0.59	0.49
Bolivia	0.02	0.02	0.02	0.04
Brazil	1.17	1.29	1.45	1.99
Chile	0.14	0.08	0.06	0
Colombia	1.64	1.32	1.22	1.51
Costa Rica	0	0	0	0.01
Dominican Republic	0	0	0	0
Ecuador	1.79	1.89	1.42	1.66
El Salvador	0	0.01	0	0
Guatemala	0.06	0.07	0.06	0.09
Honduras	0	0	0	0
Mexico	10.52	11.11	10.24	9.23
Nicaragua	0	0.04	0	0
Panama	0	0.1	0.1	0.1
Peru	0.32	0.29	0.28	0.28
Uruguay	0.04	0.02	0	0
Venezuela	12.82	11.69	11.63	10.84
Total	29.34	28.3	26.98	26.15

Source: Amjadi, Schuler, and Jammes, 2006

Although trade between China and Latin America has skyrocketed in the last decade and a half, so has China's trade with the rest of the world. The impact of China's rise as an international manufacturing powerhouse in need of raw materials has been felt everywhere. Latin America is just a minor player in this larger economic context. Sino-Latin American trade remains modest despite increases as of late, and is far closer in volume to China's trade with Africa or Oceania than with North America or Europe.[38] No country in the Western Hemisphere, with the exception of the United States, is a top-ten trading partner of China, and Latin American trade with China in 2007 was less than one-fifth of US trade with the region ($560 billion). Explaining recent surges in Sino-Latino trade as anything more than a natural consequence of China's development neglects this fact.

Various US government agencies and officials, international organizations, think tanks, and scholars have also cited investment figures that are egregiously misleading when discussing China's role in Latin America.[39] The impressive amount of FDI pouring into Latin America from China, mentioned earlier to be upwards of $20 billion to date and one half of total FDI outflows, can be deceptive if not disaggregated by country. In reality, more than 90 percent of Chinese capital is concentrated in three offshore tax havens: the British Virgin Islands, Cayman Islands, and Bahamas.[40] A great deal of this money is then sent back to China in a process known as "round tripping" which allows Chinese businesses to avoid the domestic corporate tax rate that is more than twice that of foreign corporations.[41] The actual amount of FDI devoted to natural resource extraction in Latin America is probably closer to $2 billion, although that figure is disputable as well.[42] Whatever the correct figure, it is most certainly a tiny fraction of US and European FDI stock in the region—estimated to be close to half a trillion dollars in 2002.[43]

Even Hu Jintao's infamous 2004 pledge to invest $100 billion in Latin America, one of the most frequently cited statistics in support of China's threatening role in the region, unravels upon further review. The Chinese government later corrected this statement claiming they were misunderstood or mistranslated and what the president really said was $100 billion in bilateral trade was pledged—a goal met just three years later.[44] Whether or not this re-characterization of China's commitments has damaged her reputation in the region is unknown. It most certainly, however, deflated the great sense of Chinese goodwill brought on by the pledge.

In addition to overzealous portraits of China's Latin America portfolio, her numerous energy deals have too sometimes been sold as much more intrusive than they really are. Simply from a logistical perspective, there exist sizeable geographic and technical barriers that limit Chinese exploitation of the region's energy reserves. Venezuela, Brazil, and Argentina, the three largest oil exporters to China are on the wrong side of the Panamanian Isthmus. Since most supertankers cannot pass through the Panama Canal, oil from Venezuela takes an estimated 44 days to reach China, almost 40 days longer than it takes to reach the United States. The combined costs of transporting and refining Latin American heavy crude are prohibitive, especially when superior oil can be found closer to home. As an example, suppose China has a choice between importing oil from the Middle East, Africa, and Asia at a cost of $100 a barrel or from Venezuela at, for the sake of argument, the politically reduced price of $50 a barrel. If the final cost of Venezuelan oil, including transportation and refining, is even just $1 more a barrel than nearer oil, it is not in China's economic interest to buy from Venezuela.

The problem is, of course, that Chinese demand cannot be met by just one market: when more convenient supplies are exhausted (in the short- or long-term), China must import more distant and lesser quality oil. Still, this does not automatically imply a destabilizing rise in Latin American oil imports as Chinese demand grows and world supplies dwindle. China, whether as a buyer or seller in control of oil assets through exploration and production agreements, has economic and political reasons to abide by market forces and ensure world oil exports continue to flow to their natural trading partners. It is optimal for all parties that the United States, which has lower transportation costs and the technical ability to refine heavy crude, imports oil from states like Venezuela. Every drop of Latin American oil consumed by the United States is one less drop that needs to be acquired from suppliers that are closer to China. Stated differently, why would China inefficiently compete with America in the Latin American energy market only to see an increased American presence in Eastern markets to cover the shortfall? Both states lose in this scenario because of higher transportation costs and information asymmetries. Moreover, China loses politically as the United States would interpret her actions as revisionist and hostile, likely resulting in confrontations that would harm Sino-American relations, a far more important relationship for both states. There are goods reasons why American and Chinese oil portfolios are geographically concentrated, and this will likely continue for the foreseeable future (see Figures 7.1– 7.3).

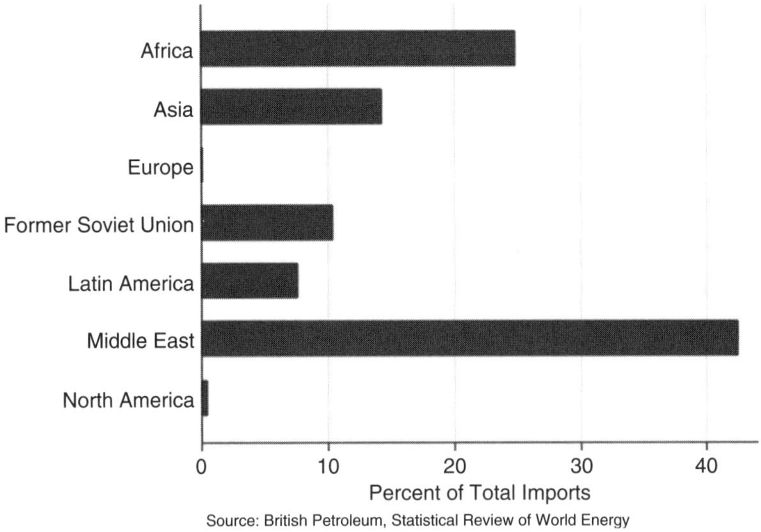

Figure 7.1 China's Oil Imports for 2008

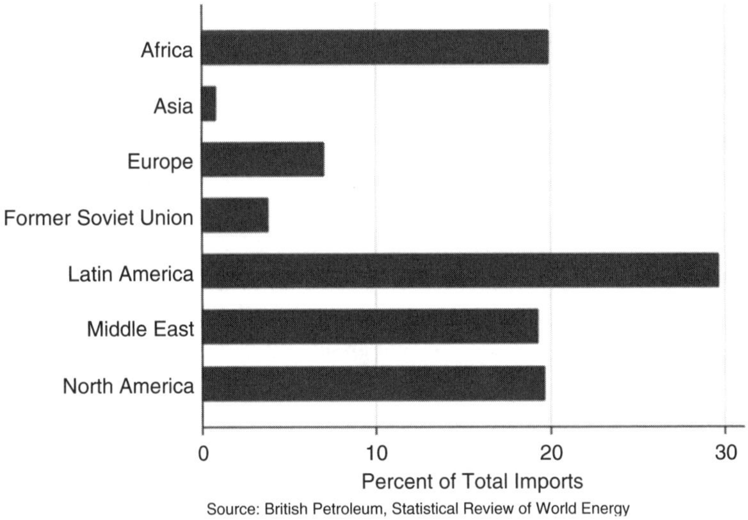

Figure 7.2 United States' Oil Imports for 2008

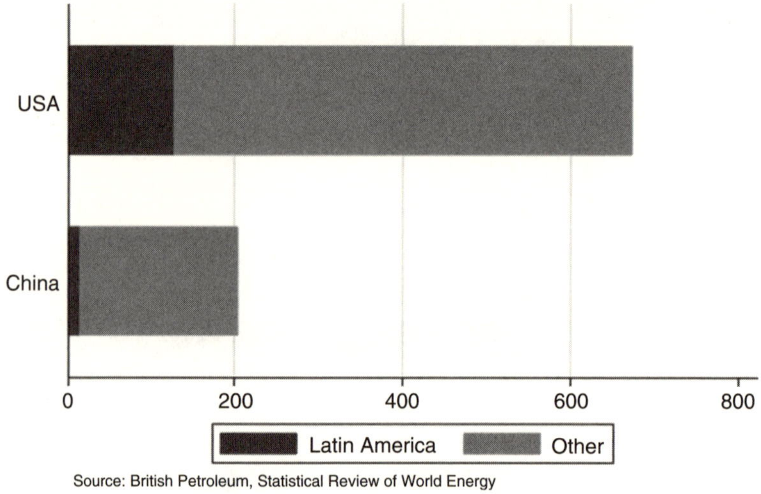

Figure 7.3 United States vs. China's Oil Imports for 2007

Yet, there has been talk of upgrading Latin America's energy transportation network, that if realized could certainly upset this argument. Chávez has spearheaded efforts to create an energy pipeline system that runs throughout South and Central America. The proposed Gasoducto del Sur (Gasur) natural gas line that would run along the East coast, from Venezuela to Brazil to Argentina has generated the most attention. This was to be part of an extensive network of natural gas and oil pipelines that Chávez hoped would unite the region, stimulate development, and improve access to Pacific ports. He has routinely hailed the 140-mile natural gas pipeline from northeastern Guajira department in Colombia to the Lake Maracaibo in the Venezuelan state of Zulia that was completed in October 2007, as the first in many pipeline projects that would send natural gas and oil to the Pacific coast via Colombia and/or Panama. Without a doubt this would make it easier for Chávez to re-direct resources to the Chinese market as shipping times would be greatly reduced.[45]

In reality, however, these are nothing more than proposals that are fraught with formidable obstacles. The Venezuelan-Colombian natural gas pipeline currently flows in the wrong direction for Chávez, as Colombian natural gas is needed to power Western Venezuelan oil facilities. Various disputes between Chávez, Colombia, and other states have soured relations as of late and render cooperation on this grand a scale improbable any time soon given the political, financial, and logistical partnerships such an undertaking would entail. The Latin American energy transportation system will likely remain uncoordinated, broken, and unable to supply Pacific ports with resources from the east for the foreseeable future. Note, even an existing transnational oil pipeline across the Andes from Argentina to Chile is reported to be non-operational at this time.[46] Furthermore, large-scale transnational infrastructure projects have a long history of difficulties in the region.

In addition to these regional constraints, political and economic factors at the state level also serve to restrict Chinese influence. Populist leaders may be the most amenable to making energy deals that benefit Chinese needs, yet these populist leaders often have somewhat tenuous holds on power, increasing uncertainty across the private sector, especially in capital intensive sectors like energy. Strong executives can change the rules of the game on a whim, if it means their political survival. Furthermore, insistence on the part of China to almost exclusively use Chinese workers in its foreign operations and a tendency to insulate themselves from local services, can lead to nationalist backlashes in these states.[47] Together this makes large-scale speculative energy investments potentially risky for China.

Perhaps unsurprisingly, China has already encountered the downsides of dealing with unpredictable populists. For example, in 2006 Venezuela ceased orimulsion production, including the joint CNPC-PDVSA, Orifules Sinoven operation, much to the annoyance of China who had built a $350 million power plant specifically for the fuel.[48] A year later newly elected Ecuadorian President Rafael Correa levied severe windfall profit taxes on oil revenue. He also used his decree authority to reduce foreign companies' role in production-sharing arrangements with Petroecuador, Ecuador's state-owned oil firm, or else restructure their energy deals into service contracts.[49] Overnight Andes Petroleum, China's $1.42 billion investment, lost control over Ecuadorian oil fields and the OCP pipeline. Similar moves by Bolivian President Evo Morales have stalled Chinese investment in Bolivia's largely untapped natural gas fields as well. In sum, political uncertainties in the region limit the attractiveness of Chinese investment in Latin American energy sectors.

Additional Complications—Energy (and Commodities) versus Industry

Until this point our main focus has been China's interest in Latin America as an energy provider. However, China's phenomenal economic development and its corresponding quest for energy have important implications beyond Latin America's energy sector. Governments across Latin America tend to see both the potential benefits and the potential costs associated with increased trade and investment relations with China. On the one hand, China's rapid industrialization provides both new markets and higher prices for Latin American commodities exports, long the strength of the region's economies. Where this has occurred, the strategic interests of the PRC and Latin American governments largely correspond with each other. Furthermore, the relationship offers an enormous potential investor to help fuel Latin America's own future development, while a small number of states see China's increased influence as a counterweight to US influence in the region.

On the other hand, many Latin American states occupy the same middle-income category China now enjoys and face stiff competition from Chinese manufacturers. A number of Latin American industries have suffered due to increased competition from Chinese manufacturing, losing both domestic and export market share. For example, the Mexican *maquiladora* industry lost hundreds of thousands of jobs due to China's comparative advantages on labor costs and other business costs.[50] Supplying a strategic economic competitor with the energy and other resources it needs in order to further develop is both economically and politically dangerous. This is reflected in the increasingly negative evaluations of China found in Latin America among government officials, manufacturers, and even citizens.[51] Moreover, China's domestic market for Latin American manufactured exports remains minuscule. Taken together, domestic leaders in Latin America are keenly aware that, in the extreme, China's rise may simply portend a new form of neo-dependency. In this section we will briefly address the strategic implications of China's economic development and growing energy demands from Latin America's perspective.

China's quest for energy and other commodities in Latin America simply reflects a long-standing economic pattern. The region has long served as the supplier of primary products used by other countries in their process of industrialization.[52] For Latin American states with small manufacturing sectors or with manufacturing sectors that do not compete with Chinese producers, China's economic boom largely matches the country's own economic interests, though with some downsides. An Organisation for Economic Co-operation and Development (OECD) analysis of Chinese import-export structures shows that Bolivia, Chile, and Venezuela have very little to fear from Chinese trade competition.[53] The fact that China's economic interests correspond with the interests of two states with large energy reserves, and one that supplies much of the world's copper, has clear benefits for China. Also as primary product exporters, China's economic boom inflated commodities prices which produced stronger than expected economic performance.

However, even these states may approach their relationship with China with some caution for two reasons. First, Latin America has considerable experience with commodities booms due to its "natural resource curse."[54] These booms are almost inevitably followed by busts due to the development of alternatives, emergence of new suppliers, or economic slowdowns in export markets. The precipitous decline in world oil and copper prices due to the global recession may portend trouble ahead for these economies. Second, the so-called Dutch Disease, or surges in income due to spikes in commodities prices also threatens non-commodities exports, especially manufacturers.[55] If governments and firms in these states are able to parlay petro-dollars into human capital accumulation, technological innovation, and infrastructure improvements China's boom may also produce long-term economic growth and increased stability in these states. Few governments, however, have successfully used petro-dollars to fuel economic development.[56] Furthermore, Chinese investment in the region, particularly outside industries directly related to energy production and commodities, is quite limited, so these states have not thus far been able to use Chinese investment to fuel development. Thus, while China's energy and other commodities demands produce economic benefits for states like Bolivia, Chile, and Venezuela because they do not compete directly with Chinese manufacturing, these benefits may be short term and are unlikely to produce long-term development.

While China's thirst for energy and commodities has clear benefits for some Latin American states, it has clear negative consequences for some other states in the region.[57] States with little energy and few commodities like those found in Central America, or with an impenetrable energy sector like Mexico also tend to be the states that most directly compete with China in the manufacturing of low-skill, labor-intensive products like textiles.[58] As a result, these states have not benefited from the region's energy boom and have undergone de-industrialization as manufacturers have shifted production to China.[59] Though, this relationship is largely confined to Mexico and Central America.

The stark contrast between Latin American states that have largely gained from China's energy and commodities demands and those that have clearly lost to Chinese manufacturers is not the norm. Instead a large number of states occupy an intermediate position, benefiting from China's thirst for energy and commodities, but also losing out economically in manufacturing sectors. As mentioned in the previous section, China struck energy deals with Argentina, Brazil, Colombia, Ecuador, and Peru and relies upon these and other states for key raw materials and food. For example, Argentina and Brazil supply a majority of China's soybean imports. China has also invested heavily in mining in a number of South American states, while investing in Latin America's leading steel producer—Brazil. As a consequence, certain economic sectors in these states have clearly benefited from increased trade with China.

Yet, within each of these states there are a number of traditionally powerful economic sectors that are threatened by China's phenomenal growth. These states all have export profiles that put a number of economic sectors in direct competition with Chinese exports.[60] While productivity is generally higher in Latin American states such as Brazil, China's low wages, access to cheap capital, and other investor-friendly incentives for export-oriented business increasingly put manufacturing in these states at a distinct disadvantage. Furthermore, neoliberal economic reforms adopted in Latin America during the 1980s and 1990s reduced state intervention in the manufacturing sector and left governments in the region with few resources to protect domestic producers. Textiles manufacturers in Colombia and Peru are rapidly losing market share both at home and abroad to Chinese producers, and Peruvian producers have asked the government to investigate whether China is dumping clothes at below market prices.[61] Government officials throughout these states have repeatedly complained that Chinese investment has been slow in coming and access to Chinese markets for non-commodities is largely blocked.[62] Brazil's Foreign Minister was famously quoted in the *Financial Times* that Brazil had been "deceived" when agreeing to recognize China as a "market economy." In short, large portions of the manufacturing sector in these states are losing market share both at home and abroad to low-wage producers in China.[63] Without major investments in human capital and technology industrial sectors in these states are poorly positioned to compete with Chinese manufacturing.

As a consequence, states that occupy this intermediate position see China's rapid growth as a double-edged sword. China's search for energy, raw materials, and food to fuel its continued economic expansion help commodities-based sectors in their economies. Yet this boom in the commodities-based sectors of their economies is, at least in some cases, undermining economic development in manufacturing. In fact, manufactured goods once accounting for 30 percent of GNP in the Southern Cone of Latin America now account for less than 20 percent.[64] While China's ascension to full membership in the World Trade Organization may reduce some of China's enormous advantages in light manufacturing, it is hard to escape the conclusion that countries that occupy this intermediate position (exporting both commodities and manufactured goods) are undermining their own long-run economic development by providing China with the energy and other resources it needs to maintain its phenomenal growth.

Conclusion

The overall tenor of the US Congressional hearings mentioned at the outset mirrors most analyses of Chinese energy relations with Latin America. While there is a select group of elected officials and scholars who believe China to be an imminent threat to American interests in the region, the prevailing opinion is one of cautious optimism. Deepening Sino-Latin American ties are a natural consequence of China's economic development and should not be interpreted as aggressive or imperialistic behavior. Moreover, China is at a competitive disadvantage compared to the United States when it comes to the region.

Throughout this chapter we demonstrate that although a number of Chinese-owned energy concerns have struck deals across Latin America, the size and scope of these agreements is actually quite limited once put in context. In addition the technical demands of extracting Latin American oil, difficulties involved in transporting energy resources largely concentrated in the Atlantic to the Pacific coast, restrictions placed on foreign involvement in most Latin American states, and domestic politics all curb China's ability to exploit the region's energy reserves. A final complicating factor for China is that her industrialization threatens manufacturing in many energy-producing states. In short, while China's energy interests in Latin America have increased as of late, there is a plethora of factors that will likely prevent a significant Chinese presence for the foreseeable future.

Our findings have important implications for those who conceive energy security in the region as a zero-sum game—where every barrel of oil obtained by the Chinese is one less barrel for the United States. This model drastically oversimplifies a globalized world, and furthermore, seems to presuppose an American claim to all energy resources on the planet. Reflexive Cold War-era thinking, that replaces ideology with energy and prescribes that the United States prevent the Latin American dominoes from falling once again, is not only empirically inaccurate but dangerous and counterproductive. China is not the semi-autarkic Soviet Union. As perhaps confirmed by the current recession, the economic well being of China and the United States depends on a healthy American export market buttressed in part by Chinese debt financing. Since accessible and affordable energy are part and parcel of economic growth, China and the United States necessarily have a stake in each other's energy security.

These economic and energy interdependencies should be cultivated so that the costs of conflict rise and China is further integrated into the status quo. The decline of fossil fuel resources is a global problem requiring collaborative solutions. China, the United States, and Latin America can all jointly benefit from the development of the region's energy reserves if it is done so in a way that is transparent, market driven, and sustainable. The American government can help ensure this by revitalizing diplomatic relations with its Southern neighbors and encouraging the improvement of democratic institutions. Continued Sino-American dialogue regarding one another's interests and intents in the region will also keep potentially hazardous misunderstandings and misperceptions to a minimum.[65] Finally, the United States and China must start to think long term about global energy needs and begin cooperating on alternative fuel technologies. For if Latin America ever becomes ground zero in an energy conflict between the two powers, everyone involved will have already lost.

Appendix

Table 7.1A Latin American Oil, Natural Gas, and Coal Exports (2008)

	Oil Exports	Natural Gas	Coal
	(Value in billions of U.S. $)		
Latin American Exports	179.1	5.1	5.3
World Exports	1561.5	266.1	106.8
Percent of World Total	11.47	1.92	4.96

Source: Amjadi, Schuler, and Jammes, 2006
Note: Bolivia accounts for 61.7 percent of the region's natural gas exports, while Colombia accounts for 94.8 percent of the region's coal exports.

Notes

1 It could be argued that these hearings reflected a general anxiety over US energy security more so than Chinese involvement with Latin America per se.

2 President Obama and Secretary of State Clinton have promised a much more active U S-Latin American policy than was seen during the Bush years.

3 OECD (2008) *Investment Policy Review: China 2008*. Organization for Economic Co-operation and Development, page 135. Retrieved from http://www.oecd.org/document/40/0,3343,en_2649_34893_41735656_1_1_1_34529562,00.html.

4 "China's Policy Paper on Latin America and the Caribbean," *Chinese Government's Official Web Portal*. Retrieved from http://www.gov.cn/english/official/2008–11/05/content_1140347.htm, accessed January 14, 2009.

5 Chietigj Bajpaee (2005) "Chinese Energy Strategy in Latin America," *The Jamestown Foundation*, China Brief 5 (14). Retrieved from http://www.jamestown.org/programs/chinabrief/single/?tx_ttnews%5Btt_news%5D=3870&tx_ttnews%5BbackPid%5D=195&no_cache=1.

6 British Petroleum (2008) "Statistical Review of World Energy 2008." Retrieved from http://www.bp.com/productlanding.do?categoryId=6929&contentId=7044622. Exports of these fuels pale in comparison to oil (see Appendix) and although China's consumption of national gas is increasing it represents only 3 percent of her total energy supply (IEA, 2008). Furthermore, a lack of infrastructure prohibits large-scale exports of liquefied natural gas from Latin America at this time. Therefore, fuels other than oil will only be discussed on a case-by-case basis as they relate to China.

7 Energy Information Administration. Statistical Agency of US Department of Energy. Various country profiles and years, http://www.eia.doe.gov.

8 Most notably, Chávez stated in December 2005 that, " . . . these have been 100 years of domination by the United States. Now we are free, and place this oil at the disposal of the great Chinese fatherland." See Juan Forero (2005) "China's Oil Diplomacy Lures Latin America," *International Herald Tribune*, March 2, 2005, http://www.iht.com/articles/2005/03/01/business/oil.php.

9 R. Evan Ellis (2008). Statement to US House of Representatives Subcommittee on the Western Hemisphere of the Committee on Foreign Affairs, June 11, 2008, http://foreignaffairs.house.gov/110/42905.pdf, page 7.

10 See Economist Intelligence Unit (2007) "China/Latin America Industry: Growing Energy Nexus," *Economist Intelligence Unit Views Wire*, April 19, 2007.

R. Evan Ellis (2005) "U.S. National Security Implication of Chinese Involvement in Latin America," *Strategic Studies Institute*, U.S. Army War College. Retrieved from http://www.hacer.org/pdf/ChinaLATAM.pdf, 8.

11 Juan Forero (March 2, 2005) China's Oil Diplomacy Lures Latin America. International Herald Tribune. Retrieved from http://www.iht.com/articles/2005/03/01/business/oil.php

12 Chávez, during his fifth trip to Beijing in October 2008, promised to increase exports to 200,000 barrels a day. See David Shambaugh (2008) "Beijing's Thrust into Latin America," *International Herald Tribune*, November 20, 2008, http://www.iht.com/articles/2008/11/20/opinion/edshambaugh.php. Other reports have put Venezuelan oil exports to China at 350,000 barrels a day in 2007 with plans to increase that amount to 500,000 in 2008 (Crowe 2007) and 1,000,000 by 2012 (Bull 2008). These numbers, however, are highly suspect and come from government rather than independent sources. See Warren Bull (2008) "Venezuela Signs Chinese Oil Deal," *BBC News*, September 25, 2009, http://news.bbc.co.uk/2/hi/americas/7634871.stm; and Darcy Crowe (2007) "Venezuela, China Create $6 Billion Joint Development Fund."

Market Watch, November 6, 2007, http://www.marketwatch.com/news/story/venezuela-china-create-6-billion/story.aspx?guid=%7BA11A6BCC-6EFD-438D-8603–57246D6F29B5%7D.

13 Bull, 2008.

14 Crowe, 2007.

15 Daniel Cancel and Matthew Walter (2009) "Chavez Seeks to Boost Oil Production With China Deal," *Bloomberg.com*, September 17, 2009, http://www.bloomberg.com/apps/news?pid=20601072&sid=aVilWho7oX_E.

16 The US Government Accountability Office explored the possibility of reduction in the Venezuelan oil supply at the behest of Congress in a 2006 report available at: http://www.gao.gov/products/GAO-06–668.

17 EIA, 2008.

18 Dumbaugh and Sullivan, 2005, 3.

19 Economist, 2007.

20 Bajpaee, 2005.

21 EIA, 2008.

22 Luft, 2005.

23 Crowe, 2009.

24 EIA, 2008.

25 Economist, 2009. "The Dragon in the Backyard," *The Economist*, August 13, 2009, http://www.economist.com/displaystory.cfm?story_id=14209932.

26 Marinho and Goodman, 2009.

27 Some have also argued that Argentina sees China's financial commitments to the country as a way to shore up its short-term debt obligations

and eventually extricate itself from International Monetary Fund (IMF) supervision (Ellis, 2005). See also Wenran Jiang (2007) "China's Energy Engagement with Latin America," *The Jamestown Foundation*, China Brief 6 (16). Retrieved from http://www.jamestown.org/programs/chinabrief/single/?tx_ttnews%5Btt_news%5D=3967&tx_ttnews%5BbackPid%5D=196&no_cache=1.

28 CSIH is a subsidiary of the Angolan state-owned oil company Sonangol. See Jorge I. Domínguez (2006) "China's Relations with Latin America: Shared Gains, Asymmetric Hopes," *Inter-American Dialogue*, Working Paper. Retrieved from http://www.thedialogue.org/page.cfm?pageID=32&pubID=321; and Florencia Jubany and Daniel Poon (2006) "China and Latin America: Historic Opportunity," *Latin America Business Chronicle*, August 14, 2006, http://www.latinbusinesschronicle.com/app/article.aspx?id=224.

29 Manuel Baigorri (2009) "China Eyes Repsol YPF's Argentine Unit," *BusinessWeek.com*, August 13, 2009, http://www.businessweek.com/globalbiz/content/aug2009/gb20090813_124217.htm.

30 Economist, 2007.

31 Ellis, 2005.

32 Energy Information Administration. Statistical Agency of U.S. Department of Energy. Various country profiles and years, http://www.eia.doe.gov.

33 Jiang, 2007.

34 Economist, 2007.

35 EIA, 2008.

36 India Times (2006) "ONGC, Sinopec Bag Colombian Co for $850mn," *The Economic Times–India Times*, September 22, 2006, http://economictimes.indiatimes.com/news/news-by-company/o-companies/ongc/ONGC-Sinopec-bag-Colombian-co-for-850-mn/articleshow/2015746.cms.

37 For contrasting perspectives on China's overall relations with Latin America and what they might mean for the United States, see Stephen Johnson (2005) "Balancing China's Growing Influence in Latin America," *The Heritage Foundation*, No. 1888. Retrieved from http://www.heritage.org/research/latinamerica/bg1888.cfm; de Louise Rosario (2003) "China's FDI Merry-Go-Round," *Foreign Direct Investment Magazine*, April 2, 2003, http://www.fdimagazine.com/news/fullstory.php/aid/215/China_92s_FDI_merry-go-round.html; and Domínguez et al. (2006).

38 Domínguez, 2006, 10.

39 These fallacies were corrected by Mr. Daniel P. Erikson of the Inter-American Dialogue during his testimony to the House Subcommittee on the Western Hemisphere in June 2008. Whether they continue to misinform future dialogue on this subject remains to be seen.

40 OECD, 2008, 135.

41 Morck et al. (2008), in their thorough investigation of China's outward FDI, explain this can also be a method of "spontaneous privatization"—converting state-owned assets into personal holdings. See Randall Morck, Bernard Yeung, and Minyuan Zhao (2008) "Perspectives on China's Outward Foreign Direct Investment," *Journal of International Business Studies*, Volume 39 (3) 337–350; Ellis, R. Evan (2006) "The New Chinese Engagement with Latin America: Understanding Its Dynamics and the Implications for the Region," *Air and Space Power Journal* 18 (3); and de Rosario, 2003.

42 Painter, James (2008) "China Deepens Latin America Ties," *BBC News*, November 21, 2008, http://news.bbc.co.uk/2/hi/americas/7737554.stm.

43 OECD, 2005, 29.

44 One could certainly argue that the whole episode was intentional. If investment deals fell through or the government changed their mind, perhaps due to unanticipated US attention, China could always claim they were misquoted and therefore avoid reneging. See Painter, 2008.

45 It is estimated that it would take about twenty days less for Venezuelan oil to reach China via Colombia, about twenty-four days, still longer than it takes sources outside Latin America to reach China (Economist, 2007).

46 EIA, 2008.

47 See Economist 2007 and Kerry Dumbaugh and Mark P. Sullivan (2005) "China's Growing Interest in Latin America." Congressional Research Service Report, April 20, 2005, Order Code: RS22119. Retrieved from http://www.italy.usembassy.gov/pdf/other/RS22119.pdf.

48 Ellis, 2008.

49 Monohan, 2007.

50 Rosen, 2003.

51 See Ellis, 2006; Domínguez, 2006; and Center for Hemispheric Policy (2007) "China Undermines U.S. in Latin America." Chronicle Special based on final report of the China-Latin America Task Force of the *Center for Hemispheric Policy*. Retrieved from http://www.latinbusiness chronicle.com/app/article.aspx?id=1297.

52 Skidmore and Smith, 2005.

53 Javier Santiso (2006) "China: A Helping Hand for Latin America?" *Policy Insight No. 23. Paris:* OECD Development Centre. Retrieved from http://www.oecd.org/dataoecd/33/13/37293128.pdf.
54 Mesquita Moreira, 2007.
55 OECD, 2007.
56 Easterly and Levine, 2003.
57 Megan Davy (2008) "What does China's Growth Portend for Latin America?", American Enterprise Institute, *Development Policy Outlook Series No. 2, July 2008.*
58 See Kevin P. Gallagher, Juan Carlos Moreno-Brid, and Roberto Porzecanski (2008) "The Dynamism of Mexican Exports: Lost in (Chinese) Translation?", *World Development* 36 (8): 1365–1380; Jamie Heine (2008) "China's Claim in Latin America: So Far, a Partner not a Threat," *Council on Hemispheric Affairs*, Research Analysis, July 25, 2008, http://www.coha.org/2008/07/china's-claim-in-latin-america-so-far-a-partner-not-a-threat/; and Daniel H. Rosen (2003) "How China is Eating Mexico's Lunch: The Maquiladora System's Comparative Advantage is Being Challenged Head On," *The International Economy*, Spring: 22–25.
59 Ernst Hillebrand (2003) "South-South Competition: Asia versus Latin America?", Dialogue on Globalization Conference Report. Friedrich Ebert Stiftung. Retrieved from http://library.fes.de/pdf-files/iez/global/02027.pdf; and Mauricio Mesquita Moreira (2007) "Fear of China: Is There a Future for Manufacturing in Latin America?" , *World Development* 35 (3), 355–376.
60 See Rodríguez Bláquez and Santiso (2006); OECD (2007); Santiso (2006); OECD (2005) *International Investment Perspectives, 2005 edition.* Organization for Economic Co-operation and Development: New York, and OECD, 2007. *Latin American Economic Outlook 2008.* Organization for Economic Co-operation and Development: New York. Retrieved from http://www.oecd.org/document/40/0,3343,en_2649_34893_41735656_1_1_1_34529562,00.html.
61 Murphy, Swann, and Drajem, 2007.
62 Center for Hemispheric Policy, 2007.
63 The one exception to this trend is Brazil's steel industry. China's Metallurgical Construction Group invested heavily to increase Brazil's steel making capacity (Ellis, 2006).
64 Hillebrand, 2003.
65 Gonzalo S. Paz (2006) "Rising China's 'Offensive' in Latin America and the U.S. Reaction," *Asian Perspective*, 30 (4), 95–112.

CHAPTER EIGHT

A Strategic Game: China's Energy Relations with Japan and India

Jian Yang

Introduction

As the world's second, third, and sixth largest energy consumers respectively, China, Japan, and India have engaged in intensive interactions in their effort to secure energy supplies. In studying China's energy relations with Japan and India, analysts have paid particular attention to China's energy security per se. Few have made serious efforts to examine the relations in a broad context of China's overall relations with these two giant neighbors. This chapter attempts to fill the gap and outline the general patterns of China's energy relations with Japan and India. It should be noted that much of the analysis is based on Chinese analysts' observations. While they do not necessarily represent the Chinese government's policy, they highlight the complexity of China's energy relations with Japan and India.

This chapter starts with an overview of China's energy relations with Japan and India, followed by an examination of the strategic interests that underline Sino-Japanese and Sino-Indian energy competition. The chapter then analyses China's energy relations with Japan and India as a part of China's grand strategy. It argues that Beijing's strategic priority is to enhance its comprehensive national power based on economic development. For that reason, Beijing is prepared to defuse tensions and to cooperate with Japan and India on energy issues.

Cooperation and Competition

Sino-Japanese Energy Relations

The first high-profile rivalry between China and Japan over energy centered on Russia's decision to build a pipeline from Angarsk in eastern Siberia to China's declining oil capital of Daqing, a distance of 2,500 km. Millions of tons of Russian oil would flow through the pipeline and would give a large boost to Chinese energy security. Having Daqing as the destination for the oil would allow Russian oil to gradually take the place of Chinese oil, which is no longer sufficient on its own to sustain the infrastructure in place in Daqing, thereby saving the Chinese government problems, such as unemployment, caused by an economic downturn associated with a reduction in activity in Daqing.[1] The two governments signed an agreement to investigate the project in September of 2001 and in 2002 an agreement was signed between China and the Russian oil giant YUKOS to construct the pipeline.

The project collapsed with the arrest of Mikhail Khodorkovsky, the head of YUKOS, and the seizure of the assets of the company by the Russian government. In 2003, Japan lobbied Russia for a rival pipeline to the Pacific Port of Nakhodka near Vladivostok—closer to Japan and outside Chinese territory, where the oil would be shipped to Japan and other East Asian countries. To sweeten the deal, Japan offered to provide $5 billion USD, which was later increased to $9 billion,[2] of low-interest loans for the project. For a while, Japan's intensive political and considerable financial lobbying seemed successful. But China subsequently intensified its diplomatic maneuvering and bargaining and regained much of its lost position. In April 2005, the Russian government announced that the first stage of the pipeline would originate at Taishet and end at Skovorodino, a town that borders China and a branch line to Daqing would be built. The second stage would continue on from Skovorodino to Perevoznaya Bay, just south of Vladivostok, where oil would flow to Skovorodino by 2008 and Perevoznaya by 2012.[3]

A potentially more explosive issue involving energy security between China and Japan is the dispute over exploitation of undersea oil and gas deposits straddling what Japan says is the border line between the two countries' exclusive economic zones (EEZs) in the East China Sea. It has been estimated that the East China Sea holds 6–7 billion tonnes of oil and gas, much of which lies to the west of the center line.[4] Under the UN's Convention on the Law of the Sea, an EEZ can extend up to 200 nautical miles from a country's shoreline. But the East China Sea between China and Japan is only about 360 nautical miles at its very widest. Japan says the boundary should be the median line between the two countries. However, China insists that its EEZ should extend to the edge of its continental shelf, which brings it close to Okinawa. The convention does not give specifics of how overlapping EEZ and continental shelf claims should be resolved. While China says that its drilling is in an undisputed area, Japan claims that China's activities could suck gas from its side of the line.[5] The dispute is not new,[6] but it escalated in 2004 when Japanese media's attention to China's Chunxiao field (known by the Japanese as Shirakaba) suddenly surged.[7] In September 2005, the

Chinese navy made a dramatic appearance near a Chinese drilling platform at the Chunxiao field. It deployed five vessels, including a new Sovremenny class missile-equipped destroyer purchased from Russia.

Another major territorial dispute related to energy between China and Japan is over the Diaoyu Islands (also called Diaoyutai or the Senkaku Islands). The dispute was intensified after the United Nations Economic Commission for Asia and the Far East suggested possible large hydrocarbon deposits in the waters off the Islands in 1969, although no oil has ever been found. The dispute attracted much public attention inside and outside China after a Japanese rightist group built a lighthouse on the disputed territory in July 1996. Tens of thousands of overseas Chinese in North America and people in Taiwan and Hong Kong protested against the Japanese act.

Despite these conflicts, Chinese analysts acknowledge that opportunities for cooperation between China and Japan on the energy issue do exist. Some suggest that as two major oil importers in the world, China and Japan could bargain jointly in the world oil market for better deals.[8] Others point to cooperation in areas like oil transportation safety, energy efficiency, nuclear power, and oil reserves.[9] In April 2007, Chinese and Japanese energy ministers held the first policy dialogue in Tokyo, and Japan's Ministry of Economy, Trade and Industry and China's National Development and Reform Commission announced a joint statement on "Enhancement of Cooperation between Japan and the People's Republic of China in the Energy Field." Japan was prepared to help the Chinese effort for energy conservation. The two countries agreed to promote cooperation on the utilization of clean-coal technology, the construction and safe operation of nuclear power plants, and the development of new and renewable energy sources. In addition the promotion of energy security and efficient energy use within a multilateral framework was stipulated.[10]

A major breakthrough in Sino-Japanese energy relations and indeed the overall relationship is an agreement the two sides reached in June 2008 to jointly develop the gas fields in the East China Sea. During the May 2008 summit between Hu Jintao and Yasuo Fukuda, China and Japan decided to put a temporary end to the territorial dispute and agree on joint gas field development. Beijing subsequently agreed to allow Japan to invest in its gas exploration in return for a share of the profits.

Sino-Indian Energy Relations

Compared with its energy cooperation with Japan, China's energy cooperation with India has been more substantial. The oil industries of the two countries share some similarities. They both have multiple state oil companies and both consider overseas investment a vital aspect of energy security. And increasingly they are targeting the same assets in the same host countries, such as in Angola, Kazakhstan, Ecuador, and Burma.[11] The oil companies of the two countries often bid against each other to the benefit of the third country.

In January 2006, the two countries signed a "Memorandum for Enhancing Cooperation in the Field of Oil and Natural Gas," in which they identified key areas for partnerships, including upstream exploration and production, refining and marketing of petroleum products and petrochemicals, research and development, conservation, and promotion of environment-friendly fuels. The agreement also allows trading in oil and joint bidding in third countries that will help both countries reduce the burden on the exchequers. The five major oil companies from both countries also signed five company-specific memoranda of understanding (MoUs). The two MoUs that India's Gas Authority of India Limited signed with the China Petrochemical Corporation and the China National Offshore Oil Corporation (CNOOC) specifically envisage cooperation in exploration in the two countries and other parts of the world. The China National Petroleum Corporation (CNPC) also signed a MoU with India's ONGC Videsh Ltd for timely exchange of information. The MoUs were acclaimed as "a key step towards enhanced energy cooperation."[12]

The cooperation has resulted in tangible results. In February 2006 a 50:50 joint venture company (Himalaya Energy, Syria) covering 36 production fields in Syria was set up by subsidiaries of OVL and CNPC International. The company was set up to purchase the entire production shares of Canadian oil company Petro-Canada. It was the first time that the two companies joined forces to acquire an oil asset.[13] In the same year, India expressed its support for a Chinese suggestion for creating an Asia Energy Agency to coordinate the long-term energy import policies of major oil importers in the region.[14] The two countries also vowed to promote bilateral civil nuclear energy cooperation although Beijing has not been as enthusiastic, since India has thus far refused to sign the Nuclear Non-Proliferation Treaty.[15]

These results notwithstanding, the Sino-Indian energy relationship is still better characterized as competitive rather than cooperative. The two countries' state-owned oil companies have been rivaling each other for contracts to produce oil in many countries. In Angola for instance, a Chinese company outbid India's and acquired a 50 percent stake in BP-operated Block 18, purchased from Shell in 2004. In 2005, ONGC was outbid by CNPC in a competition to acquire Canadian oil company Petro Kazakhstan, which has some 550 million barrels of reserves in the Turgai basin region of Kazakhstan.[16] Worried about China's relative gains, Indian Prime Minister, Manmohan Singh said in January 2005 that his government would restructure state-owned oil firms to enable them to compete with China over oil.[17]

The January 2006 memoranda have enhanced the cooperation between Chinese and Indian companies but have not stopped the competition between them. In August 2008 a bid battle broke out between Indian and Chinese companies over London-listed energy group Imperial Energy. In the end, ONGC outbid China Petroleum and Chemical Corp (SINOPEC) with an offer which was 62 percent higher than ONGC's earlier offer.[18]

India is also apprehensive of Chinese entrepreneurial activities in its neighbor Pakistan's south-western Makran coast of Balochistan, where Chinese businesses are involved in the Gwadar Port project. The Gwadar Port is only 72 km away from Iran, and about 400 km away from the Strait of Hormuz, the only sea passage to the open ocean for large areas of the petroleum-exporting Persian Gulf states. The Chinese hope that they will one day ship Persian Gulf oil from Gwadar overland through Pakistan to China. That will cut transport by 12,000 miles (19,308 km), shaving a month off the journey's time and 25 percent off the fees.[19] Perhaps more importantly, it would give China an alternative to the Malacca Strait, an increasingly busy and dangerous Strait which is plagued by pirates and is vulnerable in times of great power conflicts. This is especially true now that the United States has significantly enhanced its ability to cut off Chinese supplies of oil with new bases in Central, South, and West Asian countries after the 9/11 terrorist attacks.[20]

Pakistan had the plan to develop the Gwadar Port early in 1964, and had talks with US companies but was not successful. In 2000, the isolated Musharraf government which came to power through a coup, proposed the plan to Pakistan's long time ally China. Beijing decided in 2001 to provide \$198 million in funds and offered technical and construction assistance.[21] The port finally became functional on December 21, 2008.[22]

Burma is another place where China and India have been competing for energy resources. China's three major oil companies, CNOOC, SINOPEC, and CNPC, all are involved in Burma. What is significant is the plan of PetroChina, which is controlled by CNPC, to build a gas pipeline from the A-1 block in the Shwe field off the coast of Rahine State to Kunming, capital of China's Yunnan Province. The Shwe field is of unconfirmed size and the A-1 block is estimated to be the largest block, containing 2.88 trillion to 3.56 trillion cubic feet of gas. PetroChina signed a memorandum of understanding with Burma in 2005 to buy 6.5 trillion cubic feet of gas from the block for thirty years starting from 2009.[23] China and Burma subsequently started a feasibility study of a gas pipeline from the western coast of Burma to Kunming, capital of China's Yunnan province. More importantly, the two sides are also investigating the possibility of building an oil pipeline with the same route as the proposed gas pipeline. The oil pipeline would enable China to obtain access to the Indian Ocean through Burma, thus reducing China's dependence on transport through the Malacca Strait and the South China Sea.[24]

On the other hand, India also made great efforts to secure Burma's gas from the same A-1 block. The two countries had been negotiating about building a gas pipeline from Shwe, through Bangladesh to India's eastern city Calcutta. However, India could not conclude a deal with Burma due to its problems with Bangladesh over India's proposed overland pipeline through Bangladesh. After losing the A-1 block to China, India offered more favorable conditions to Burma. India would guarantee earnings every year to Burma even if it is not able to access the gas. It would be more costly for India to build a Burma-Bangladesh-India gas pipeline now as the pipeline starting from the A-2 block would be 150 km longer.[25] Meanwhile, in 2004 an agreement was signed in Yangon by the foreign ministers of India, Burma, and Thailand to develop transport linkages between the three countries, including a 1,400 km highway connecting North-eastern India with Mandalay and Yangon, and on to Bangkok.[26]

Strategic Security and Energy Relations

Japan

Japan's aggression and atrocities committed in China in the first half of the twentieth century continue to bedevil Sino-Japanese relations although it is now clear to the Chinese government that the history issue "no longer has traction in Japan, and its pressure over history can be counterproductive."[27] China did make conciliatory gestures to Japan; however, they were perceived as measured and fragile. In the first half of this decade, with Koizumi continuing to visit the Yasukuni shrine, Beijing believed that it had little room to maneuver. The past might not be that important if Japan were not so powerful. As Barry Buzan pointed out some time ago: "One has to ask . . . how much of this sensitivity is actually to do with the war and how much of it simply uses the symbolism of the war to reflect more contemporary worries."[28]

The Chinese media and some analysts continue to warn the Chinese public that Japan is powerful not only economically but also militarily, raising suspicions about Japan's intentions.

The landmark victory of the Democratic Party of Japan in the August 2009 parliament elections is an opportunity for China and Japan to strengthen their strategic cooperation. Yukio Hatoyama, Japan's new Prime Minister, has made it clear that he will pursue a diplomatic course more independent of the United States than his predecessors. Hatoyama has emphasized that, as a key element of his Asia-oriented diplomacy, Japan must come to terms with China's rise and cooperate with China to build the East Asian community. On the other hand, with China overtaking Japan as the world's second-largest economy in the near future, the Chinese have become increasingly confident in dealing with Japan, which may well enable them to be more rational on the history issue.[29] Notwithstanding such optimistic prospects, strategic calculations out of mutual distrust are likely to continue in the coming years.

Sino-Japanese energy competition has been a reflection of the strategic distrust between the two countries. The rivalry between China and Japan over the pipeline from Eastern Siberia is not purely an energy issue. While Russia attempted to play China against Japan, both Moscow and Beijing intended to strengthen their bilateral relationship through the pipeline. Politically, Russia and China have moved closer since the end of the Cold War, thanks to their common interests in anti-hegemony and a multi-polar world. However, these political developments were not matched by corroborating economic relations between the two countries. Sino-Russian trade fluctuated in the 1990s, without substantial improvement. Trade in 1992 was $5.962 billion and it reached $7.68 billion the following year. In April 1997, Yeltsin and Jiang agreed to try to increase the trade to $20 billion by the year 2000.[30] By 2000, however, the trade was a mere $5.73 billion, compared with Sino-American trade of $74.46 billion and Sino-Japanese trade of $83.16 billion.[31] Both sides have had the concern that the "strategic partnership" would not go very far without compatible economic intercourse between the two countries.[32] To "commercialize" China-Russia relations was a challenge of strategic importance, and a pipeline to China would be a big step forward.

It is widely accepted in China that strategic consideration was a key reason Japan was determined to foil Sino-Russian cooperation on the pipeline. Chinese analysts note that Japan regards Russia's Far East and the Korean Peninsula as part of its traditional strategic interests. The construction of a pipeline to China's Daqing would mean not only Chinese involvement in the development of the resources in Siberia but also the consolidation of China's strategic existence. More importantly, the pipeline would become a huge strategic belt which could tighten the Sino-Russian strategic partnership. Eventually, the Korean Peninsula would be part of this strategic partnership.[33] On the other hand, if Japan succeeded in securing the Angarsk-Nakhodka route, the Russo-Japanese strategic relationship would be greatly enhanced. Japan would be fully involved in the development of the resources and economic development in Siberia. Japan could then argue that due to labor shortages in Siberia, the two Koreas should participate in the development of Siberia. As a result, China's political and economic influence in Northeast Asia would be minimized.[34]

The East China Sea dispute between China and Japan is even less an energy issue than a political issue with strategic implications. To start with, China's policy toward Japan is one of those issues which "allow the leadership less room to operate." [35] A misstep on this issue can result in political disaster for Chinese leaders and the Chinese government. Chinese public opinion of Japan has been negative. A survey in August 2005 found that 63 percent of those polled had a "very bad" or "not very good" impression of Japan.[36] The impact of the overwhelmingly negative perceptions of Japan on China's Japan policy is further strengthened by Chinese nationalism. To be perceived as soft on Japan by the public is politically risky for the Chinese leadership. In his unsuccessful visit to Japan in 1998, Jiang repeatedly called for Japan to face up to the past and it was believed that Jiang's criticisms were aimed at the audience in China.[37] In October 2000, Chinese Premier Zhu Rongji also paid a visit to Japan. Before the visit, Zhu told Japanese journalists that he would not make a big issue of history. Zhu subsequently received more than 200 letters criticizing him as being too soft on Japan. During Zhu's visit, the Chinese media kept silent on some of his conciliatory statements regarding the history issue.[38]

The Chinese navy's dramatic appearance at the Chunxiao field in September 2005 should be understood in this context. The show of force took place at a time when Sino-Japanese relations were seriously strained under Junichiro Koizumi who resisted Chinese pressure and continuously paid visits to the Yasukuni Shrine.[39] It should also be noted that Japanese maritime forces, which are non-military but are believed no less well equipped than the Chinese navy, had been to the area more than once.[40]

Chinese analysts believe that Japan's claims over the East China Sea are driven not only by sovereignty and economic interests, but also by strategic security interests. They note that the East China Sea issue is not an isolated case. It has implications for China's disputes with Japan over other territories, such as the Diaoyu Islands. Japan could extend its defense depth by claiming waters surrounding these islands.[41] On the other hand, the East China Sea is crucial to China's strategic security. It is "the road that must be taken" (*bi jing zhi lu*) in China's "go out" strategy.[42] And the Chunxiao field is perceived as China's gateway in the East China Sea.[43] "In this sense, the East China Sea disputes raised by Japan reflect not only the changes in Japan's energy policy toward China, but also the interweaving and clash of the two countries' maritime strategic interests," a Chinese analyst notes.[44]

Some Chinese analysts argue that the East China Sea dispute had been there for years and Japan did not react strongly to Chinese activities. The most important reason why the issue escalated in recent years is the emergence of the unprecedented co-existence of two great powers in Northeast Asia. These analysts argue that historically China–Japan relations have always followed the "strong-weak model" (*qiang ruo xing*). According to a Chinese calculation in 2003, the comprehensive national power between China and Japan had become almost the same (1:0.996).[45] This "strong-strong model" (*qiang qiang xing*) is new and Japan, like China, is still in the process of adjusting its strategies. Chinese analysts share the view that the trend of "China rising and Japan declining" worries the Japanese, including policy makers. Therefore Japan intends to check China's rise through its energy containment strategy.[46]

India

China's relations with India were scarred by a brief but bitter border war in 1962. After Indian Prime Minister Rajiv Gandhi's ice-breaking visit to Beijing in 1988, the two countries made considerable efforts to repair and rebuild their relations. China and India were in a process of rapprochement, albeit an "uneasy" one, before 1998. The rapprochement process was briefly interrupted by India's nuclear tests in mid-May 1998. Beijing's strong reactions were largely generated by the way New Delhi justified the tests rather than the tests themselves. The week before the tests, Indian Defense Minister George Fernandez declared China India's "potential threat No. 1." Fernandez accused China of aiding Pakistan's missile program and keeping nuclear weapons aimed at India.[47] Then, to justify the tests, Prime Minister Vajpayee sent a letter to US President Bill Clinton and identified China's nuclear weapons as the main reason why India must go nuclear.[48]

India's 1998 nuclear tests reminded Chinese analysts of India's great power dream and they acknowledged that India had the potential to be one of the most powerful countries in the world. They pointed to India's determination to become a great power, its size, population, economy, military, technology, and resources, and its geographical position as well as its rapidly growing economy.[49] A decade later, Yuan observed that "Beijing is now paying increasing attention to India's drive for great-power status through diplomatic initiatives and a military buildup."[50]

Realist calculations on balance of power carried much weight in China's policy toward India. For instance, the Chinese were concerned that the improvement of the Indo-American relationship after 1998 was achieved at the expense of US support for China's ally, Pakistan. In contrast to his five-day stay in India in March 2000, Clinton stopped in Pakistan for only five hours. Even that short stop did not come easily. Clinton decided to add a stop in Islamabad to his itinerary only after Islamabad, with the help of Beijing, had lobbied intensively.[51] Pakistan has been and will remain an important factor in China's strategic planning. It is in China's interest to have Pakistan as a strong center of power in South Asia, independent of Indian domination. Garver noted in 1996 that there was a "continuing robust Chinese support for Pakistan's efforts at national security modernization" at the time when China was improving its relations with India.[52]

Against this background, it is natural that India is concerned about Chinese activities in the Gwadar Port. What worries Indian analysts is that China is involved in the Gwadar Port not only economically but also militarily. The Sino-Pakistani defense project and cooperation on the Gwadar Port facilities is perceived in India as part of China's "maritime encirclement of India."[53] The port is said to be part of Chinese naval expansion along the Asian and African coasts called the "string of pearls" initiative, according to a US Department of Defense report.[54]

The Chinese do not necessarily see encircling India as its strategic priority. Nevertheless, they see the Gwadar Port as "the concentration of Pakistan's strategic values."[55] It could be the nearest gateway for Chinese goods and resources to go to Central Asia and an important port in the routes from the Red Sea, Arab Sea, and Persian Gulf.[56] China's activities at the Gwadar Port are linked with China's construction of the Qinghai-Tibet railway and the expansion of the Karakoram Highway. They are all parts of the grand plan, initiated by Pakistan, of making use of Pakistan's geographic importance and constructing a China-Pakistan energy channel, trade corridor, and railway.[57] The Gwadar Port will be the beginning of the energy channel. The port is so important strategically that reportedly the United States tried to pressure Pakistan to out price the Chinese from Gwadar to take over the entire facility.[58]

Chinese activities in Burma are perceived as another important part of the "maritime encirclement" and Burma is seen as another one of China's pearls. It is observed that "Burma exemplifies the difficult balance of competition and cooperation between China and India over oil and gas resources in third countries."[59] As Lixing Geng has observed

> Myanmar's [Burma] location on the tri-junction of South Asia, Southeast Asia and China is potentially important for China to achieve its strategic presence in the Indian Ocean and hence become a two-ocean power. Economically, too, Myanmar is important for China as a trading outlet to the Indian Ocean for its landlocked inland provinces of Yunnan and other south-western parts of China. Furthermore, Sino-Myanmar ties are strategically useful for China to contain the influence of India and other powers in Southeast Asia.[60]

Geng notes that by not passing through the Strait of Malacca to reach the Bay of Bengal, the PLA Navy would be able to shorten the distance by 3,000 km, reducing the voyage by five to six days. In 2003, China assisted Burma in building an 85-meter jetty to naval facilities on Great Coco Island, which lies 18 km from India's Nicobar Island. China also established a modern reconnaissance and electronic intelligence system on the island. Thus China's strategic gains in cultivating relations with Burma have long-term security implications.[61] China has not only strengthened its military and security relations with Burma, it also facilitated a joint military exercise between Burma, Pakistan, and Bangladesh.[62]

Energy, Security, and Comprehensive National Power

The above analysis demonstrates that China's energy competition with Japan and India is not just an energy security or economic issue. The competition can have strong geo-political implications. Any compromise or cooperation therefore must be based on a more comprehensive assessment of China's national interests and need to be analyzed in the context of China's overall foreign policy goals. It is thus necessary to understand China's energy relations in the context of China's grand strategy.

China's Grand Strategy

According to Michael Swaine and Ashley J. Tellis, a grand strategy is a country's "basic approach to political-military security."[63] Chinese analysts accept that security now means "comprehensive security" (*zonghe anquan*). It no longer equals to national defense and diplomacy and is no longer limited to the defense of national sovereignty and territorial integrity. In addition to traditional military security, national security now includes, among other things, economic security, political security, societal security, environmental security, human security, and technological security. The fundamental change in China's understanding of national security is the realization that without a strong economy, the military dimension of national security is not sustainable. This understanding contributed to China's concept of "comprehensive national power" (*zonghe guoli*) which has constituted the foundation of China's foreign and domestic policies. The emphasis on economic security, however, should not overshadow military security. "Military security is no less important [than economic security]. It still is an effective guarantee of comprehensive security and the last resort," said a Chinese analyst in 2003.[64]

China tried to redefine its main potential threats in the years immediately after the end of the Cold War. According to some analysts, Japan was likely to replace the Soviet Union/Russia to become the Chinese leadership's main concern.[65] China's perceptions of security threats became more complicated after 1996 when the Taiwan Strait crisis made clear the possibility of a military clash between China and the United States over Taiwan.[66] Just one month after the dangerous escalation of the Taiwan Strait crisis, US President Bill Clinton and Japanese Prime Minister Ryutaro Hashimoto held a summit meeting in Tokyo and signed the US-Japan Joint Declaration on Security for the twenty-first century. The crisis and the joint declaration as well as the subsequent revision of the 1978 Guidelines for US-Japan Security Cooperation deepened China's suspicion of US motives regarding Taiwan and, in the longer term, US strategy toward a rising China. Then came George W. Bush and Sino-US relations experienced a dramatic downturn in the first months of the Bush administration.

The September 11 terrorist attacks on America and the subsequent US "war on terror" had a strong impact on China's external security perception. Many Chinese analysts were relieved to see the improvement of Sino-US relations. In the short and medium terms, it was believed, US efforts against terrorism would help ensure the stability of Sino-US relations. Chinese leaders saw no major military clashes between China and other great powers before 2020, and they deemed the period until then "a period of important strategic opportunities" (*zhanlue jiyuqi*) for China's economic development. This does not mean that China has become relaxed with its strategic environment. For instance, some analysts have noted that Japan has become more active militarily while India is determined to seek a world power status. Both have been making changes to their military strategy to guard against the rise of China.[67]

For Chinese leaders, more imminent security concerns are not externally caused but come from within. As an undemocratically elected government in a globalized world, Beijing is acutely aware of its vulnerability. Marxism or Communist utopia is no longer appealing to the Chinese and the Chinese economy is now more capitalist than socialist. Beijing has a persistent sense of internal crisis. It faces a number of explosive issues, especially the widening gap between the rich and the poor, mass unemployment, and rampant corruption.

China's grand strategy thus consists of at least two main components—national security strategy and national development strategy. National security strategy is based on pillars of diplomacy and national defense. National development strategy is more complicated. It encompasses economic, political, technological, social, and cultural development initiatives. However both are interrelated. As mentioned earlier, the Chinese are aware that a strong economy is the foundation of the military dimension of national security. Economic development is also the key to internal stability. It remains valid to say that to develop the economy is China's "ultimate solution (*genben chulu*) to all internal and external problems."[68] Internally, to claim its legitimacy, the Chinese government has had to substantially raise the living standard. Externally, economic development is the key to comprehensive national power. The Chinese often remind themselves that the Soviet Union lost the Cold War to the West mainly because the Soviet economy was not able to sustain the conflict. Military modernization therefore must be based on economic modernization.

Energy security is closely related to China's strategic security, economic security and internal stability. This determines that China will compete with Japan and India for its energy security. On the other hand, China's national development strategy requires a peaceful environment which is conducive to China's economic development. Thus, China does have incentives to cooperate with Japan and India and to defuse the tensions over energy competition.

Japan

China has a lot of interest in a stable relationship with Japan. Japan has been one of the most important players in the Chinese economy since the late 1970s when China began its economic reforms. By 2003, Japan had been

China's biggest trading partner for thirteen years. It was replaced by the European Union (EU) in 2004 after the EU's enlargement. The two-way trade between China and Japan surpassed $200 billion for the first time in 2006 and reached $236 billion in 2007.[69] By October 2004, Japan had invested in 31,000 projects in China with an agreed investment of $65 billion and an actual investment of $46.1 billion, which was the third largest after Hong Kong and the United States. About 62 per cent of Japan's over forty-five thousand overseas enterprises are located in China, employing one million Chinese.[70]

Japan is important to China not only economically but also politically. First, as a strong ally of the United States, Japan plays a key role in US strategy toward China. How to deal with Japan is crucial in China's strategy toward the United States. Second, a strained relationship with Japan is not helpful in promoting the concept of "China's peaceful rise" or "China's peaceful development." Third, cold politics may eventually have an impact on hot economics, meaning it is impossible to separate political considerations from economic activity.

China's energy relations with Japan reflect this complex relationship. On the one hand, China competes with Japan in securing its energy supply. On the other hand, it has made sure that its energy competition with Japan will not derail the bilateral relationship. A good example is China's handling of the East China Sea dispute. As mentioned earlier, in September 2005, Beijing drove home its tough policy on the issue by sending five naval ships to the area near the disputed Chunxiao field. In June 2008, however, the two sides agreed to jointly develop some gas fields in the East China Sea. Beijing subsequently agreed to allow Japan to invest in its gas exploration in return for a share of the profits. As James Manicom observes, the evolution of the dispute is in line with the changes in Sino-Japanese relations. The Chinese navy's show of force took place at a time when Sino-Japanese relations were seriously strained under Koizumi. And the June 2008 breakthrough was achieved when Beijing wanted to strengthen Sino-Japanese relations under the more moderate Fukuda. Manicom notes that China permitting Japanese entities to invest in the Chunxiao field "appears to be a political concession made by China" as CNOOC does not require further investment to bring the Chunxiao field online.[71]

On the Diaoyu Islands, while Beijing was firm in claiming sovereignty over the islands, it is careful not to whip up Chinese nationalism against Japan. Tong Zeng, perhaps the most prominent anti-Japan campaigner in China, was sacked because of his activism in 1996. Beijing's restraint partly lay in its realization that nationalism is a double-edged sword and demonstrations against Japan could turn into anti-government protests. Equally important, Beijing did not want to let the issue overshadow the big picture of Sino-Japanese relations.[72]

Japan is also important to China's sustainable economic growth, an indispensible part of China's economic development strategy. Air and water pollution is already costing China between 8 and 15 percent of its GDP. China uses seven times more natural resources than Japan to produce $10,000 worth of goods, six times more than the United States, and even three times more than India.[73] For every $1 of GDP produced, China spends three times the world average on energy. Beijing is anxious to build a more energy-saving economy. Japan, as the most energy-efficient nation, can play an important role. Japan's GDP of $4.7 trillion in 2005 was two and a half times higher than China's ($1.9 trillion). Yet China's energy consumption of 45.5 quadrillion Btu in 2003 was twice as high as Japan's (22.4 quadrillion Btu). Hence Japan gets five times more than China out of its energy. China, although relying on oil for only 25 percent of its energy consumption (as against 65 percent coal) now consumes more oil than Japan even though Japan relies on oil for as much as 50 percent of its energy consumption (against 18 percent coal). In 2004, the Chinese oil consumption was 6.53 million bbl/d, while Japan's did not even exceed 5.43 million bbl/d in 2005.[74]

India

Despite its balance of power approach toward South Asia, Beijing resumed its rapprochement with India one year after the nuclear tests and the bilateral relationship came back on track before long. Indian Defense Minister George Fernandez paid a weeklong visit to China in April 2003. Fernandez was followed by Prime Minister Atal Bihari Vajpayee in June 2003. During the visit, Beijing and New Delhi vowed not to view each other as security threats and reaffirmed their determination to resolve disputes through peaceful means. Then in April 2005, Chinese Premier Wen Jiabao visited India. More importantly, President Hu Jintao paid a visit to India in November 2006, the first such visit by a Chinese head of state in a decade. During Hu's visit, the two governments signed more than a dozen agreements to strengthen cooperation in trade, investment, energy, and cultural and educational exchanges.

China's rapprochement policy toward India is determined by a number of factors. First, China regards India as "a crucial key in preventing external intervention in Tibet."[75] Second, it can be argued that China does not see India as a threat in the near future. Chinese analysts tend to emphasize that India is still relatively weak in terms of comprehensive national power. Third, India could help other great powers to check a rising China. The talk of "axis of democracy" in Asia, involving the United States, Japan, Australia, and India was a concern to China. It was believed that the "axis of democracy" was primarily aimed at keeping China in check.[76] India has reassured Beijing that it would never agree to be part of the "axis of democracy."[77] On the other hand, India has been trying to build its leverage against China, and improving its relations with the United States is a key step. Clinton's visit to India in March 2000 deepened Chinese concerns. The visit amounted to de facto acceptance of India's status as a nuclear power. In New Delhi, Clinton told the Indians that the Indo-American relationship was "too important to ever fall into disrepair again" and that "India and America should be better friends and stronger partners."[78] Another major progress in US-Indian relations is the March 2006 US-Indian agreement on nuclear cooperation which was announced at the summit between President George W. Bush and Prime Minister Manmohan Singh.[79] What is even more important is the October 2008 US-Indian civilian nuclear deal, also known as the "123 Agreement." The deal treats India as an exception in US non-proliferation policy and discriminates against China's traditional ally Pakistan by refusing to offer it similar arrangements.

Most importantly, however, China's rapprochement policy is in accordance with China's strategy of creating an international environment conducive to its economic development, a foundation for its comprehensive national power. India also offers economic opportunities to China. Observers have pointed out that China is stronger in hardware while India's strength is in software. China is stronger in commercial markets, while India excels in financial markets. In the short space of five years, Sino-Indian trade has expanded from $5 billion to $38.7 billion in 2007; it is projected to reach $60 billion by 2010.[80]

Compared with Japan, India is more likely to cooperate with China in the energy sphere. Politically, history is not as big a factor in Sino-Indian relations and border conflicts are slowly being resolved. Unlike policies toward Japan, policies toward India are much less sensitive in China. Chinese leaders have much more political freedom in strengthening China's energy cooperation with India. And both countries can provide useful political leverage to the other in order to enhance their energy security. For instance, China could use its relationship with Pakistan to help India in its pursuit of

Central Asian energy, while India might use its closer relationship with Japan and the United States to help China on issues like the East China Sea dispute.

Economically, China and India share a similar identity as they are at similar levels of development and face similar challenges, such as moving away from dependence on coal. Such a similar identity could increase competition between the two most populous countries in the world. Arguably, a similar identity may well encourage the two countries to focus on their common interests. Unrestrained competition at this point could have negative political consequences which could damage both countries' interests and their economies. For instance, with a population of 1.05 billion and a mere 0.4 percent of the world's oil reserve, energy security is a much bigger challenge to India. The Indians have become tired of being outbid by deep-pocketed Chinese oil companies. India's concerns over energy security may have driven it closer to Japan and the United States, which in turn could be an incentive for China to increases its military aid to Pakistan. Each outcome is bad for China and India, and it is not worth what would be gained in the energy security sphere.

Technically, it is also easier for China and India to cooperate. Both countries have strong control over their oil companies which, unlike Japan, are state-owned. And in contrast to Japan and the United States, China and India have a strong preference for state-owned oil acquisitions because of lack of trust in market forces (largely dominated by non-Asian companies). Therefore there are more possibilities or incentives for cooperative joint-bidding by Chinese and Indian state-owned oil companies.

Conclusion

Sino-Japanese energy relations have been characterized by stiff and even dangerous competition. The two countries have engaged in a fierce rivalry for an oil pipeline from eastern Siberia in Russia. Their dispute over Chinese gas and oil fields in the East China Sea could escalate into military conflicts if not well managed. Meanwhile, Chinese and Japanese oil companies have been competing for energy projects worldwide and particularly in Asia although opportunities for cooperation do exist. For instance, they could cooperate in areas like oil transportation safety, energy efficiency, nuclear power, and oil reserve.

Compared with Sino-Japanese energy relations, Sino-Indian energy relationship is more promising in terms of cooperation. Like Japan, India has also engaged in a worldwide competition with China over energy resources. Unlike Japan, India has already cooperated with China on a number of oil and gas projects in countries like Kazakhstan, Sudan, Syria, Iran, Russia, and Colombia. India also invested in a Chinese oil company and has exchanged bidding information on overseas oil and gas projects. On the other hand, although the bilateral relationship has improved in recent years, India still is concerned about China's rise and Chinese support for Pakistan.

Energy relations should be viewed as a component of Chinese strategic relations with Japan and India. The East China Sea dispute, the Diaoyu Islands dispute, and the Chinese involvement in the Gwadar Port and Burma, all have strong implications for the strategic security of the parties involved. At the moment, mutual suspicion is still a driving force behind Sino-Japanese and Sino-Indian relations. Strategic competition determines that China will continue to compete with Japan and India in the energy sphere. Prime Minister Manmohan Singh admitted in June 2008 that India would face "increasing competition" from China in the area of energy security, while emphasizing the need for a peaceful neighborhood for the country's growth and prosperity.[81]

Nevertheless, the deal reached between China and Japan on the East China Sea dispute demonstrates that careful leadership can overcome mutual suspicion to reach mutually beneficial outcome. As Manicom puts it, "Chinese and Japanese elites overcame domestic and structural impediments to arrive at the cooperative agreement; hence they may be able to do so again in the future."[82] The key driving force for China to defuse the strategic competition and to cooperate with its energy security rivals is its commitment to economic development which is believed to be the foundation of China's comprehensive national power.

Notes

1 Philip Andrews-Speed, Xuanli Liao, and Roland Dannreuther (2002) *The Strategic Implications of China's Energy Needs* (New York: Oxford University Press), p. 64.
2 All currency estimates are in USD unless otherwise indicated. Wang Weijun, "shixi Riben de guoji nengyuan zhanlue" (An Analysis of Japanese International Energy Strategy), *Shijie Jingji Yanjiu* (*World Economic Studies*), No. 3, 2006, p. 88.
3 N. J. Watson, "Russian Oil Pipeline Takes a Tentative Step Forwards," *Petroleum Economist*, Vol. 72, No. 12 (December 2005), pp. 14–15. The first stage of the Eastern Siberia-Pacific Ocean (ESPO) oil pipeline was completed in December 2009. A branch of the pipeline from Skovorodino to Daqing is expected to become functional in October 2010.

4 Pak K. Lee, "China's Quest for Oil Security: Oil (Wars) in the Pipeline?", *The Pacific Review*, Vol. 18, No. 2 (June 2005), p. 284.

5 "Oil and Gas in Troubled Waters," *The Economist (US)*, Vol. 37, Iss. 8447 (8 October 2005), p. 53.

6 Reinhard Drifte, *Japan's Security Relations with China since 1989: From Balancing to Bandwagoning?* (London and New York: RoutledgeCurzon, 2003), pp. 55–60.

7 Zhang Sanbao, "Zhongri Donghai zhengduan yu chulu" (Sino-Japanese East China Sea Dispute and Solutions), *Guoji Ziliao Xinxi* (*International Material and Information*), No. 10, 2007, pp. 18–23.

8 Masahiro Atsumi however, thinks differently. Atsumi notes that Japan relies on market forces while China is more prone to using state intervention. Masahiro Atsumi, "Japanese Energy Security Revisited," *Asia-Pacific Review*, Vol. 14, No. 1 (2007), pp. 28–43.

9 Zhang Jifeng, "ZhongRi liangguo zai nengyuan lingyu de jingzheng yu hezuo" (Sino-Japanese Competition and Cooperation in the Energy Sphere), *Riben Xuekan* (*Japanese Studies*), No. 4, 2004, pp. 111–125.

10 Shoichi Itoh, "China's Surging Energy Demand: Trigger for Conflict or Cooperation with Japan?" *East Asia* 25 (2008), p. 85; Sun Bingbing, "lun ZhongRi Donghai zhengduan yu nengyuan hezuo" (On Sino-Japanese East China Sea Dispute and Energy Cooperation), *Taipingyang Xuebao* (*The Pacific Journal*), No. 6, 2005, pp. 88–96.

11 "China, India Sign Energy Agreement," *China Daily*, January 13, 2006. <http://www.chinadaily.com.cn/english/doc/2006-01/13/content_511871.htm>. Accessed January 19, 2009.

12 Siddharth Varadarajan, "India, China Primed for Energy Cooperation," January 13, 2006. <http://www.thehindu.com/2006/01/13/stories/2006011318821400.htm>. Accessed January 19, 2009.

13 Stein Tonnesson and Ashild Kolas, *Energy Security in Asia: China, India, Oil and Peace: Report to the Norwegian Ministry of Foreign Affairs*, April 2006, p. 52. http://www.prio.no/files/file47777_060420_energy_security_in_asia__final_.pdf. Accessed January 24, 2009.

14 Anil K. Joseph, "India, China Plan Asia Energy Agency," January 13, 2006, http://www.rediff.com///money/2006/jan/13oil.htm. Accessed February 4, 2009.

15 June Teufel Dreyer, "A New Era in Sino-Indian Relations or Deja-vu All Over Again?", January 19, 2008, <http://www.strategycenter.net/research/pubID.178/pub_detail.asp >. Accessed February 3, 2009.

16 Tonnesson and Kolas, pp. 50–51.

17 Lee, p. 287.

18 CNN-IBN, “India Beats China to Imperial Energy Co Bid,” August 27, 2008.<http://ibnlive.in.com/news/india-beats-china-to-imperial-energy-co-bid/72294–3.html>. Accessed January 24, 2009.

19 David Montero, “China, Pakistan Team Up on Energy,” *The Christian Science Monitor*, April 13, 2007.

20 Dreyer.

21 Lin Xixing, “Zhongguo ying goujian Nanya nengyuan ‘shuang tongdao’” (China Should Construct Energy “Double Channels” in South Asia), *Zhongguo Xinwen Zhoukan* (*China News Weekly*), p. 52.

22 Saleem Shahid, “Gwadar Port Becomes Fully Functional,” December 22, 2008, http://www.dawn.com/2008/12/22/top2.htm. Accessed February 3, 2009.

23 Lixin Geng, “Sino-Myanmar Relations: Analysis and Prospects,” *Culture Mandala*, Vol. 7, Iss. 2 (2007), p. 1; Lin Xixing, “Miandian-Zhongguo: xin shiyou liuxiang” (Burma-China: A New Direction of Oil Flow), *Zhongguo Shiyou Shihua* (*China Petro and Petrochemistry*), No. 7 (1 April 2006), p. 29.

24 Lin Xixing, “ZhongMian shiyou guandao sheji zhong de MeiYin yingsu” (The US and India Factors in the Proposed Sino-Burmese Oil Pipeline), *Dongnanya Yanjiu* (*Southeast Asian Studies*), No. 5 (2007), p. 32.

25 Lin Xixing, “Miandian-Zhongguo: xin shiyou liuxiang” (Burma-China: A New Direction of Oil Flow), pp. 28–29.

26 For a detailed analysis, see Tonnesson and Kolas, pp. 66–92.

27 Ming Wan (2006) *Sino Japanese Relations: Interaction, Logic, and Transformation* (Washington D.C.: Woodrow Wilson Center Press; Stanford, CA: Stanford University Press), p. 111.

28 As quoted in G. V. C. Naidu, “Japan and the Asia-Pacific Region,” *Strategic Analysis*, Vol. 16, No. 11 (1992), p. 1301.

29 Exchange with a Chinese analyst from China Academy of Social Sciences in Hong Kong in June 2009.

30 “Russian Nuclear Fusion,” *China Economic Review*, Vol. 8, No. 8 (August 1998), p. 1.

31 National Bureau of Statistics of China, *China Statistical Yearbook, 2001.*

32 Yu Bin, “Sino-Russian Relations: NATO’s Unintended Consequence: A Deeper Strategic Partnership . . . Or More,” *Comparative Connections: A Quarterly E-Journal on East Asian Bilateral Relations*, Vol. 1. Iss. 1 (July 1999), p. 68.

33 Liu Xinhua, Qin Yi, “diyuan zhengzhi, diyuan jingji yu ZhongE shiyou guandao fengbo” (“Geopolitics, Geoeconomics and the Sino-Russian Oil Pipeline Issue,” *Shiyou Daxue Xuebao—Shehui Kexue Ban*) (*Journal*

of the China University of Petroleum—Social Sciences Edition), Vol. 20, No. 3 (June 2004), p. 3; Zhang Shaodong, Guo Xinge, "Riben jiaozu duochong guojia liyi de Elosi shiyou guandao zhizheng" (The Rivalry for the Russian Oil Pipeline—Japan's Pursuit of Multiple National Interests," *Siboliya Yanjiu* (*Siberian Studies*), Vol. 33, No. 4 (August 2006), pp. 52–54.

34 "Riben zhankai nengyuan zhengduozhan, zhuzhi ZhongE shiyou guanxian jiancheng" (Japan begins its war over energy and blocks the construction of the Sino-Russian oil pipeline), October 9, 2003. http://news.xinhuanet.com/newscenter/2003–10/09/content_1115516.htm. Accessed February 5, 2009.

35 David M. Lampton (2001) "China's Foreign and National Security Policy-Making Process: Is it Changing, and does it Matter?" in David M. Lampton (ed.), *The Making of Chinese Foreign and Security Policy in the Era of Reform, 1978–2000* (Stanford, CA: Stanford University Press), p. 12.

36 *BBC News Online*, "Polls find Chinese wary of Japan," August 24, 2005.

37 Kyodo, "President Jiang's criticism of Japan aimed at Chinese audience," November 30, 1998.

38 Author's interview with a specialist in Chinese Academy of Social Sciences, Beijing, December 2002.

39 For more information, see Jian Yang, "Of Interest and Distrust: Understanding China's Policy towards Japan," *China: An International Journal*, Vol. 5, No. 2 (September 2007), pp. 250–275.

40 Feng Yifen, "Donghai youtian: ZhongRi hezuo kaifa de nanti" (East China Sea Oil Fields: Challenges to Sino-Japanese cooperative development), *Zhongguo Xinwen Zhoukan* (*China News Weekly*), September 26, 2005, p. 48.

41 Zheng Ran, "cong diyuan zhengzhi jiaodu kan ZhongRi Donghai zhizheng" (Geopolitics and Sino-Japanese dispute over the East China Sea), *Fazhi yu Shehui* (*Legal System and Society*), No. 6, 2007, p. 810; Zhu Fenglan, "ZhongRi Donghai zhengduan jiqi jiejue de qianjing" (Sino-Japanese East China Sea Dispute and Possible Solutions), *Dangdai Yata* (*Contemporary Asia Pacific*), No. 7, 2005, p. 12; Jiang Xinfeng, "kai youtian: Riben Donghai zai tiao shiduan" (Open up an oil field: Japan makes troubles again in the East China Sea), *Sijie Zhishi* (*World Affairs*), No. 16, 2005, p. 28.

42 Wang Shan, "cong Donghai youqitian zhengduan kan Riben dui Hua nengyuan zhengce" (The Dispute over the East China Sea Oil and Gas Fields and Japan's Energy Policy towards China), *Xiandai Guoji Guanxi* (*Contemporary International Relations*), No. 12, 2005, p. 42.

43 Feng Yifen, p. 49.
44 Wang Shan, p. 42.
45 Hu Angang (ed.), *Zhongguo Dazhanlue* (*China's Grand Strategy*), Hangzhou: Zhejiang renmin chubanshe (Hangzhou: Zhejiang People's Publishing House), 2003, p. 68.
46 Sun Zhi, "ZhongRi Donghai haiyu huajie wenti beihou de ZhongRi liang qiang bing li xin gejiu" (Behind the Demarcation Issue in the East China Sea: The new order in an era of China and Japan both as great powers), *Shijie Jingji yu Zhengzhi* (*World Economics and Politics*), No. 11, 2007, p. 60. This energy containment strategy theory is also applicable to analyzing Japan's intervention in the Russian pipeline. Yin Xiaoliang and An Chengri, "Zhong Ri E zai Dongbeiya diqu de nengyuan boyi" (The Energy Game in Northeast Asia between China, Japan, and Russia), *Ribenxue Luntan* (*Japanese Studies Forum*), No. 3, 2006, pp. 31–32.
47 Dexter Filkins and Maggie Farley, "New Nuclear Cloud Looms over Old Kashmir Dispute," *Los Angeles Times*, May 15, 1998, p. A-1.
48 For a full text of Vajpayee's letter to Clinton, see *New York Times*, May 13, 1998, p. A14.
49 Sun Shihai, "Yindu de jueqi: qianli yu juxian" (The Rise of India: Potential and Limitations), *Dangdai Yatai* (*Contemporary Asia-Pacific*), No. 8, 1999, pp. 3–14. Wang Chuanbao, "Yindu de daguomeng: jiyu yu tiaozhan" (India's Big Power Dream: Opportunities and Challenges," *Shijie Jingji yu Zhengzhi Luntan* (*Forum of World Economy and Politics*), No. 5, 1999, pp. 32–33.
50 Jing-dong Yuan, "The Dragon and the Elephant: Chinese-Indian Relations in the 21st Century," *Washington Quarterly*, Summer 2007, p. 135.
51 Nayan Chanda, "Coming in from the Cold," *Far Eastern Economic Review*, March 30, 2000, p. 22.
52 John W. Garver, "Sino-Indian Rapprochement and the Sino-Pakistan Entente," *Political Science Quarterly*, Vol. 111, No. 2 (1996), p. 333.
53 Tonnesson and Kolas, pp. 88–89; James R. Holmes and Toshi Yoshihara, "China's Naval Ambitions in the Indian Ocean," *The Journal of Strategic Studies*, Vol. 31, No. 3 (June 2008), pp. 378–379.
54 "China Builds Up Strategic Sea Lanes," *Washington Times*, January 18, 2005, http://www.washingtontimes.com/news/2005/jan/17/20050117-115550-1929r/. Accessed January 20, 2009.
55 Huang Junbao, et. al., "cong zhanlue gaodu renshi he shenghua yu Bajisitan de quanmian hezuo" (Understanding and Deepening Comprehensive Relations with Pakistan from a Strategic Perspective), *Yatai Jingji* (*Asia Pacific Economy*), No. 2, 2008, p. 64.
56 Ibid.

57 Ibid; Yuan Ying, "Guadaergang zhishi nengyuan zoulang de diyibu" (The Gwadar Port is only the first step towards the energy channel), *Shangwu Zhoukan* (*Business Weekly*), September 20, 2006, pp. 42–44.

58 Citing diplomats, an Indian magazine reported that Pakistan raised the cost of Chinese participation to $3 billion in addition to the $1.5 billion yearly payment. The Pakistani government dismissed the report. Yet, a leading Chinese expert noted that the United States tried to price out China but was turned down by Pakistan. See Sudha Ramachandran, "China's Pearl Loses its Luster," *Asia Times Online*, January 21, 2006, http://www.atimes.com/atimes/South_Asia/HA21Df03.html. Accessed January 20, 2009; Lin Xixing, "Guadeer xiangmu de YuLiang qingjie" (The Complexity of the Gwadar Project), *Nan Feng Chuang* (*Nanfengchuang Magazine*), March (second half) 2006, p. 11.

59 Tonnesson and Kolas, p. 66.

60 Lixin Geng, p. 1.

61 Ibid.

62 Lin Xixing, "Zhongguo ying goujian Nanya nengyuan 'shuang tongdao' " (China Should Construct Energy "Double Channels" in Southeast Asia), p. 53.

63 Michael D. Swaine and Ashley J. Tellis (2000) *Interpreting China's Grand Strategy: Past, Present, and Future* (Santa Monica, CA: RAND), p. ix.

64 Geng Mingjun, "China's National Security under Globalization," *Dangdai Shijie yu Shehui Zhuyi* (*Contemporary World and Socialism*), No. 2, 2003, p. 57.

65 Chu Shulong, "The PRC Girds for Limited, High-Tech War," *Orbis*, Vol. 38, No. 2 (Spring 1994) pp. 180–183; David Shambaugh, "The Insecurity of Security: The PLA's Evolving Doctrine and Threat Perceptions towards 2000," *Journal of Northeast Asian Studies*, Vol. 13, No. 1 (Spring 1994), p. 6.

66 For more information, see Jian Yang (2000) *Congress and US China Policy, 1989–1999* (New York: Nova Science).

67 Wei Ling (2003) "An Analysis of the Current Security Soundings of China," *Renmin Daxue Xuebao* (*Journal of Renmin University*), No. 3, pp. 133–135.

68 Chu Shulong and Wang Zaibang, "dui guoji xingshi he woguo duiwai zhanlue ruogan zhongda wenti de sihao" (Thoughts on Some Major Issues in International Situation and Our External Strategy), *Xiandai Guoji Guangxi* (*Contemporary International Relations*), No. 8, 1999, p. 6; Yan Xuetong, "International Environment and Thoughts on Diplomacy,"

Xiandai Guoji Guangxi (*Contemporary International Relations*), No. 8, 1999, p. 10.

69 "China, Japan Need Mutually Beneficial Economic Development," *Xinhua News Agency*, April 6, 2007.

70 Feng Zhaokui, "ZhongRi guanxi zoudao le shizi lukou" (Sino-Japanese Relations at Crossroads), *Riben Yanjiu* (*Japanese Studies*), No. 1 (2005), p. 8. Japan's actual investment in China reached US$58 billion by April 2007. See "China, Japan Need Mutually Beneficial Economic Development," *Xinhua News Agency*, April 6, 2007.

71 James Manicom, "Sino-Japanese Cooperation in the East China Sea: Limitations and Prospects," *Contemporary Southeast Asia*, Vol. 30, No. 3 (2008), p. 468.

72 Erica Strecker Downs and Phillip C. Saunders, "Legitimacy and the Limits of Nationalism," *International Security*, Vol. 23, No. 3 (Winter 1998), pp. 114–146.

73 Reuters, "Environment woes to slow China growth, official says," March 5, 2005.

74 Tonnesson and Kolas, p. 20.

75 Dawa Norbu, "Tibet in Sino-Indian Relations: The Centrality of Marginality," *Asian Survey*, Vol. 37, No. 11 (November 1997), p. 1093.

76 Hisane Masaki, " 'Axis of Democracy' Flexes its Military Muscles," *Asia Times Online*, March 31, 2007. http://www.atimes.com/atimes/Japan/IC31Dh01.html, Accessed January 21, 2009.

77 Dreyer.

78 Chanda, p. 22.

79 Jing-dong Yuan, p. 137.

80 Dreyer.

81 IANS, "India will face more competition from China on energy: PM," *Thaindian News*, June 11, 2008. http://www.thaindian.com/newsportal/uncategorized/india-will-face-more-competition-from-china-on-energy-pm_10059180.html. Accessed January 24, 2009.

82 Manicom, p. 471.

PART III

Challenges for the Future

CHAPTER NINE

Pipelines versus Sea Lanes: Challenges and Opportunities for Securing Energy Resources

Andrew S. Erickson and Gabriel B. Collins[1]

Introduction

Chinese oil demand, growing rapidly, has reached 8.5 million barrels per day (mbtd) even amid the global recession. China became a net oil importer in 1993 and will likely become a net gasoline importer by the end of 2009. While still a very significant oil producer, China is now the world's second-largest oil user. It now imports half of its crude oil, with imports reaching a record 4.6 million bpd in July 2009. Seaborne imports, which overland pipelines will not reduce, constitute more than 80 percent of this total. At present, therefore, 40 percent of China's oil comes by sea.[2]

Chinese security analysts and policy makers worry about their nation's "excessive" reliance on seaborne oil shipments. Many believe that by investing in pipelines to deliver oil from neighboring oil producers and building additional lines to "bypass" the Malacca Strait, China can protect its oil imports from possible interdiction during a conflict.

A robust internal debate is being waged within China at multiple levels and across a number of disciplines regarding how to ensure access to oil supplies. At stake is the extent to which China should cooperate with international economic institutions versus seeking unilateral military solutions. Also at stake is: should China develop as a maritime versus continental power, or should it focus on defending against state, as opposed to non-state, actors? Despite this diversity of opinion, a wide variety of influential Chinese experts, including scholars, policy analysts, and members of the military, believe that the United States can sever China's seaborne energy supplies at will and in a crisis might well choose to do so. It is widely claimed, for instance, that "whoever controls the Strait of Malacca effectively grips China's strategic energy passage, and can threaten China's energy security at any time."[3] Such views are widely cited to justify pipeline construction.

Yet as this chapter will demonstrate, China's overland oil supply plans may largely be unrealistic, driven by a combination of a misunderstanding of global oil market mechanisms, incomplete assessment of security issues, and the lobbying by local commercial and political interests of a massively overtaxed national energy policy-making apparatus. Some projects—such as the planned line from Russia and an existing line from Kazakhstan—are indeed economically viable overland projects that will bring at least limited diversity to China's oil supplies. Others, however, like the proposed lines through Burma and Pakistan, make much less economic and security sense.

In the end, pipelines are not likely to increase Chinese oil import security in quantitative terms, because the additional volumes they bring in will be overwhelmed by China's demand growth; the country's net reliance on seaborne oil imports will grow over time, pipelines notwithstanding. If we estimate Chinese oil-import demand growth conservatively at an average of 3 percent annually over the next five years, Beijing's imports will still increase by a total of roughly 500,000 barrels a day—the combined volume that the pipelines from Russia and Kazakhstan will likely be able to bring in by 2013. Of that total, the 300,000 bpd from Russia will not be "new" overland supplies, but rather, a transfer from rail to pipe as the crude volumes previously carried into China by rail are moved into the pipeline instead. The proposed Burma–China and Pakistan–China lines are simply "shortcut" routes, not true overland supply routes; oil will still have to be carried by sea in tankers to the pipelines' starting points.

A total figure for these two sources of 500,000 bbl/day may seem low, but it reflects the reality that China's neighbors have limited capacity to offset its seaborne oil imports. Their reserves are limited in key potential supply areas (e.g., eastern Siberia), and politics further complicate the picture. Kazakhstan, for its part, is pursuing a three-vector oil export policy. It entails shipping oil through the Caspian Pipeline Consortium line to the Russian Black Sea port of Novorossisk; to China through the Atasu–Alashankou line; and, soon, through the $1.5 billion Kazakhstan Caspian Pipeline System to a port on the Caspian Sea, from which it will be carried by tanker to Azerbaijan, there to enter the Baku–Tbilisi–Ceyhan pipeline. The third route may ultimately be able to pump up to fifty-six million tons a year of oil.[4]

Russia, meanwhile, may prioritize oil supplies to the East Siberia–Pacific pipeline, feeding the port of Kozmino, on the Sea of Japan near Nakhodka;

from there it can be exported to Japan, South Korea, China, the United States, and other Pacific Basin consumers, not China alone. A spur pipeline from Russia to China is now under construction and is scheduled to enter service in the second half of 2010.

Pipelines are more vulnerable to sabotage and military interdiction than seaborne shipping is. Projects designed to help seaborne shipments bypass choke points (e.g., the Burma–China pipeline) are expensive, can be blockaded, and are vulnerable to weather and other physical disruptions. Seaborne shipping, by contrast, is very flexible and can be routed around disruptions. For this reason, pipeline plans predicated on the idea that bypassing the Strait of Malacca increases oil security are fundamentally flawed. Even if Malacca were completely sealed off by blockade or accident, tankers could be diverted through the Sunda, Lombok, or other passages with little disruption in deliveries and at an additional cost of as little as one or two dollars per barrel. Some Chinese analysts now share this conclusion, one noting that "SLOC security is much more important than pipeline transport lines."[5]

Finally, as Figure 9.1 demonstrates, pipelines are far more expensive than tankers in terms of what must be spent to move a given volume of oil a given distance. Certain pipelines—such as the Pakistan, and possibly the Burma, projects—will likely require substantial subsidies if they are to compete with seaborne imports. Much of the cost of supporting such uneconomical projects, which are driven more by politics than profits, will fall on the Chinese government, which already faces substantial energy-subsidy costs as well as the demands of its new four-trillion-RMB stimulus package, of which more than 25 percent may come from central government funds.

Mode	Route	Distance (km)	Cost (US$/bbl)	cost/US$/bbl/ 1000 km
Tanker[a]	Ras Tanura–Ningbo	7000	1.25	0.18
Pipeline[b]	Angarsk–Daqing	3200	2.41	0.75
Train[c]	Angarsk–Manzhouli	1000	7.19	7.19

Notes:

a. VLCC at $150k/day charter, 2 million bbl/day cargo.
b. Transneft tariff of 15.41 rubles/ton/100 km.
c. Based on weighted average of Russian Railway's oil tariffs to Zabaikalsk and Naushki.

Figure 9.1 Sample Oil Transport Costs to China

The first section of this chapter will examine operational and prospective pipelines oriented toward China. The projects are arranged chronologically in the order that they have, will, or might become operational. At present, the Kazakhstan–China pipeline is operating at partial capacity, a Russia–China line could become operational within eighteen months, the China–Burma pipeline project is now under construction, and a China–Pakistan pipeline remains entirely aspirational.

The second section will examine Chinese views of how pipelines might enhance China's oil security and assess the potential for, and utility and disadvantages of, a pipeline-centric oil-security strategy. The final, and concluding, section will suggest how China might enhance its energy security at lower financial and diplomatic cost.

Pipeline Options

In the outline that follows of current and possible pipeline projects, fear that non-state actors or foreign navies could interdict oil shipments to China will be prominent as a factor that impels the national government to support overland supply projects. Yet it should be noted at the outset that provincial and local level officials appear to be playing on that fear, the sense of oil insecurity among high-level decision makers, in order to secure projects that could create substantial local investment and jobs.

Indeed, if one averages labor-demand numbers for sample refinery expansion and new-build projects in the West and the developing world, the proposed 200,000-bbl/day refinery near Kunming could create ten thousand or more construction and engineering jobs while it is being built and at least several hundred permanent positions to run the plant thereafter. Building the pipeline itself and associated storage and pumping facilities would create additional temporary and permanent jobs.

Pipeline and associated refinery construction brings local governments tangible benefits; such local interests must be differentiated from overall Chinese national energy-security interests, which often diverge. In this sense, significant portions of China's push for pipelines mirror the "Going Out" oil security strategy, in which the state oil companies cultivated fears of oil insecurity in Beijing and then turned around and wrapped themselves in the flag as they sought overseas oil projects. These projects have boosted their incomes and reserves but have done little to enhance China's oil security on the national level; these firms have even damaged China's image abroad, through their dealings with Sudan and other pariah states.

Kazakhstan-China Pipeline

The Kazakhstan–China pipeline is currently the PRC's only operational overland oil pipeline project. China previously imported Kazakh crude by rail through the entry port of Alashankou, Xinjiang Province. To move larger volumes and lower shipping prices, however, both sides desired a pipeline. In September 1997, the Chinese and Kazakh governments signed the General Agreement on the Project of Oil Deposits Development and Pipeline Construction.[6] The initial stage of the line was built from Kenkiyak to Atyrau during 2002–2004, the second stage during 2004–2006 from Atyrau to the Chinese border at Alashankou. The China National Petroleum Corporation (CNPC) funded the construction cost of $806 million for the thousand-km leg from Atasu to Alashankou, as well as a 252-km extension from Alashankou to the refinery at Dushanzi, also in Xinjiang.[7]

The pipeline is operated by a joint stock company called MunaiTas North-West Pipeline Company CJSC, which is backed by China National Petroleum Corporation and KazMunaiGaz. Its current capacity is approximately 200,000 bbl/day. In 2008, however, China imported an average of only 115,000 bpd of crude oil from Kazakhstan by pipeline and rail.[8] In December 2007, the pipeline carried an average of 102,600 bpd—only about half of its total capacity—due to pricing disputes and problems with supply availability that created gaps, only partially filled with Russian crude from western Siberia. Figure 9.2a–9.2b shows the current pipeline and future planned additions.

Now that the segment from Kemkiyak to Kumkol is completed, Kazakhstan's Caspian Sea production (in the Tengiz and Kashagan fields) can enter a pipeline network reaching deep into China. In August 2007, CNPC opened a 400,000-bbl/day capacity crude oil pipeline from Shanshan in Xinjiang to the refining center at Lanzhou, in Gansu Province.[9] This line, and a parallel oil products pipeline, will allow crude and refined products from Xinjiang to be shipped to Lanzhou and then into CNPC's existing network pipeline network serving central and southwestern China. This will permit Kazakh crude to penetrate deep into China, because as crude oil and products from the Dushanzi refinery can be shipped farther east, boosting oil supplies to the inland regions that will be a focus of Beijing's development program, meant to reduce regional economic disparities. The Kazakhstan–China pipeline will also be integrated with a new strategic petroleum reserve site under construction near Urumqi, which will store fifty-one million barrels of crude once completed.[10] The line could reach a maximum throughput

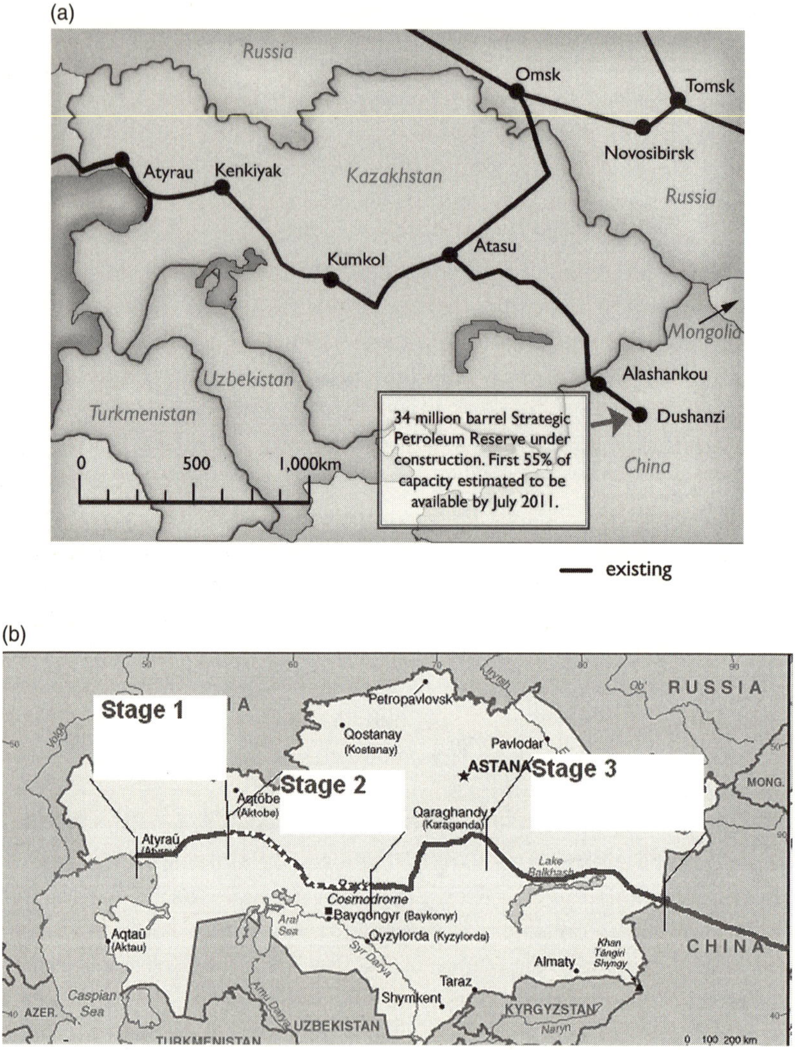

Figure 9.2a and 9.2b Kazakhstan–China Oil Pipeline

capacity of 400,000 bbl/day in 2011, if its final stage, from Kenkiyak to Kumkol, is finished and reaches its full capacity at that time.

While this pipeline project originated in part due to oil-supply security concerns, it is easily justifiable as the most economic way to bring Kazakh crude oil into the western Chinese market. China wins, because it gains what it sees as "secure" oil supplies; Kazakhstan gains a crude export route independent of Russia and a new market for its oil; and Russian companies gain an additional route for getting West Siberian crude oil production into the Chinese market.

A Russia–China Pipeline

China views Russia as a rich and secure oil source capable of delivering crude overland, far from US Navy–patrolled sea routes. China and Russia first began discussing a pipeline in 1994. Yukos unveiled plans in 2001 to construct a pipeline from Angarsk to Daqing. These plans were suspended during the Kremlin's 2004–2007 assault on Yukos and have been superseded by Transneft's massive East Siberia–Pacific Ocean (ESPO) pipeline. The ESPO's first section, from Taishet to Skovorodino, is complete and can now pump crude, although as of September 2009 the line was running in reverse, moving crude into the existing West Siberian pipeline network. The second half of the line runs 2,100 km from Skovorodino to Nakhodka, on the Sea of Japan, and the entire line may not be fully operational until 2025.[11] Figure 9.3 shows oil pipelines existing, under construction, and planned from Russia.

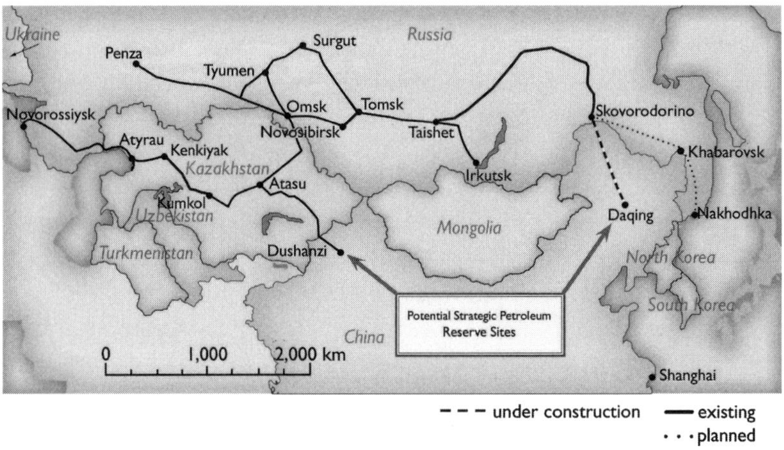

Figure 9.3 Russian and Eurasian Oil Pipelines

In the meantime, China has been importing increasing volumes of crude from Russia by rail (as well as smaller volumes through the Kazakhstan–China pipeline). In 2007 and 2008, China imported an average of more than 300,000 bbl/day of Russian crude.[12] Shipping crude by rail can cost twice as much as shipping it by pipeline, however.[13] Driven by this reality and by the fact that regional rail infrastructure likely cannot handle China's ultimately desired crude volumes, CNPC and Sinopec (the primary Chinese buyers of Russian crude) pushed for construction of a spur pipeline from Skovorodino to Daqing, in Heilongjiang Province. The entire spur line will run roughly a thousand km (70 km on the Russian side and 965 km on the Chinese side) and will cost around $436 million.[14] The Chinese side is financing the majority of the spur's length, as it lies largely on Chinese soil. Initial capacity is slated to be fifteen million tons per year (300,000 bbl/day), with the possibility of later expansion to thirty million tons annually (600,000 bbl/day).[15]

While the China–Russia pipeline deal is presently on track, there are still a number of potential friction points. Rosneft may still worry that near- and medium-term production from eastern Siberia cannot fill the spur line and ensure adequate supplies to the new 400,000 bbl/day refinery that the company plans to build near the Pacific port of Nakhodka.

Perhaps of greatest concern to Beijing, Moscow has and will have options to divert oil from China if it so desires. While the initial capacity of Russia's line to China will be 300,000 bbl/day, and could rise to 600,000 bbl/day, an alternative pipeline to the Pacific coast (perhaps available within ten years; and spurred by potential 400,000 bbl/day Rosneft refinery on the Pacific Coast near Nakhodka) could ultimately offer Moscow oil diversion alternatives that it might possibly use to pressure China. Russia can also move sufficient volumes of crude oil by rail to the Pacific Ocean to allow it to cut off a substantial portion of pipeline exports to China in the event of a dispute. Transneft does not operate under the normal economic incentives US and European pipeline operators do, meaning that if ordered by the Kremlin, the company will favor achieving political objectives over the need to keep capacity utilization high to maximize earnings and please shareholders.

A Burma–China Pipeline

The proposed Burma–China oil pipeline aims to reduce China's reliance on oil shipped through the Malacca Strait. The idea of the pipeline was first articulated publicly in 2004 by Yunnan University professor Yang Xiaohui. Yang argued that given Burma and Southeast Asia's historical collective role as a "backdoor" supply line for China, a China–Burma line would reduce reliance on Malacca and help secure Chinese oil imports.[16]

National and local economic development interests then sought additional backing for the project. The Yunnan provincial government subsequently professed its support, and in early 2006 the Sino–Burma pipeline emerged on the national radar screen when the National Development and Reform Commission's (NDRC's) 2005 "Refining Industry Development Overview" named it one of four key oil import channels.[17] Figure 9.4 shows the proposed pipeline route and facilities that might be associated with the project.

Beijing will likely finance the bulk of the line's construction costs, in addition to supporting infrastructure. By 2010 CNPC may construct an oil wharf capable of berthing tankers of 300,000 deadweight tonnage, as well as storage facilities capable of holding more than four million barrels of crude.[18] The project will be a key element of China's plans to promote inland economic development, as its southwest provinces often have difficulty receiving stable fuel supplies from the refining centers at Lanzhou and Guangzhou.[19]

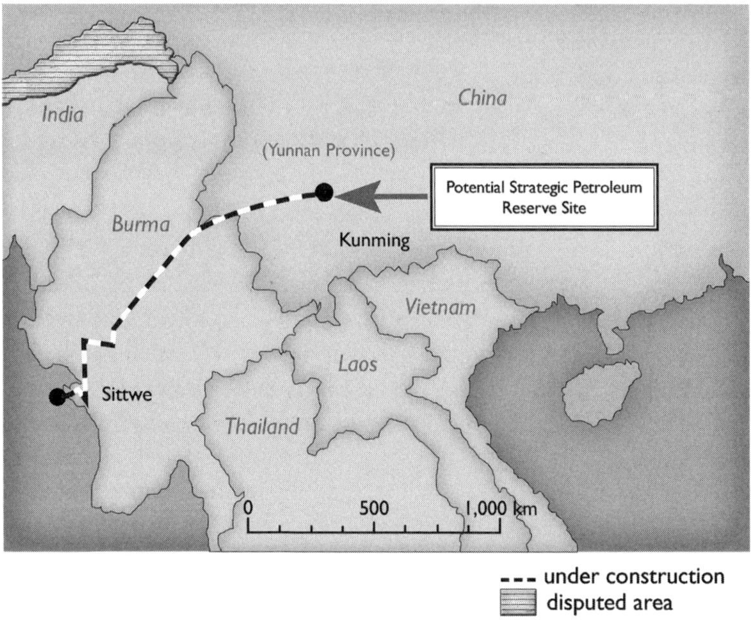

Figure 9.4 Burma–China Oil Pipeline

One proposal includes constructing a 400,000 bbl/day refinery and a colocated million-ton-per-year ethylene plant near Kunming, Yunnan Province.[20] Chongqing Municipality, with the support of Sinopec, has also proposed extending the line to Chongqing and building refining facilities there.[21] The pipeline's initial capacity is slated to be 200,000 bbl/day, but if it is expanded to 300,000 or 400,000 bbl/day both Kunming and Chongqing could build refineries of significant size.

From the economic perspective, a China–Burma pipeline may make sense, as the costs of piping crude to inland refineries in southwest China and then distributing refined products through the expanding pipeline network likely approximate those of shipping crude by tanker to southeast China, refining it there, and then shipping products by pipe or rail to southwest Chinese consumers. The Sino–Burma pipeline would also provide an impetus for enhancing crude and product supplies by building more regional refineries and expanding the area's product pipeline networks. Oil-product demand in southwest China is forecast to grow by 8 percent annually from now until 2010, reaching yearly consumption of 22.56 million tons, 21.81 million of which will have to be imported from other areas unless southwest China's refining capacity expands.[22] Expanding regional oil-processing capacity will also create significant employment, through construction work and, later, for manning the facilities.

From the security perspective, however, a Sino–Burma pipeline largely fails the test. It would allow around 200,000 bbl/day of oil imports to bypass the Malacca Strait, yet it would be exposed to major security risks in Burma, which is ruled by a capricious junta and still struggles with ethnic separatism in regions through which the pipeline would likely pass. Separatism still smolders in Burma's hinterlands, as evidenced by the August 2009 clashes in Burma's Kokang region that sent at least 30,000 refugees streaming into Yunnan Province. Transit countries hosting pipelines gain significant strategic leverage, as manifested in calculated strategic moves or in disputes over other factors, such as pricing and transit payments. China would also be seen as directly financing the Burmese junta's rule and its repression of the population, since an operational oil line would likely generate direct transit payments of at least fourteen million dollars a year. Furthermore, in the event of conflict, the oil port/pipeline terminus at Sittwe would be a concentrated target set, highly vulnerable to blockade or precision strike.

A proposed canal across Thailand's Kra Isthmus, now stalled, appears unrealistic. Zhang Xuegang, a scholar at the China Institutes of Contemporary International Relations, maintains optimistically that it "could . . . provide a strategic seaway to the Chinese navy" through which "fleets could . . .

ORPHAN HOLD
DO NOT SHIP

H1 – 000000000673

ISBN 9781441141040

CLIENT	Alternate Sourcing
STATION	TPP Receiving Station 01
HELD	2026 – 10 – 12 13:49

SHELF

If its order arrives, scan this label at a receiving station.

more easily protect the nearby sea-lanes and gain access to the Indian Ocean."[23] But a canal across the isthmus could cost twenty billion dollars or more to build and, like the Burma–China pipeline, would simply concentrate the target set for potential blockaders.

A Pakistan–China Pipeline?

Chinese analysts have also suggested the possibility of building an "energy corridor," including oil pipelines, from Pakistan into western China to diversify China's oil import routes and avoid the Malacca Strait.[24] Yet Chinese analysts increasingly recognize that geographic and security barriers render a Pakistan–China oil pipeline unfeasible in the near and medium terms.[25]

These Chinese analysts express grave reservations about the security situation in Pakistan in light of the country's perpetual violence and rising political instability, along with the rise of Islamic fundamentalism and terrorist attacks against outsiders. Indeed, Chinese workers have been kidnapped and killed in at least three separate incidents in western and northwestern Pakistan, the regions that would be traversed by a Pakistan–China pipeline.[26] In addition to security problems, there would also be serious financial barriers, since oil transport costs could run to at least ten dollars a barrel to achieve payout plus a 10 percent rate of return.

Even at prices above a hundred dollars a barrel, a transport cost of nine to ten dollars a barrel is very high compared to that of seaborne shipping. If a Chinese oil company chose to move 200,000 bbl/day of crude through the Burma–China pipeline and 250,000 bbl/day through the Pakistan–China line, it could lose roughly a billion dollars a year compared to what it would have earned moving the oil by sea to eastern China. Beijing would likely have to subsidize such operations, either directly or indirectly. A billion dollars is roughly 6.8 billion RMB at today's exchange rates and exceeds by 30 percent the Chinese government's total of 4.9 billion RMB in subsidy payments to refiners in 2007.

If the Chinese government allowed fuel to be sold at market prices, companies might have a much higher incentive to build pipelines into remote areas like western and southwestern China; regional fuel deficits could allow them to charge premium rates for fuels produced by refineries at the end of the pipeline. Under these conditions, pipeline plans might be more financially attractive than they are now, with Chinese oil product prices lagging international market prices by 15–20 percent during times of high crude oil prices, such as those of mid-summer 2008.

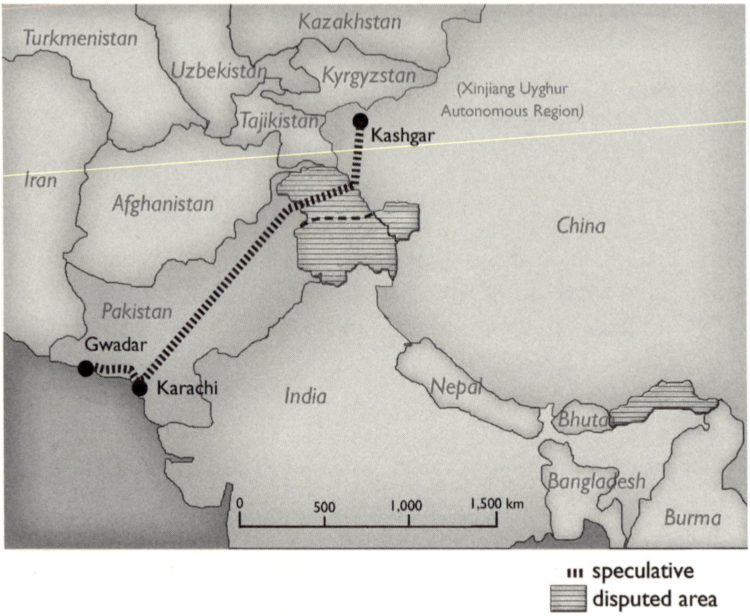

Figure 9. 5 Pakistan–China Oil Pipeline

Geography and cost alone would pose major challenges, however, even under the best of conditions. The pipeline would have to be constructed in some of the world's most challenging terrain and lift oil from sea level at Gwadar up to the 15,400-foot-high Khunjerab Pass, over 6,000 feet higher than the world's highest existing pipeline. This would require massive pumping power and steady electrical supplies in remote areas vulnerable to insurgent activity. Figure 9.5 shows the currently proposed route of a Pakistan–China oil pipeline.

Despite the major challenges, Chinese strategists and policy makers appear enthusiastic about the latent strategic value of the new port at Gwadar, in western Pakistan along the Arabian Sea, a likely starting point for any Pakistan–China oil pipeline. Yet barring a major shift by the Chinese side, it appears that the main impetus for establishing an "energy corridor" is coming from the Pakistani side.[27] President Pervez Musharraf pushed the idea in June 2006 and raised the issue again during talks with President Hu Jintao during the April 2008 Boao Forum.[28]

Disadvantages

The enthusiasm with which some Chinese analysts contemplate these pipeline projects is based, as we have seen, on a conviction that they will reduce China's reliance on seaborne oil imports, which, they fear, may be easily interdicted in time of crisis. Too many of the (relatively few) analyses of these issues produced thus far have, however, failed to consider the physical and economic realities of oil transshipment, which greatly complicates seaborne oil blockade operations.

Transport and Construction Costs: High

Importing oil into southwest China through a Burma–China pipeline rather than through an expanded pipe network serving existing oil ports at Maoming and elsewhere in South China will be very costly. Pipelines are expensive to build in frontier regions like Burma, and new deepwater oil-import jetties and associated storage facilities will have to be constructed at the pipeline start point on the Burmese coast. Pipeline shipping will also be very expensive relative to maritime shipping, as pumping oil through the planned Burmese line could cost more than four dollars a barrel, assuming that CNPC seeks at least a 10 percent internal rate of return in operating the line.

In contrast, shipping oil by sea from the Persian Gulf to South China can cost as little as US $1.00 per barrel for transport costs, and piping it to interior refineries in areas likely to be served by the Burma–China line would cost an additional two or three dollars a barrel. This represents a substantial cost savings over moving crude through the proposed Burma–China line to refineries in Yunnan. To lower "stated" project costs, the NDRC might subsidize project financing or take other measures to reward CNPC, any of which would cost the Chinese government more than if it relied on seaborne imports to South China for supplying pipelines to the interior.

At today's new-build prices for very large crude carriers (VLCCs), roughly $140 million per vessel, one could build fourteen ships for the two-billion-dollar estimated price of the Burma–China pipeline. Given that each VLCC carries roughly two million barrels of crude and that the round-trip from the Persian Gulf to Southeast China takes thirty total days, fourteen additional supertankers could deliver an average of 666,000 bbl/day of crude, versus 200,000 bbl/day for the planned pipeline. The cost disparity between maritime and pipeline shipping would be even greater for the Pakistan–China line, which could cost up to 10 dollars to move a barrel of oil to Ürümchi in western China. After reaching Ürümchi, the oil would have to be piped an additional three or four thousand km to reach major east coast demand centers, meaning that transport costs from the Persian Gulf to Chinese end users could exceed fifteen dollars a barrel, as opposed to closer to US $2.00/bbl for oil transported from the Gulf to Eastern China on supertankers as of March 2009 (the peak equivalent approached $4–5/bbl in July 2008; during this time, however, pipeline operators raised rates as well).[29]

Demand in Pipeline Terminus Region: Low

A Burma–China pipeline would not be feeding into a major demand center. One might argue that building pipelines into southwest China could ensure stable oil supplies in the region, which lags coastal China in economic growth and does not have access to a pipeline network so developed. Driven by earthquake reconstruction in Sichuan, the rapid development of Chongqing, and other regional growth, oil product demand in interior Southwest China is on the upswing and will continue to grow strongly as the government promotes further growth of domestic consumption. Building more local refining capacity and expanding the domestic pipeline system into underserved areas would be a safer and cheaper way of ensuring oil and product supplies while still creating jobs.

Physical Security Risks: High

Pipelines face substantial physical security risks. In fact, with the Burma and Pakistan pipelines, there would be a twofold vulnerability. First, oil would have to be brought by sea to the pipeline terminus via long sea-lanes, concentrating the target set for an enemy force. Then, it would have to be pumped through a long line traversing remote terrain in potentially insecure areas.

Pipelines are typically more vulnerable to sustained disruptions than are ships. Tankers at sea can be rerouted, while pipelines are fixed links between a producer and consumer. Pipelines offer a wealth of targeting options to non-state actors and opposing militaries.

During an interstate conflict, however, the dynamics would be quite different. Modern military forces equipped with precision-guided munitions could target pump stations and other vital points and rapidly disable pipelines carrying oil or gas into China. A maritime blockade, on the other hand, would be extremely difficult to conduct effectively. Oil cargoes in normal commerce may change ownership ten or more times while a ship is at sea, which reduces the effectiveness of a distant blockade since it is challenging to identify a cargo's final destination. Moreover, if implementing a close blockade of the Chinese coast would solve the destination identification problem, it would bring the blockader's forces within range of numerous and capable Chinese access-denial systems, including aircraft, supersonic anti-ship cruise missiles, mines, and submarines.[30] In short, the flexibility of modern maritime oil transport confers far greater oil-supply security benefits than would pipelines supplied by sea or traversing unstable regions.

An Indicator of China's Overall Security Approach?

Pipeline development will likely be insufficient to offset China's rising seaborne oil import demand. A simple comparison of planned oil pipeline supply additions to China's likely overall demand growth in coming years bears this out, as demand growth will very likely outstrip overland supply additions under even the most optimistic scenarios.

Some projects (e.g., the Burma line) make sense from local and corporate perspectives but not that of national oil security. The Burma line will be expensive to build. The numbers can be "massaged" to ensure that officially stated project costs remain near the stated figure of two billion dollars, but the real costs could be much higher. Also, given Burma's high political risk and the fact that placing a pipeline terminus along the poorly defensible Burmese coast might invite interdiction during wartime, relying on shipments through the Burma line would not enhance China's oil security.

A more sensible and more secure approach might entail building a more comprehensive pipe grid connecting southern Chinese oil ports in Guangdong to the interior southwest provinces. Construction costs will likely be similar (possibly lower, without the political and security risks inherent in Burma). In addition, the immediate and long-term economic benefits could be high, since enhancing China's internal oil and products transportation grid will boost and stabilize fuel supplies to Guangxi and other relatively impoverished inland provinces in which Beijing hopes to catalyze development.

Other lines are simply unviable from nearly all perspectives. The Pakistan line, with its formidable geography, regional instability, and absence of a major demand center at its terminus exemplifies this chimera. That is not to say that there is no logical role for pipelines in China's oil import portfolio. Some pipeline projects are driven by geographic reality (e.g., the line from

Kazakhstan and the planned line from Russia). The fields filling these lines are so far from the sea that an overland line is the most effective way to transport their oil into the Chinese market. Pipelines move oil much more cheaply than rail can. But, as happened in the early years of China's "Going Out" strategy, special interests are apparently playing the security card to benefit themselves in the face of more rational, comprehensive calculations of national interest.

Conclusion

A continued quest for higher overland oil deliveries will not enhance China's oil supply security substantially but will represent a barometer of Chinese trust in global oil markets and maritime oil transport security. As this chapter has demonstrated, however, Chinese decision makers will ultimately have to face the fact that their nation's dependence on seaborne oil imports is likely only to increase. This reality and China's other growing overseas interests have already stimulated debate concerning the extent to which China should develop a blue-water navy to defend its commerce on the high seas.

Before Beijing commits firmly to such a substantial investment, which is likely to have tremendous geopolitical ramifications—some of them likely to involve counterbalancing by regional nations discomfited by such ambitious Chinese naval growth—it would be wise to see if China and the United States can reach a better understanding of their respective roles in the Asia-Pacific as well as work to clarify areas ripe for mutually beneficial energy security cooperation. Such strategic dialogue will be difficult to carry out, and it would not in itself resolve the substantial differences in national interests. But the economic interdependence between the two nations and the potential costs of miscommunication are so high that repeated efforts must be made.

This is a critical time in China's naval development, and the events of the next few years will have disproportionate influence. A good first step would be to encourage Beijing to join two related international organizations. Washington should take the lead in bringing Beijing into the International Renewable Energy Agency (IRENA); as well as the International Energy Agency (IEA), as it meets the requirement to store 90 days of import reserves, so that SPR inventories can be tracked and reported.

The October 2007 issuance of a new maritime strategy by the US sea services suggests that Washington is eager to support cooperative, collective approaches to maritime energy security. Discussion between China, the

United States, and other key energy market stakeholders may facilitate adoption of energy security measures far more effective and mutually beneficial than expensive, limited, and vulnerable pipelines.

Notes

1 The ideas expressed in this chapter are those of the authors alone. They do not represent the official policies or estimates of their respective employers. Unless otherwise specified, calculations were performed by the authors, and are available upon request.

2 Grant Smith and Christian Smollinger, "Crude Oil Rises in New York on Speculation of Inventory Decline," *Bloomberg*, June 11, 2008, www.bloomberg.com/.

3 Li Xiaojun, "On the Influence of Sea Power upon China's Oil Security," *International Forum* 6, no. 4 (July 2004), p. 18.

4 "Kazakhstan Prepares to Build a Pipeline for Exporting Its Oil across the Caspian," *Oil and Capital*, June 7, 2008, www.oilcapital.ru/.

5 Li Jie, "Oil, China's Requirements, and Sea-Lane Security," *Naval & Merchant Ships* (September 2004), p. 12.

6 "'MunaiTas' North-West Pipeline Company Joint Stock Company," www.munaitas.com.

7 Isabel Gorst, "Welding New Relations: Pipelines; Kazakhstan," *Petroleum Economist*, February 1, 2006.

8 *Argus China Petroleum* 2, no. 2 (February 2008), p. 23.

9 Winnie Lee, "CNPC Opens 400,000 b/d Oil Line to Gansu; Gathers Crude from 3 Major Fields in Xinjiang," *Platts Oilgram News*, August 6, 2007.

10 "China's CNPC Starts Building Xinjiang Reserve," *Platts Oilgram News*, March 11, 2008.

11 Ibid.

12 Energy Intelligence Group, "China Oil Import Data 2007," *Energy Intelligence*, www.energyintel.com/.

13 Author's models.

14 "Variables in Construction of China–Russia Oil Pipeline," *Zhongguo Tongxun She*, BBC, December 16, 2007.

15 Lyudmila Podobedova, "Bogdanchikov Tells Chinese to Wait," *RosBisnesConsulting*, September 6, 2007, www.rbcdaily.ru.

16 Yang Xiaohui, "Chinese Oil Strategy's Southwestern Orientation," *Contemporary Asia-Pacific* no. 3 (2004), p. 13.

17 Yin Zhenmao, "Sino–Burmese Pipeline Will Achieve High Capacity," *China Petroleum & Petrochemical*, February 15, 2007, p. 29.

18 Yin Zhenmao, "Sino–Burmese Pipeline Will Achieve High Capacity," p. 29.

19 Zhang E, "A Visitor to the Energy Corridor," *China Petroleum & Petrochemical*, March 1, 2006, p. 29.

20 Lin Xixing, "Two Difficult Choices Facing China's New Oil Passage," p. 33.

21 Lin Xixing, "China Must Build an Energy 'Double Passage' in South Asia," *China News Weekly*, March 20, 2006, p. 52.

22 Yin Zhenmao, "Sino–Burmese Pipeline Will Achieve High Capacity," p. 29.

23 Zhang Xuegang, "Southeast Asia: Gateway to Stability," *China Security* 3, no. 2 (Spring 2007), p. 26.

24 Wen Chou, "People Look Forward to the Implementation of the Sino-Pakistani 'Energy Corridor'," *China Petroleum & Petrochemical*, May 15, 2006, p. 65.

25 See for example, Wu Yongnian, "A Discussion of China and Pakistan Opening Up a New 'Trade-Energy' Corridor," *World Economic Research*, no. 11 (2006), p. 86.

26 "Three Chinese Dead in Pakistan 'Terrorist Attack'," *Reuters*, July 8, 2007, www.reuters.com/.

27 "Gwadar–China Oil Pipeline Study Underway," *Pakistan Observer*, September 4, 2006, pakobserver.net/.

28 "Pakistan Proposes Building Oil and Gas Pipelines to China to Diversify Maritime Energy Delivery Routes," *Oil and Capital*, April 14, 2008, www.oilcapital.ru.

29 "OPEC Output Cuts Send VLCC Rates to Seven-Year Low," *Lloyd's List*, March 19, 2009, via Lexis-Nexis.

30 See Gabriel Collins and William Murray, "No Oil for The Lamps of China?" *Naval War College Review* 61, no. 2 (Spring 2008), pp. 79–95.

CHAPTER TEN

China's Energy Relations with the Global South: Potential for Great Power Realignment

Charles E. Ziegler

Introduction

China's expanding economic and diplomatic involvement in the global south is strongly influenced by its growing demand for energy, but Beijing's global presence is also shaped more broadly by expanding trade relations and investment in the Middle East, Africa, and Latin America, and by skilled diplomacy. Beijing's political influence has grown, and China is increasingly viewed as a rising global power independent of the energy issue. The foundations of China's rise are more economic than military, though military modernization has accompanied China's economic expansion. This chapter draws on the studies presented in this volume to assess the significance of energy in China's foreign policy. To what extent are China's foreign relations shaped by its need to secure reliable energy supplies? Will China's search for energy resources in the global South lead to conflict with other energy-consuming great powers such as the United States, as realist theory would predict? Or will China's energy needs push the regime to engage in new forms of multilateral cooperation leading to energy interdependence, as the liberalist approach would suggest? Finally, what role will energy issues play in the possible realignment of global power away from the United States and toward China?

China at a Crossroads

In many respects, China is a country poised between two worlds—the developed and the developing. China has gleaming, modern cities filled with an affluent middle class, yet half of its population consists of poor people living in rural villages. The country's rapid development, initiated over thirty years ago by Deng Xiaopeng, has unleashed tremendous growth and even greater potential, but it has also created massive problems, most of which are domestic. In foreign policy, though, China's "rise" has been mostly a success story.[1] For the past 150 years the country had been occupied, exploited, and humiliated by the great powers. Now China has eclipsed all of them, with the exception of the United States, and the academic and journalistic literature is filled with speculations on when the PRC will definitively surpass America as the dominant power.[2] It will indeed be difficult for the United States to stem the long-term decline brought about by the financial crisis of 2008–2009, and to extricate itself from military overextension. Throughout the George W. Bush administration Chinese leaders consistently criticized American unilateralism, advocating a multilateral world more suited to China's ascendancy. China's rise will make multilateralism a reality.

No country other than China is likely to challenge the United States for the position of global leadership. The European Union is an economic powerhouse, but as a confederation (and a contentious one at that) it is hard-pressed to conduct an effective, coherent foreign or security policy. Japan is still bound (at least for now) by its peace constitution and its alliance with the United States; perhaps more importantly, the country's continued economic stagnation and its graying population make a reassertion of Japanese power unlikely, notwithstanding periodic nationalist rumblings. Russia is temporarily resurgent under the ambitious Putin-Medvedev team, but its prominence is largely illusory, based on volatile energy prices and constrained by acute demographic problems and an inability to diversify its resource-based economy. India has great potential, and nascent global ambitions, but is constantly scrambling to stay even with its northern neighbor.

China's growing international presence rests on its dynamic economy, which was barely affected by the global recession of 2008–2009. Nobel Prize-winning economist Robert Fogel estimates that by 2040 China's gross domestic product (GDP) will reach an astounding $133 trillion, with a per capita GDP of $85,000, if current trends continue. At that point China will account for 40 percent of global GDP, far outstripping the United States (at 14 percent) and the European Union (at 5 percent).[3] While Fogel's projects may prove to be greatly exaggerated, virtually all analysts foresee continued high levels of growth in the coming decades. China's huge economic engine will consume vast amounts of hydrocarbons, even if the country succeeds in shifting a fifth to a quarter of its energy demand to renewable sources (in 2009 renewable energy accounted for just 8 percent of China's total energy demand). Securing reliable energy supplies can indeed be described as the current leadership's "biggest challenge" in foreign and security policy.[4]

How well positioned is China to handle the energy demands of the twenty-first century? Jean Garrison suggests that China lacks a coherent energy strategy, with policy fragmented among a number of competing bureaucracies and subject to disruption by regional authorities. Steven Lewis of the Baker Institute echoes this assessment by illustrating the regional nature of energy investments and the widely differing forms of energy administration across Chinese localities.[5] China's economy is energy intensive, and while Beijing's leaders are enacting conservation measures and pushing renewable energy, Garrison finds China's current energy policy to be unsustainable. Granted, China's companies are developing renewable energy technologies like wind and solar power, and hydroelectric and renewables are an increasing share of the country's electricity production, but coal will continue to generate the bulk of China's electric power well into the twenty-first century. China holds about 13 percent of the world's coal reserves, but it has only 1.2 percent of the world's oil reserves, and an equally small percentage of global natural gas. China cannot avoid relying on coal to generate electric power. Moreover, the transportation sector, which now constitutes a relatively small share of China's energy demand, will grow as automobile consumption expands, and that will inevitably translate into increased oil consumption.

Of the five rivals for global great-power status, four, like China, are net energy importers. In recessionary 2009 the United States imported about 50 percent of the oil it consumed, the European Union imported over 80 percent of its oil needs, and India imported about 68 percent of its total oil requirements.[6] Japan has virtually no domestic reserves, and so is entirely dependent on imported oil. Although natural gas has in recent years been touted as a cleaner alternative to coal and oil, and nuclear power and renewable hold promise, oil is uniquely suited to today's transportation infrastructure; consequently the global energy balance is not expected to shift dramatically over the next quarter century.[7] Overall levels of consumption are likely to increase, barring global economic collapse, major technological breakthroughs, or the enactment of stringent conservation measures. Much of the world's "easy oil" has already been tapped, and the discovery of large fields has slowed, so that growing competition for limited supplies of the world's oil and gas is to be expected. The bulk of the world's old oil is controlled either by powerful national oil companies (NOCs), and access is restricted by resource nationalism, or the international oil majors have long ago secured the most lucrative properties. Late entrants to the global oil market—most notably China and India—are forced to scramble for the few remaining assets, many of which are located in remote, hard to develop, and unstable locations in the global South. China's search for energy security has frequently meant establishing close relationships with fragile and authoritarian regimes in Africa, Asia, or Latin America where Western influence is limited.

China is already deeply imbedded in the world economy: in 2008, the country's GDP was $3.86 trillion, with foreign trade accounting for nearly three-fourths of the total, or $2.86 trillion.[8] A liberal perspective would suggest that despite China's growing economic and military strength, and resurgent nationalism, the country's leaders should be taken at their word when they profess a desire for international stability and harmony. In its 2007 White Paper on energy, the Chinese government emphasized its goal of strengthening international cooperation through various intergovernmental organizations (ASEAN+3, APEC, and the International Energy Forum), while working with the International Energy Agency and OPEC, and encouraging foreign investment in China's energy sector.[9] China's need for international markets, its enormous dollar holdings ($2.2 trillion in late 2009), and its critical need to access raw materials, above all oil, improve the chances that China will remain a status quo power for the near future.

China's growing dependence on imported energy is a key limiting factor in its global rise. Energy security is vital to continued economic development, which in turn is critical for ensuring domestic stability, and so Beijing's energy policy seeks dependable supplies and minimal price fluctuations. Chinese leaders would prefer not to be overly reliant on imported energy, but while China has sufficient coal reserves (and coal accounts for about 70 percent of the country's energy balance), China has only 16 billion barrels of proven oil reserves, or just over 1 percent of the world's total reserves. China's natural gas reserves, at 80 trillion cubic feet, are also just over 1 percent of the world total. With one-fifth of the world's population, and consuming 7.8 million barrels of oil per day in 2008 (second largest after the United States), domestic crude production cannot meet China's needs.[10] China's energy position is no worse than that of its fellow great powers (with the notable exception of Russia), and its domestic energy reserves are far superior to those of Japan or India. But China, like the United States and other major powers, cannot escape its vulnerability in terms of energy dependence on foreign sources. The question is how this interdependence will play out in the country's relations with the global South, as well as those with the industrial north.

Looking to the South

China's relations with the Middle East are critical for its energy security, since two-thirds of the world's oil reserves are located in the Persian Gulf region, and at present about half of China's oil imports come from Middle Eastern countries. In addition, the International Energy Agency estimates that non-OPEC oil production will peak in 2010, so that increases in oil production over the next two decades will come largely from OPEC countries, accentuating the critical nature of the Middle East.[11] Beijing's leaders are justifiably concerned with the stability of the region. The perennial Israeli-Palestinian conflict, Islamic extremism and terrorism, Iran's quest for nuclear weapons, the fragility of oil-based autocracies, and the half-century dominance of American power (culminating in the occupation of Iraq) make this region problematic for oil importing nations. As Manochehr Dorraj and Carrie Liu Currier emphasize in their chapter, China is a pragmatic, status quo power in the Middle East. Beijing's ties with Riyadh have developed over the past two decades, while US-Saudi relations became more strained after the 9/11 terrorist attacks. But Saudi Arabia's oil sector, a monopoly of state-owned Saudi Aramco, is largely closed to foreign investment, limiting the ability of Chinese companies to acquire equity stakes. The Saudis have invested in a number of projects in China, while China has sold weapons and consumer goods to the Saudis and Chinese businesses have been allowed limited access to the Saudi economy. Riyadh is also interested in the political benefits from stronger ties with China, as well as India, to balance pressure from Washington over issues of democratization and funding terrorism, since these countries are traditionally reluctant to press their political ideas on other countries.[12]

Iran is a different story. China's extensive energy deals with Iran have complicated Washington's efforts to isolate Teheran, promote democracy in Iran, and force the Iranian government to give up its nuclear weapons program. Beijing has consistently resisted sanctions against Iran, in part because of its need for Iranian oil and gas, and in part because of its general opposition to sanctions as a foreign policy instrument. President Barack Obama made Beijing's support for his administration's policy on Iran a top priority during his November 2009 Asia trip, but elicited little more than agreement that Iran should "engage constructively" with the P5+1 (permanent members of the UN Security Council plus Germany) and "cooperate fully" with the International Atomic Energy Agency.[13] China and Iran share a geopolitical perspective that is uncomfortable with American domination of the post-Cold War international system, but this has not crystallized into shared strategic principles.[14] China is concerned about investing in Iran as long as the level of international tension over Iran's nuclear weapons' program remains high, but since Iran holds about 11 percent of global oil reserves (and about 15 percent of the world's natural gas), Beijing can ill afford to shun Teheran.

In Africa, the old revolutionary approach of the Mao era has given way to pragmatic, commerce-driven policies free of ideology or the moralizing tone of Western democracies. Africa has key reserves of new oil, attracting the attention of major importers around the world. Zhao Hong shows how China has rapidly expanded trade with key energy producers, including Angola, Sudan, Republic of Congo, and Equatorial Guinea, and has ramped up foreign direct investment in South Africa, Nigeria, and elsewhere, in its search for petroleum, metals, and other raw materials. Over 700 Chinese companies, both private and state-owned, are now operating in Africa. Through infrastructure development these companies are able to maintain close relations with African governments and to secure lucrative state contracts. China is less risk-averse in its engagement strategy than many Western nations, and China has provided representation for African nations in the UN, furthering Beijing's long-standing ambition to become a leader of the developing world.

But China's economic and diplomatic successes in Africa should not be overstated. Chinese investment without strings attached has a downside—it prolongs the failures of poorly governed African nations and feeds corruption, since Beijing does not make good governance demands on host countries as do Western aid agencies. China's willingness to deal with brutal regimes makes for cordial state-to-state relations, but reports of poor working conditions in Chinese companies and undercutting of domestic industries raise the possibility of an anti-Chinese backlash among Africans.[15] Zhao Hong detects changes in Beijing's approach to Sudan in recent years, reflecting an understanding that the instability of civil war and genocide is not in China's interest. While China provides much-needed aid and expertise, its national oil companies do not have the deep-water extraction technology to compete with US firms in Gulf of Guinea. Furthermore, as Zhao notes, Chinese investment in Africa's oil industry is a fraction of that supplied by Western companies, and its aid to the continent is far behind that provided by the United States, Europe, and Japan.

Russia and Central Asia are promising sources of hydrocarbons, as described by Gregory Gleason in Chapter five. These states have ample supplies of oil and natural gas, and they have the advantage of being geographically contiguous to China. Transportation by pipeline requires major investments, but the result is a more diversified network that is less susceptible to interdiction than seaborne tankers. The down side is that pipelines, whether oil or natural gas, established interdependencies that make both producers and consumers vulnerable to political manipulation. Moreover, China's high-growth coastal regions are distant from Central Asian and Siberian reserves, making it generally more efficient to supply these regions by tanker. Beijing is seeking oil and gas from its neighbors to the West, but its experiences with Russia have been less than rewarding. Russian resource nationalism under Vladimir Putin's leadership has resulted in a neomercantilist approach to energy that makes the Russian-Chinese energy relationship more competitive than cooperative.[16]

Central Asia is more open to Chinese energy investments. Bordering as it does on China's restive Xinjiang province, Central Asia is within Beijing's sphere of vital interests. Central Asia's authoritarian rulers are closely attuned to China's growing influence, and engage with Beijing bilaterally and multilaterally through the Shanghai Cooperation Organization (SCO). Russia is still the dominant power in the region, but its influence is gradually slipping as China expands trade links and seeks investment opportunities in Central Asian oil, gas and hydroelectric projects. A major oil pipeline from Kazakhstan to Xinjiang (the Atasu-Alashankou route) went online in summer 2006, with a capacity of 200,000 barrels per day. Completion of the Kenkiyak-Kumkol segment of the pipeline in summer 2009 provides the final link connecting Caspian Sea oil to China. Turkmenistan began pumping gas to Western China in December 2009 through a pipeline that, at full capacity, will deliver 30 billion cubic meters of gas per year. Plans for Kazakh gas to supplement Turkmen supplies could raise this figure by a third.

In Central Asia, China is competing with Russia for access to the region's energy wealth. As Vitaly Kozyrev has argued, Beijing views the post-1991 world as anarchic, comparable to the "Warring States" period of 476–221 BCE. This would suggest that Chinese leaders are following a purely realist strategy, based on the belief that they are on their own when it comes to energy.[17] Although the weaker Central Asian states have proved skillful at preserving good relations with all the larger powers (through their "multi-vectored" foreign policies), China is viewed in the region as the greatest long-term challenge because of its demographic weight and growing economic presence. Already many of the larger Central Asian cities have Chinese markets, the countries have been flooded with Chinese goods, and large numbers of legal and illegal Chinese workers have moved into the region. Central Asians fear the demographic threat posed by China. In December 2009 a rumor that Kazakhstan's President Nursultan Nazarbayev was planning to make large plots of agricultural land available to immigrant Chinese farmers sparked a vocal reaction in this tightly controlled country.[18]

As in Africa, Chinese energy investment and trade with Latin America have expanded dramatically over the past decade. Gregg Johnson and Jesse Wasson address the possibility that China may challenge Washington's long-standing hegemony in South America. Several years ago Peter Hakim, President of the Inter-American Dialogue, posed the question "is Washington losing Latin America?"[19] Certainly, the United States appears to have lost influence in the first decade of the twenty-first century. As a partner, China presents an alternative to American political and economic hegemony in the continent, and its neomercantilist model of development presents an appealing contrast to the largely discredited Washington Consensus. As in Africa, China's leaders have been especially attentive to South America's energy giants—Venezuela and Brazil—signing a number of energy and infrastructure deals in recent years. China's close relations with Venezuela under Hugo Chavez have been particularly galling to the United States. President Chavez has periodically threatened to cut off shipments to the United States, heralding China as a friendlier power free of American imperial intentions. News that China and Venezuela had signed a $16 billion oil exploration agreement followed an announced $20 billion deal with Russia, and emphasized Chavez's close ties with Washington's major competitors.[20]

But geography limits the potential for energy cooperation with South America's major energy producers. Supertankers cannot fit through the Panama Canal, there are currently no east- to-west pipelines to the Pacific Ocean, and shipping around the southern tip of the continent makes costs prohibitive. Venezuela under Hugo Chavez has been eager to deal with America's competitors, striking energy and arms deals with China and Russia, but Chavez will lose influence (and possibly his office) as the country's economy flounders under his ill-considered policies. Although China and Venezuela share a neomercantilist approach to energy, and resist American dominance of the global order, Venezuela's petroleum infrastructure is closely tied to the US refinery complex on the Gulf of Mexico. In addition, PDVSA (the Venezuelan National Oil Company Petroleos de Venezuela) has major downstream operations in the United States in the form of Citgo's refineries and retail gasoline stations. Chavez's socialist policies and the 2002 strikes have caused serious damage to PDVSA's production capacity, and investors in the country's petroleum market face considerable risk.

China has extensive trade relations with Brazil, and has provided loans to Brazil's hydrocarbon sector. While Brazil's investment climate is more promising than Venezuela's, state-owned Petrobras still controls over 95 percent of crude production in the country, leaving little room for foreign investors.[21] As Johnson and Wasson point out, though China's trade with Latin America has skyrocketed in recent years, it is still only a fifth of overall US trade with the region.

China is effectively excluded from Mexico, the third largest oil producer in the Western Hemisphere (and the seventh largest producer in the world), since upstream petrochemical assets are nationally owned and the Constitution severely restricts foreign investment in hydrocarbons. In any event, Mexico's relations with China have traditionally been tense, since Mexico's imports compete with China's for the US market. Johnson and Wasson note that similar tensions exist in China's relations with Central America. As middle-income countries in South and Central America lose domestic and US market share to Chinese companies, new forms of dependency may generate resentment and hinder energy cooperation.

China's Global Reach

As a number of the authors in this volume note, the rapid expansion of Chinese trade with Africa, Latin America, or the Middle East should be viewed in the context of the dramatic overall expansion of Chinese trade and investment throughout the world. In many cases in the global South, Chinese investments and trade have been targeted toward oil—in 2007, for example, Chinese oil imports from Angola accounted for over half of all the value of all Chinese imports from sub-Saharan Africa, and four of China's five largest trading partners in sub-Saharan Africa were oil suppliers.[22]

China has traditionally been a land power but, as the country has become more integrated into the global economy, and finds itself increasingly dependent on imported oil, the role of sea power in guaranteeing the country's security will grow. No longer concerned solely with coastal defense and preventing Taiwanese independence, China is expanding the People's Liberation Army Navy (PLAN) gradually, and is seeking a greater presence in the Western Pacific and Indian Oceans, the principle energy and trade routes vital to China's prosperity (some 70 percent of the world's traffic in petroleum transits the Indian Ocean). As China's naval interests move beyond the Taiwan Straits into the Pacific and Indian Oceans, Beijing finds itself challenging an established naval power (the United States) and an ascendant one (India). China and India share some common interests, as in keeping the sea lanes open and combating terrorism and piracy, but overall the relationship between these two powers appears competitive. New Delhi is suspicious of Chinese motives in developing the so-called string of pearls facilities in the Indian Ocean.[23] Beijing denies it has any grand strategy in the waters around South Asia, but its presence in Bangladesh, Burma, Thailand, Cambodia, and Pakistan seems designed to secure the vital oil shipping lanes.

China cannot be complacent about the security of its maritime commerce. Pipelines from Russia and Central Asia can diversify China's oil and gas imports, but the 500,000 barrels per day that the East Siberia Pacific Ocean (ESPO) and Kazakh pipelines will supply by 2015 would account for only 6 percent of China's oil demand (about 12 percent of imports) as of late 2009. The only other possible pipelines, following the Burma–China and Pakistan–China routes, face serious political and logistical obstacles and may not be economically viable, as Andrew Erickson and Gabriel Collins find in Chapter Nine. That does not mean that they will not be built, since energy security often trumps profitability in the calculations of major powers. Nonetheless, the overwhelming proportion of China's imports will continue to be supplied by tanker, and most of that will transit the Indian Ocean and the Strait of Malacca. For that reason, keeping sea lanes open will become even more important in Chinese foreign policy, and that will mean naval expansion.

As China develops its naval presence in the Pacific and Indian Oceans it is likely to spark a reaction among its large Pacific neighbors, Japan and India. Beijing recognizes that its overriding goal achieving "comprehensive national power" must be realized through economic development paired with military security. These two forms of security are best served by lowering tensions and promoting cooperation with its two major Asian competitors, but as Jian Ying argues, realizing this strategy has proved difficult. Sino-Japanese tensions run deep, and growing nationalism on both sides fuels suspicions and distrust, which flare up periodically over disputed territories, the Yasukuni shrine, and the lingering residue of Japanese colonialism. However, trade has ballooned to the point that conflict between the two would be very costly. China's bilateral trade with Japan surpassed $266 billion in 2008, with China displacing the United States as Japan's biggest trading partner.[24]

China has a troubled past with India, but the relationship appears more manageable than that with Japan. Their economies have different strengths, so they are not competing for the same markets, as is the case with much of

Latin America. According to the International Energy Agency, the bulk of growth in energy consumption over the next two decades will be accounted for by these two Asian giants. India's hydrocarbon reserves are smaller than China's, and while there are a few instances of energy cooperation, the two countries' NOCS have been competing for many of the same energy assets, with India's Oil and Natural Gas Company lagging behind its Chinese counterparts. As Yang rightly notes, China's close ties to Burma and especially Pakistan are troubling to India's leaders. China's investments in the port of Gwadar and its broader naval expansion in the Indian Ocean raise alarm bells in New Delhi. The expansion in the Indian Ocean is part of the general growth of China's naval power in recent years, much of which is linked to Beijing's concerns over the vulnerability of energy shipments.

A recent study by Asia specialists at the US Naval Institute found Chinese naval writings reflected growing concern with China's vulnerability to an oil embargo. Yet Chinese publications do not reflect a consensus on how to deal with energy insecurity. A neomercantilist strain in the writings of Chinese naval strategists stresses China's naval weakness and the possibility that the United States, Japan, or India could interdict the sea lanes of communication, thus severing China's energy lifeline. A second economic liberal school, by contrast, rejects such zero-sum thinking, focusing instead on possibilities for cooperation, both multilaterally and bilaterally with the United States. Neither approach appears to dominate state policy.[25]

It bears noting that the global South, or at least parts of it, is also rising along with China—Brazil, India, Turkey, South Africa, and Indonesia are only some of the most notable examples. Together with China, these countries will account for most of the increase in energy demand over the next two decades and, as supplies tighten, energy competition among these developing nations may heat up. In a very few cases—India, most notably—China's ties are more competitive than cooperative. But in the remainder of the global South, China has very good, businesslike relations. To the extent that China becomes more closely aligned with the South in its search for energy, America's preeminent position in the world will erode even more quickly. The United States will very likely suffer a loss of position and influence in the global South relative to China. Growing energy demands from China, India, and the United States empower the smaller energy-exporting countries such as Nigeria, Kazakhstan, and Venezuela that would otherwise have little claim to world prominence.[26]

There is broad agreement that China is a rising power, that America is in long-term but gradual decline, and that no other power on the horizon has a realistic chance of supplanting either in the foreseeable future. There is also considerable agreement that the rise of the global South, and the inability of the United States to craft a sustainable energy policy will place unprecedented demands on the world's reserves of fossil fuels over the next few decades. The alignment of forces in world politics will depend in large part on which great power is the more creative and effective in meeting the energy challenge. Does China's technocratic authoritarian system confer an advantage over America's consumer-driven democracy? In both countries leaders are responsive to popular demands for continuous improvements in living standards, though in the US, leaders at the national, state, and local levels are virtually paralyzed by powerful lobbies and an aversion to taxes. Some states and locales have enacted progressive energy policies, but the national government seems unable to craft effective energy legislation that would lower consumption, reduce waste, and enhance energy independence.

China's national government appears more forward-looking, but local and provincial governments often frustrate central objectives. While the central government may address the long-term needs of the nation, local governments are focused on short-term economic goals. China's domestic energy production has resulted in negative economic impacts on vulnerable segments of the population, which has been exacerbated by the operation of local governments in the oil, coal, and hydroelectric sectors.[27] Local government officials tend to be perceived as more unresponsive and concerned with their own interests, while central government policies have generated higher satisfaction levels among the population.[28] And local officials are pressured and rewarded for following a strategy of "growth at any cost" that neglects sustainability and efficiency in energy production and harms the environment. Local officials fear instability or measures that will disrupt revenue flows more than they fear energy insecurity or environmental degradation.[29]

Conflict or Cooperation?

China is a rising power. The question is what does this mean for world politics, and specifically for the purposes of this volume, what does it mean for international energy politics? Part of China's increased global presence can be attributed to its search for stable supplies of oil and natural gas. But energy also constrains China. Beijing's foreign policy options are limited by its dependence on imported oil, just as its domestic development strategies are shaped and constrained by its limited supplies of oil and gas, and the increasingly serious environmental consequences of fossil fuel consumption.

The chapters in this volume agree that China's foreign policy is flexible, adaptable, and highly pragmatic. In its search for reliable supplies of energy, Chinese companies have sought equity stakes around the world, struck deals for upstream and downstream operations, and concluded auxiliary agreements on building infrastructure and developing non-energy sectors, all of which has expanded Beijing's global reach. Since much of the available oil China seeks is "new oil" in the global South, China's energy strategy has focused on that part of the world. While vaguely reminiscent of the Cold War competition for presence and influence in the Third World, the current competition is not driven by ideology, nor has it taken the form of proxy wars. Diversifying supplies and bringing more oil onto the international market is in the interests of all major energy consumers, by contributing to stable flows and moderating prices. There is a strong incentive for major energy consumers to cooperate, if they can move beyond a mercantilist mindset that views the world energy market in terms of relative gains.

The Chinese state invariably acts on its national interests, defined largely in terms of maintaining domestic growth and social stability. However, China is not a unitary actor. When it comes to energy there are two deep divisions of interest within the country—between national energy interests and those of the state energy companies that produce oil and gas; and between the central government in Beijing and the regional and local governments. In the first instance, the energy component of China's "going out" strategy has involved a search for equity oil, which has enhanced profitability for Chinese oil companies but achieved little in the way of enhanced energy security for China. And while central authorities may enact progressive conservation measures or mandate efficiency standards and pollution controls, their decrees are often frustrated by self-interested or corrupt local officials.

China's quest for energy security encompasses both cooperative and competitive elements. As a regional power that is gradually developing a global presence, China's energy and security concerns are most acute around its periphery. In part, this focus derives from the lessons of China's "century of humiliation" and the exploitation of the Middle Kingdom by foreign powers. China's restive minority populations share space with the country's major oil and gas deposits—in Xinjiang, the Northeast and Inner Mongolia—and development of these fields has sparked unrest, particularly among the Uighurs. Central Asian and Siberian oil and gas pipelines will transit China's border regions, making these areas doubly important for Beijing's national security. China's offshore deposits are located in the Bohai Bay and South China Sea, areas that bring Beijing into potential conflict with its historic enemy Japan. This suggests that China's quest for energy will be competitive in regions closer to China's borders, and where historical tensions influence relations. And yet competition is not the sole form of energy interaction—in recent years China has struck agreements with both India and Japan for exploration and development projects, and has worked out energy cooperation arrangements with the Association of Southeast Asian Nations (ASEAN).

Viewed through the prism of energy needs, China's foreign policy appears to be rational, based solely on national interests. Offensive realism would see in China's rise the prospects for conflict, but there is as yet little evidence of this in China's international behavior, even over a vital strategic commodity such as oil.[30] In many respects China's energy diplomacy has been less competitive or conflict oriented than that of the United States, and Chinese leaders (at least in their public pronouncements) claim not to view security in terms of relative power. But China's national identity clearly is shaped by a nineteenth-century view of absolute sovereignty that meshes well with realist theory, relying as it does on self-help in an anarchic world, and rejecting interference in the country's internal affairs. And yet China has acquired membership in literally hundreds of international organizations, including such sovereignty-limiting bodies as the World Trade Organization.

Oil presents a "security dilemma" in China's relations with other major energy importing nations—oil is a strategic commodity, and if one side perceives the other as seeking to deny it access to stable supplies this could lead to conflict. There is good evidence that Chinese leaders recognize the potential for a security dilemma in energy competition, and will continue efforts to avoid conflict with the other major powers. Over a decade ago Robert Ross, arguing from a realist perspective, concluded that since China was basically a land power and the United States a naval power, the absence of overlapping spheres of influence would result in a bipolar stable order.[31] A constructivist perspective such as that outlined by the editors in the introduction would suggest that the direction of China's foreign energy policy will depend on how the leadership defines its identity and interests, and how China's major potential rivals define theirs.

However, if Beijing and the other major powers continue or intensify their neomercantilist approaches to energy security, dominated by zero-sum thinking and efforts to secure relative gains, the chances of an "energy arms race" would increase. Pressures for protectionism and neomercantilist measures grew in the wake of the 2008–2009 global recession, although the drop in demand for oil and gas and subsequent decline in energy prices moderated reactions. As the global economy emerges from the recession energy demand will increase, and the major energy-importing nations will likely be faced with short supplies and escalating prices. Unless these countries succeed in coordinating their energy policies, either through bilateral negotiations or through multilateral forums such as the International Energy Agency (of which neither China nor India is a member), then the possibility of conflict over energy is real. At present China cooperates with the IEA, but legally only members of the OECD can join the organization, so either China would need to bolster its democratic credentials, or the IEA would have to revise its constitution. Clearly, the stakes are high enough that the United States should find creative ways to integrate China into the IEA and the G-8 mechanisms, giving Beijing a seat at the table and encouraging it to be a responsible stakeholder in energy issues.[32]

While China's foreign policy is wholly pragmatic, American foreign policy remains heavily ideological.[33] To the extent that the constructivist argument is persuasive, much then rests on the ability of Washington to shape American identity and interests vis-à-vis energy security and China in such a way that cooperative approaches will surmount American distaste for China's repressive authoritarian regime. If American leaders deny China's legitimate interests in securing needed energy supplies in the global South, we can expect a nationalist backlash well beyond the upper echelons of the Chinese Communist party. The United States has viewed China's energy forays into the global South with suspicion, convinced that Beijing is trying to displace America's unipolar moment. American reactions to China's energy search, together with condemnations of Chinese human rights abuses, censorship, trade surpluses, and currency valuation, confirm China's perceptions that Washington is trying to deny it a rightful place in the global order. By encouraging Beijing's participation in bilateral and multilateral energy arrangements, the United States can strengthen the cooperative elements in China's quest for energy security, encourage conservation, and avoid a natural resource rivalry in the global South, while seeking to enlist Beijing's support for humanitarian and development projects.

Notes

1 References to China's "rise" raised alarm bells among observers outside the country, leading Chinese officials and scholars to refer instead to China's "peaceful rise" and then to its "peaceful development," in keeping

with the country's commitment to a "harmonious world." See Bonnie S. Glaser and Evan S. Medeiros, "The Changing Ecology of Foreign Policy-Making in China: The Ascension and Demise of the Theory of 'Peaceful Rise,'" *The China Quarterly*, Issue 190 (June 2007), pp. 291–310.

2 See, for example, C. Fred Bergsten, Charles Freeman, Nicholas R. Lardy, and Derek J. Mitchell (2009) *China's Rise: Challenges and Opportunities* (New York: Peterson Institute for International Economics); Robert G. Sutter (2006) *China's Rise in Asia: Promises and Perils* (Lanham, MD: Rowman & Littlefield); Susan Shirk (2008) *China; Fragile Superpower* (New York: Oxford University Press).

3 Robert Fogel, "$123,000,000,000. *China's Estimated Economy by the Year 2030. Be Warned," *Foreign Policy* (January/February 2010), accessed at http://www.foreignpolicy.com/articles/2010/01/04/123000000000000?page=0,0

4 Willy Wo-Lap Lam, "China's Petroleum Diplomacy: Hu Jintao's Biggest Challenge in Foreign and Security Policy," in Guoguang Wu and Helen Landsdowne, eds. *China Turns to Multilateralism: Foreign Policy and Regional Security* (London: Routledge, 2008).

5 Steven W. Lewis, "China and Energy Security in Asia," Korea Economic Institute (May 6, 2008), accessed at http://www.bakerinstitute.org/publications/ASIA-EnergySecurity-050608.pdf

6 During the boom era of the mid-2000s imported oil accounted for nearly 60 percent of total consumption.

7 Adam E. Sieminski (2005) "World Energy Futures," in Jan H. Kalicki and David L. Goldwyn, eds, *Energy & Security: Toward a New Foreign Policy Strategy* (Baltimore: Johns Hopkins University Press).

8 World Trade Organization Country Profile—China, accessed at http://stat.wto.org/CountryProfile/WSDBCountryPFView.aspx?Country=CN&Language=E

9 *China's Energy Conditions and Policies*, December 26, 2007, accessed at http://www.china.org.cn/english/environment/236955.htm#8

10 In 2008 China imported fully half of its petroleum needs. Data are from the US Energy Information Administration, Country Analysis Brief—China, accessed at http://www.eia.doe.gov/emeu/cabs/China/pdf.pdf

11 International Energy Agency, World Energy Outlook 2009, Executive Summary (accessed at http://www.worldenergyoutlook.org/docs/weo2009/WEO2009_es_english.pdf).

12 Harsh V. Pant, "Saudi Arabia Woos China and India," *Middle East Quarterly*, Vol. 13, No. 4 (Fall 2006), 45–52; Chas. W. Freeman, Jr. "The

Arabs Take a Chinese Wife: Sino-Arab Relations in the Decade to Come," speech to the World Affairs Council of Northern California at Asilomar, May 7, 2006, accessed at the SUSRIS website, http://www.saudi-us-relations.org/articles/2006/ioi/060601-freeman-sino-arab.html

13 Xinhua, November 17, 2009.

14 Ahmed Hashim (2008) "China's Evolving Relationship with Iran," in *China's Energy Strategy: The Impact on Beijing's Maritime Policies*, Gabriel B. Collins, Andrew S. Erickson, Lyle J. Goldstein, and William S. Murray, eds (Annapolis, MD: Naval Institute Press), p. 174.

15 Clifford Shelton, "The Energy Component of China's Africa Strategy," in *China's Energy Strategy*, pp. 192–195.

16 See Charles E. Ziegler, "Neomercantilism and Energy Dependence: Russian Strategies in East Asia," *Asian Security*, Vol. 6, No. 1 (2010), pp. 74–93.

17 Vitaly Kozyrev, "China's Continental Energy Strategy: Russia and Central Asia," in *China's Energy Strategy*, p. 205.

18 Bruce Pannier, "Prospect of Chinese Farmers Brings Controversy to Kazakh Soil," Radio Free Europe/Radio Liberty (December 17, 2009) accessedathttp://www.rferl.org/content/Prospect_Of_Chinese_Farmers_Brings_Controversy_To_Kazakh_Soil/1906896.html

19 Peter Hakim, "Is Washington Losing Latin America?", *Foreign Affairs*, Vol. 85, No. 1 (January/February 2006), pp. 39–53.

20 Chinadaily.com.cn (September 18, 2009); Marketwatch (September 17, 2009), accessed at http://www.marketwatch.com/story/venezuela-and-china-agree-16-billion-oil-deal-2009–09-17.

21 Sam Fletcher, "Pemex, PDVSA, Petrobras: How Strategies, Results Differ," *Oil & Gas Journal* (August 3, 2009).

22 Evan S. Medieros (2009) *China's International Behavior: Activism, Opportunism, and Diversification* (Santa Monica, CA: RAND Corporation), pp. 149–150.

23 Robert D. Kaplan, "Center Stage for the Twenty-First Century: Power Plays in the Indian Ocean," *Foreign Affairs*, Vol. 88, Issue 2 (March/April 2009), 16–32.

24 Japan External Trade Organization, Trade and Investment Statistics 2008, accessed at http://www.jetro.go.jp/en/reports/statistics/

25 The United States, Japan, and India each have the capability to cut China's oil supply lines, but only the United States has the power and nerve to blockade China at the present time. Gabriel B. Collins, Andrew

S. Erickson, and Lyle J. Goldstein, "Chinese Naval Analysts Consider the Energy Question," in *China's Energy Strategy*, especially pp. 302–306, 312–325.

26 Richard N. Haass, "The Age of Nonpolarity: What will Follow U.S. Dominance," *Foreign Affairs*, Vol. 87 (2008), pp. 44–56; Michael Klare, *Rising Powers, Shrinking Planet: The New Geopolitics of Energy* (New York: Metropolitan Books, 2008).

27 See Philip Andrews-Speed and Xin Ma, "Energy Production and Social Marginalization in China," *Journal of Contemporary China*, Vol. 17 (55), May 2008, pp. 247–272.

28 Tony Saich, "Citizens' Perceptions of Governance in Urban and Rural China," *Journal of Chinese Political Science*, Vol. 12, No. 1 (2007), pp. 1–28.

29 *China's Rise*, pp. 78–79.

30 On offensive realism, see John. J. Mearsheimer (2001) *The Tragedy of Great Power Politics* (New York: Norton).

31 Robert S. Ross, "The Geography of Peace: East Asia in the Twenty-first Century," *International Security*, Vol. 23, No. 4 (Spring 1999), pp. 81–118.

32 Kenneth Lieberthal and Mikkal Herberg, "China's Search for Energy Security: Implications for U.S. Energy Policy," *NBR Analysis*, Vol. 17, No. 1 (April 2006), p. 6.

33 Aaron L. Friedberg, "The Future of U.S.-China Relations: Is Conflict Inevitable?" *International Security*, Vol. 30, No. 2 (Fall 2005), p. 32.

Index